PENGUIN BOOKS
# TRAGIC NATION BURMA

Amitav Acharya is a distinguished professor and the UNESCO Chair in Transnational Challenges and Governance, School of International Service, American University, Washington, DC. His major works on Southeast Asia include: *The Quest for Identity: International Relations of Southeast Asia* (Oxford, 2000); *Constructing a Security Community in Southeast Asia: ASEAN and the Problems of Regional Order*, 3 edns. (Routledge, 2001, 2002, 2014), *Whose Ideas Matter: Agency and Power in Asian Regionalism* (Cornell, 2009); *Civilizations in Embrace: The Spread of Ideas and the Transformation of Power* (Singapore: ISEAS, 2012); *The Making of Southeast Asia* (Cornell, 2013); and *East of India, South of China: Sino-Indian Encounters in Southeast Asia* (Oxford, 2017). His articles and op-eds have appeared in *International Organization, International Security, International Studies Quarterly, International Affairs, World Politics, Financial Times, Foreign Affairs, Washington Post, International Herald Tribune/ Global New York Times, Times of India, Australian Financial Review*, and *YaleGlobal Online*. He has been interviewed by BBC, CNN, CNBC, and National Public Radio (NPR) and other world media.

T0017735

## ADVANCE PRAISE FOR *TRAGIC NATION BURMA*

'A fresh, insightful, provocative and outstanding account of Burma's/Myanmar's political destiny.'

—Kavi Chongkittavarn, Leading Thai journalist, former editor of *Myanmar Times* and former president of the jury for the UNESCO/Guillermo Cano World Press Freedom Prize

'If you are after the most comprehensive historical survey of the processes that have produced today's crisis in Myanmar, this is the book you need to read. Isolated and with a complex unique history, unravelling the intertwining threads of Myanmar's political destiny is no easy task. Here, the author presents all the necessary information in one book, with a coherent analysis of the chains of cause and effect that have interacted to create the zigs and zags of Myanmar's tragic experiments in democracy. Need to understand Myanmar now: read this book.'

—Max Lane, author of *Indonesia Out of Exile: How Pramoedya's Buru Quartet Killed a Dictatorship* and translator of the four novels of Pramoedya starting with *This Earth of Mankind*, now known as the *Buru Quartet*

'A bold effort to analyse contemporary Myanmar after the 2021 coup drawing on the lessons of recent history and contemporary voices.'

—Michael Vatikiotis, writer, broadcaster and journalist, and former editor, *Far Eastern Economic Review*

'Exceptional. I can't thank the author enough for this wonderful piece of work. I would like to encourage everyone to give this book a try so that you can get a sneak peak of what the citizens living in Myanmar had to and have to go through over the past decades.'

# Tragic Nation Burma
## Why and How Democracy Failed

Amitav Acharya

**PENGUIN BOOKS**
An imprint of Penguin Random House

PENGUIN BOOKS

USA | Canada | UK | Ireland | Australia
New Zealand | India | South Africa | China | Southeast Asia

Penguin Books is part of the Penguin Random House group of companies
whose addresses can be found at global.penguinrandomhouse.com

Published by Penguin Random House SEA Pte Ltd
9, Changi South Street 3, Level 08-01,
Singapore 486361

First published in Penguin Books by Penguin Random House SEA 2022

Copyright © Amitav Acharya 2022

ISBN 9789815017762

Typeset in Adobe Caslon Pro by MAP Systems, Bangalore, India

www.penguin.sg

# A Dedication to Burma's Young
## *Thought Warriors*

I have been thinking of writing a book on Burma's experience with democracy since the 2010 elections. I visited the country many times and had two stints of teaching at Yangon and Mandalay universities. But for personal and professional reasons, progress in writing had been slow. When I finally started to write this book, in 2019, events quickly overtook my plan. The twin evils of COVID and the Coup struck, and made it impossible to visit the country during the actual process of writing, which is always critical to me.

The only alternative was to research by stealth. With the help of some friends, my initial plan was to conduct some face to face interviews with the people taking part in the struggle for Burma's soul. But my contacts were rightly afraid—of not only being caught by security forces but also of catching the virus during Burma's calamitous second wave.

Much of the inspiration and a fair amount of the information, for this book comes from a secret survey I conducted with the help of a group of young people inside Burma. They are young, mostly but not all students, who identify themselves with Burma's Civil Disobedience Movement (CDM) against the coup. A few are CDM activists but are employed. And there is one who identifies simply as 'adult unemployed'.

I call them *Thought Warriors*. While rejecting violence and weapons, they carry out their struggles, just as effectively in my view, with their mind and thought. They are anonymous yet energetic, passionate yet wise, restless but not reckless. Ultimately, Burma's democratic transformation depends on its *Thought Warriors*, as much, perhaps more than it does on armed insurgents or seasoned politicians.

All the quotes in the book that are in italics are the actual words of the *Thought Warriors*. They mostly communicate in English, although a few of them use Burmese only; those are translated into English. I have not altered their original expressions, but sometimes cut the length.

While I never met, and perhaps never will meet, them in person, they remain very special in my heart and mind. It is to them that I dedicate this book.

# Contents

## Ethnic Map of Burma

Figure 1

Source: International Crisis Group, 'Myanmar's Coup Shakes Up Its Ethnic Conflicts', 22 January 2022, https://www.crisisgroup. org/asia/south-east-asia/myanmar/319-myanmars-coup-shakesits-ethnic-conflicts

# Chronology of Major Political Developments in Burma Since Independence

### Compiled by Shagun Gupta

1948: Burma gains independence from British colonial rule. U Nu, leader of the Anti-Fascist People's Freedom League (AFPFL), becomes prime minister.

1958–1960: A temporary caretaker government is formed, led by Chief of Staff General Ne Win and his Burma Socialist Programme Party (BSPP), against a backdrop of internal power struggles within the AFPFL and a rise in insurgencies led by ethnic armed groups.

1960: U Nu's faction wins a decisive victory in the election.

1962: General Ne Win overthrows U Nu's government in a military coup and abolishes the federal state system under the 1947 Constitution. He introduces the 'Burmese Way of Socialism' in a one-party state under the BSPP, with a nationalized economy and a ban on independent media.

1974: The new Constitution comes into force: it transfers power from the military to the People's Assembly, which is headed by General Ne Win and other military leaders.

1981: General Ne Win steps down from the presidency and is replaced by a retired military general, San Yu, but remains chairman of the BSPP.

1982: The Burma Citizenship Law is introduced. It states that anyone who arrived in the country after 1823 is not considered a citizen. It specifically targets ethnic minorities, such as the Rohingya, who are classified as 'associate citizens', thereby denying them rights afforded to full citizens, including the right to hold public office.

1988: Thousands of people are killed during anti-government protests. Ne Win resigns, and the State Law and Order Restoration Council (SLORC) is formed under General Saw Maung, who seizes power. Simultaneously, Aung San Suu Kyi rises to prominence and becomes the General Secretary of the National League for Democracy (NLD).

1989: SLORC declares martial law. It also changes the country's name from Burma to Myanmar, and the capital Rangoon to Yangon. Aung San Suu Kyi is placed under house arrest for the first time (until 1995).

1990: The NLD wins a decisive victory in the 1990 General Elections, but the SLORC does not accept the result.

1991: Aung San Suu Kyi is awarded the Nobel Peace Prize.

1992: General Saw Maung steps down as chairman of the SLORC, and General Than Shwe assumes power as prime minister and defence minister.

1997: Burma is admitted to the Association for Southeast Asian Nations (ASEAN). The SLORC is renamed the 'State Peace and Development Council' (SPDC).

2000: Aung San Suu Kyi is placed under house arrest a second time (until 2002).

2001: The government releases over 200 political prisoners in a bid to improve the country's international image as it faces sanctions from various countries.

2003: Khin Nyunt becomes prime minister and proposes a convention for drafting of a new constitution as a pathway to democracy. Meanwhile, Aung San Suu Kyi is placed under house arrest for a third time following an attack on a NLD convoy by pro-government supporters.

2004 (January): An informal ceasefire between the Tatmadaw and the Karen National Union ends hostilities in one of the most significant developments in the country's decades-long civil war.

2004 (May): The National Convention on a new constitution begins and is boycotted by the NLD.

2004 (October): Khin Nyunt is replaced by Soe Win as prime minister following reports of an internal power struggle. The former is placed under house arrest.

2005: The capital is officially moved from Yangon to the central town of Pyinmana, later named Nay Pyi Taw.

2007: The National Convention is formally closed by the military. Anti-government protests led by monks spark the Saffron Revolution, leading to a brutal military crackdown. Aung San Suu Kyi makes her first public appearance since 2003. General Thein Sein takes over as prime minister.

2008: The SPDC proposes a new constitution, which reserves 25 per cent of seats in Parliament for the military, and bars

Aung San Suu Kyi from holding the office of president. Cyclone Nargis hits the Irrawaddy Delta in southern Myanmar, killing approximately 140,000 people. The referendum on the new Constitution continues despite the humanitarian crisis.

2010: Government announces new election laws. The military-backed Union Solidarity and Development Party (USDP) claims resounding victory. The NLD boycotts the election, amid widespread claims of fraud. The government marks the election as the country's official transition from military rule to civilian democracy. Aung San Suu Kyi is released from house arrest.

2011: Thein Sein is sworn in as president of a new, quasi-civilian government. The NLD re-registers as a party ahead of the parliamentary by-elections.

2012: NLD candidates win the by-elections, and Aung San Suu Kyi is elected along with other NLD members. She officially becomes the Leader of the Opposition in Parliament. The government also lifts a ban on independent media. Renewed communal clashes between Buddhist and Muslim communities in Rakhine State.

2013: Riots break out between Muslim and Buddhist communities in Meiktila in Mandalay Region. Six Muslims are jailed.

2015 (March): The National Ceasefire Agreement is signed between the government and sixteen rebel groups.

2015 (November): The NLD-led by Aung San Suu Kyi wins a landslide victory in the General Elections.

2016: U Htin Kyaw is sworn in as president, and a new office of the State Counsellor is created for Aung San Suu Kyi, given the ban on her holding office of the president under the 2008 Constitution.

2017: Rohingya militants attack police outposts in Rakhine State, triggering a brutal crackdown by military forces that results in over 700,000 Rohingya fleeing the country and taking refuge in Bangladesh.

2018: U Htin Kyaw resigns, and U Win Myint is sworn in as president.

2020: The NLD wins the general elections again, defeating pro-military USDP candidates. The military claims voter fraud and irregularities in voter lists.

2021: Talks allegedly between the NLD and the military breakdown over the issue of voter fraud, and the military overthrows the newly elected government before it is able to take oath in Parliament on 1 February. Senior General Min Aung Hlaing takes over, declaring a one-year state of emergency. Senior NLD leaders, including Aung San Suu Kyi, are detained.

# Chapter 1

## Prologue: A Tragic Nation

From the Thought Warriors:

*I woke up around 6 a.m. on February 1 as my mother was talking on the phone and the first news I heard was that the military council had taken power. At that time, all telephone lines, TV channels and internet lines were cut off. At around 10 a.m., they announced that they would retain the country for one year. In the 21st century, this kind of situation is completely unacceptable and unbelievable. We already knew that there was no way for a bunch of dictators who had ruined the country for three generations to maintain the country for one year into better progress.*

*Coup in the 21st century? That's so unacceptable. The world is moving forward and the juntas keep pulling us backwards. We can't stand the coup.*

*Is Min Aung Hlaing insane? Why did he lead a coup while tons of benefits were getting through his unjustly founded businesses? His military folks will be mad at him for being a power-mad person and blocking their businesses.*

*1. People die.*
*2. Economy is downgraded.*

3. *Military-owned businesses are boycotted.*
4. *The sense of revolution (which should have been within us for a very long time) grows bigger.*

\* \* \*

The signs of a major political earthquake in Burma emerged around 3 a.m. on Monday, 1 February 2021, when reports came in of disruptions in telecommunications. Internet was down throughout the nation.[1] Around 7 a.m. came reports that Burma's Presidential power had been assumed by then First Vice President and Former General Myint Swe.[2] Sometime at this point, the news agency *Reuters* reported hearing directly from National League for Democracy (NLD) Spokesman Myo Nyunt, over the phone, that State Counsellor Aung San Suu Kyi, Burma's most famous leader, President Win Myint, and other NLD leaders had been taken into custody.[3]

As tanks and military vehicles patrolled the streets of Yangon, the Office of the Commander-in-Chief of Defence Services of the Tatmadaw, as Burma's military is known, released a brief six-paragraph statement. It read:

1. The Union Election Commission failed to address a large difference over the voting list used in the multiparty general election held on 8 November 2020. Although the request was made to call for the special session of the Second Pyidaungsu Hluttaw, it was failed to do so. The President refused the submission for two times to hold the National Defence and Security Council meeting.
2. The Union Election Commission will be re-constituted to continuously take appropriate measures, including checking the voting lists in accord with the law.
3. Prevention of the current outbreak of the COVID-19 pandemic will be effectively carried out with momentum.

4. Efforts will be made to recover the businesses closed by the COVID-19 pandemic as quickly as possible.
5. Emphasis will be placed as much as possible on restoring eternal peace all over the country, in accord with the Nationwide Ceasefire Agreement (NCA).
6. When these tasks have been completed in accord with the provisions of the State of Emergency, a free and fair multiparty general election will be held, and then, the assigned duty of the state will be handed over to the winning party meeting norms and standards of democracy. [4]

The statement (Notification No.1/2021) made no mention of when the aforementioned legitimate elections would be held. In August of 2021, Senior General Min Aung Hlaing, the chief architect of the coup, would extend the state of emergency until August of 2023.[5]

On 2 February 2021, a day after Myint Swe became President, approximately 400 elected members of Parliament had been placed under house arrest.[6] The next day, criminal charges were filed against both Aung San Suu Kyi and Win Myint.[7] Suu Kyi was charged with violating Burma's Export and Import Law when a search of her home on the day of the coup led to the discovery of communication devices that were allegedly imported illegally, while Win Myint was accused of violating the Natural Disaster Management Law for allegedly waving to a passing NLD convoy from outside the Presidential Palace.

Burma's decade-long opening, which Barack Obama on 19 November 2012 in Rangoon had described 'with confidence' as 'something that cannot be reversed',[8] was over. This itself was a matter of immense tragedy, and it was made worse by the considerable economic hardship and violence that followed, aggravating the misery produced by a raging pandemic.

I title this book *Tragic Nation* for a reason. It is not because Burma is necessarily prone to natural disasters or human sufferings, such as that caused by famine, war, and disease. Burma is also not a nation of sad, hopeless people. Quite to the contrary, comedy is a big part of Burma's social life and is also used as a tool of political protest. In my first ever visit to the country in the early 1990s, I attended a comedy show by the legendary Moustache Brothers of Mandalay. One of the puppets used in the show still adorns my office, along with another one I was given as a gift for a lecture I gave at the Mandalay Marionettes Theatre in 2016. In 1996, the Moustache Brothers were imprisoned for six years for their political satire against the military regime. Two years before their arrest, the country's best-known comedian, Zarganar (Maung Thura), was released after serving a five-year sentence for participating in the 8888 People Power Uprising. In August 2012, I organized a two-day workshop for Zarganar and his circle of former political prisoners to tell them about 'what was going on in the world' when they were in prison.

Burma is not a tragic nation because it lacks talent or resources to achieve progress and prosperity comparable to its neighbours. The country did have one of the most promising economies of Asia before the 1962 military coup, being the world's largest rice exporter.[9]

Burma does not suffer from a particularly unfavourable geographic location, either. Being at the crossroads of Asia's two largest civilizations and economies—China and India were historically Asia's two largest civilizations and economies, with China currently on top, followed by Japan, then India—Burma's past and present had enormous growth potential through commercial and cultural contacts. For Indians like myself, Burma historically was considered 'suvarnabhoomi' or the land of gold. The people and rulers of Burma looked to India not only for religion—Buddhism and Hinduism—but also for political and legal codes and institutions, which were adapted to the local context for their benefit. While the external environment has not always been kind to Burma—war (especially the devastating effects of the Second World War), foreign interventions, and eternally supported armed insurgencies undermined the stability of the country—Burma's relations with its neighbours, especially since the creation of the Association of Southeast Asian Nations (ASEAN) in 1967, has been generally positive and cooperative. Even though Burma did not join ASEAN until 1997, ASEAN helped shield Burma from international criticism and, to some degree, from sanctions through a 'constructive engagement' approach.

However, Burma has lost opportunities to advance due to setbacks that were mainly self-inflicted, and from forces that are mostly domestic in origin. This is the real tragedy of Burma, and the reason for the book's title. Even when its prospects looked bright, and the country seemed poised to take off, things fell apart. The February 2021 coup, which came after a decade of political and economic opening, represents the most striking example of the tragedy of modern Burma.

The sense of that tragedy can be seen in the confusion, frustration and despair that engulfed its population after the coup. They are vividly indicated in the following reactions, which I was able to document through a secret survey with the Thought Warriors inside Burma. Here are some comments from the Thought Warriors:

*I cried so hard every day for months since 1 February thinking I won't have a future that I want to live in.*

*I felt disappointed, hatred and disgust. I was heartbroken and felt upset for my dreams and intentions, which were ruined by a group of people that seek power. I also felt frustrated for not being a useful person for the revolution.*

*I felt like the world had turned upside down.*

*Still can't believe that it's the truth as I have never experienced this.*

*I was so shocked and worried about my beloved ones. I couldn't even believe it but when I looked at my phone, there was no signal and the internet data connection was cut off. I wanted to cry as*

*I couldn't make calls to my friends. I desperately wanted to tell my beloved ones to take care of themselves so bad, as if I was going to die at that moment. I still feel so anxious whenever I think about that day.*

*The world went black and I immediately got worried about my family.*

*I feel lost, sad and angry at the same time.*

*What a selfish and stupid act: destroying the future of a country for the sake of wealth and power by a small group of people, neglecting the people inside it.*

*The country became hell itself.*

The Burmese, it seemed, felt utter despair for their nation and hopeless for its future. In its seventy-three years of independence from Great Britain, Burma has had some form of military rule for fifty-three years. The 2021 coup violently punctuated any hopes for a democratic future in the largest mainland Southeast Asian nation.

## What Makes Democracy Possible?

Burma is a tragic nation, but this does not mean that its tragedy was inevitable.

There is a considerable body of writing on where and under what conditions democracy succeeds or fails in the developing world. Some scholars argue that stable democratic transitions require some background conditions, the presence of which explains successful democracies in the West and the lack thereof in the developing countries.[10] One of the background conditions that makes for successful democratization is a prior level of economic development and industrialization. For example, in 1988, South Korea's transition from a military dictatorship to a democracy was attributed to the country's rapid economic development between 1963 and 1988.[11] Another condition is the existence of a prior 'liberal' sociopolitical tradition that includes restraints on the ruler, religious tolerance, and protection of civil liberties like freedom of speech. For example, England's liberal tradition can be traced back to the enactment of the 1689 Bill of Rights that codified rules that governed freedom of speech, requirements for regular elections and restraints on the monarch's power. These changes allowed the Parliament to be more powerful than the monarch, setting the stage for the onset of democracy.

In developing countries, such conditions were absent when the end of colonial rule led to the establishment of new democracies, which then faltered quickly. There was no prior industrialization, no property rights or rule of law. Democracies were created on the basis of popular mobilization that resulted from anti-colonial movements. In short, the popular will was geared towards decolonization rather than towards democratization. When and where leaders of anti-colonial movements desired democracy after independence, it reflected in their political ideology and idealism. But it was secondary to national unity or nation-building. It was not backed by conditions like industrialization or liberal ideologies. Most developing countries started in extreme poverty, exacerbated by wars of national liberation or other forms of conflict. Another favourable condition for democracy is ethnic homogeneity, or the absence of major ethnic conflicts or cleavages. The absence of an ethnic or political group that enjoys a decisive numeric majority over other groups in the country can be helpful in maintaining democracy. In such cases, leaders would have to cultivate the support of minorities to stay in power through electoral means.

Going by these criteria, Burma had no chance of achieving stable democratic rule. Many of the conditions mentioned above that led to successful democratization were absent in Burma. Its leaders seemed to put more emphasis on national unity, and as argued by Prof. Mary Callahan, a Burma expert at the University of Washington, even to Aung San, democracy was secondary to national unity. On the eve of independence, Burma was beset with major ethnic cleavages. The largest ethnic group, the Bamars, enjoyed a clear majority and were confident of wielding power indefinitely. Did democracy even have a chance then?

On the other hand, Burma was and is hardly alone in being born into poverty and under-development; nor was it the only country that lacked the conditions identified above that led to stable democracies in the West. Many Southeast Asian countries did manage to create a modicum of democracy, even under the one-party rule. While these democracies were imperfect, or at best led to illiberal democracies, they did offer more freedom to their citizens, greater stability, and a considerable level of economic development. Burma could achieve neither democracy nor development, and while it did seem to achieve a degree of stability under different periods of military rule, it was fragile and short-lived at best.

Since its independence in 1948, Burma has had two 'democratic phases'. The first lasted from 1948 to 1962, although there was a major break in 1958 when the civilian government, facing an alarming surge in ethnic and communist rebellion, temporarily surrendered power to the military. While an elected government resumed in 1960, it was cut short by the coup led by General Ne Win in 1962, this time for an indefinite period.

The second experiment with democracy took shape in 2011, first in a limited form under a former military leader, Thein Sein, who rode to power after the 2010 elections, which were boycotted by the NLD. The NLD participated and won the 2015 election, establishing in 2016 what seemed to be a more fully instituted if flawed democratic experiment, until it was cut short by the coup of 1 February 2021.

Why did Burma's second experiment with democracy prove as short-lived as the first one after independence? This is the story of *Tragic Nation*.

The next two chapters, 2 and 3, of the book look at different, if not alternative, ways of explaining Burma's political tragedy, especially focusing on geography, culture, ethnic and racial diversity; the impact of war and foreign intervention; and the role of an isolationist foreign policy, and the self-propelling and self-fulfilling logic of military regime survival. These provide some necessary background not only to the structural conditions and context of Burma's political life, but also to international and domestic developments—some forced on the country while others from the choices made by its leaders, without which Burma might have developed in an entirely different and perhaps brighter direction.

Chapters 4 and 5 examine key political developments and turning points in Burma's politics from its independence to the 2021 coup, including the military-engineered 2008 Constitution and the two governments of the 2011–21 period that followed. Along with the previous chapters, Chapter 4 offers a window to the longer-term forces and factors behind Burma's enduring political crisis. Chapter 5 complements this with a picture of the more proximate causes behind the 2021 coup.

Chapters 6 and 7 look at the immediate fallout of the coup; how it tore into the country's domestic fabric; the way its military rulers went about imposing their authority, brutally but precariously, on the nation; the emergence of resistance to the coup by the ousted political party NLD, unarmed civilians, newly formed militias, and long-standing ethnic groups and armies in the country.

Chapters 8 and 9 look at the response of outside players, especially ASEAN and the major Western and Asian powers.

Chapter 10 provides an overview of the prospects for Burma after the coup, and speculates (yes, there can only be speculation) on the direction in which the political and military balance in the country might evolve, leading to stabilization or civil war without an end.

This is not intended to be a traditional academic book. It is not meant for a specialist audience of Southeast Asian studies scholars. Rather, it is written for a wider international audience who may have little previous knowledge of the country. I have written this book within the constraints of being unable to visit the country in the immediate period before and after the coup, due to COVID-19 travel restrictions and the disruptions caused by the coup itself. I rely much on available primary and secondary sources, including media sources that can be confusing and conflicting. There are bound to be errors and limitations, for which I fully apologize and take sole responsibility. The book's narrative ends in April 2022.

A big part of my goal in writing this book is to motivate and excite the younger generation in Burma to deploy their newfound political consciousness to chart and lead a better democratic future for their country. It is my hope that, by the end of the book, the readers will do just that.

# Chapter 2

## Explaining Burma I:
## Things That Stay the Same

### Is it Geography?

When Burma was still under military rule before 2011, I bought a book from the streets of Rangoon entitled *A First Geography of Burma*. Intended as a primary school text, it noted that if one took a bullock cart on a straight path from the northern limit of Burma to its southern tip, going fifteen miles a day, the entire journey would take a hundred days. Doing the same from the widest middle part of the country, at the same speed, would take forty days. Travelling around the coastline of Burma would take ninety days. Doing the same in the narrowest strip of Tenasserim—the long narrow southern part of the country that reaches the upper Malay peninsula—would take only five days.[12]

With a total land area of 676, 577 sq. km (261, 228 sq. miles), Burma is the size of Texas. In comparative terms, it is no small country. It is the second-largest country in size in Southeast Asia after Indonesia but the largest country in mainland Southeast Asia, eleventh largest in Asia, and fortieth largest in the whole world. The distance between the north and the south runs 2,000 km. Burma shares borders with five nations. The largest border is with China (2,185 km/1,360 miles), followed by Thailand (1,800 km/1,120 miles), India (1,463 km/910 miles), Bangladesh

(193 km/120 miles), and Laos (235 km/145 miles).[13] This makes up for 5,858 km in international borders, while its coastline stretches to over 2,800 km.[14] The majority of the population, some close to 70 per cent, lives in rural areas.[15]

Burma is not an isolated nation, even though it pursued a foreign policy of self-isolation after the 1962 coup. Lying at the crossroads between India and China, the areas of modern Burma was known to ancient India as Suvarnabhoomi. It was a major hub of trade and transmission of culture and religion, especially Buddhism but also Hinduism, between India and Southeast Asia. Some of the earliest contacts with India were established when ships sailed from India's coastal centres to Southeast Asia by hugging the coast. That changed with the advent of larger vessels, which could sail directly to Indonesia and Malaya through the Andaman Islands.

Geography is key to geopolitics. Burma has cultural and commercial connections with both mainland and maritime Southeast Asia. Mainland connections helped with the development of Burma's population through migration, while maritime connections were important for cultural development. For example, the majority ethnic group in Burma, the Bamar people, migrated from southwest China, while migrations from India's east coast, helped establish the ancient port city of Pegu. Burma's emergence as a major centre of Theravada Buddhism was a result of links with South Asia—Sri Lanka in particular.

Geography can be a blessing as well as a curse because of the different consequences it can have on a country's political landscape. In Burma's case, geography cursed the country by allowing for ethnic rebellions of groups straddling the border, who are able to conveniently retreat into neighbouring countries when attacked by the Burmese military. Cross-border insurgencies have been a major part of Southeast Asia's history, both before and after the Second World War when 'nation-states' were established. Having long borders with China, India and Thailand has been a mixed blessing. Although China formally stopped supporting communist insurgencies in Southeast Asia in the 1970s, its support to some ethnic groups in Burma still continues. This took place through the support of ethnic Chinese communities in Burma for communist and ethnic insurgencies. The continuous support for insurgencies has helped keep alive the defiance of ethnic groups such as the Wa, with its army of 20–30,000, against Burma's central authority. The long border with Thailand has seen many inter-state conflicts between the two countries, in many of which the Burmese had the upper hand. Post the Second World War, Southeast Asia witnessed many instances of spillover of the Burmese military's armed confrontation with ethnic groups, like conflict against the Karens spilling into Thailand, fight against the Chins into India and against the Rohingyas into Bangladesh.

As illustrated by these examples, geography can also become a factor that affects a country's domestic politics. Geographical factors, like location, topography, and natural resource deposits, can lead to the dominance of one ethnic group over another and make a national society resistant to change. With few exceptions, like that of Pegu in mid-16th century, Burma's centre of political gravity, and its seat of power, has been in the dry zone of upper Burma. Historians Michael Aung Thwin and Maitri Aung-Thwin labelled it as the 'dry zone paramountcy of Upper Myanmar'. As they put it, 'Whereas it provides a predictable and dependable resource base (hence a familiar and comfortable socio-psychological setting), it also tends to constrain the system from expanding beyond a certain limit ... It creates a conservative mindset that resists fundamental (structural) change, one of the major themes of the history of Myanmar.' This has the effect of limiting political change, which is a constant reality that has dogged Burmese politics since the country's independence.[16]

But geography, like culture, is not destiny. The effects of Burma's geography on its domestic politics are not unique and can be likened to Javanese dominance in Indonesia or Hindu dominance in India. Other factors matter here in turning geography into a force for instability. A key factor is the way in which Burma's *political culture* evolved in relation to its majority Bamar ethnic group, who reside in the central plains and the ethnic minorities in the hills.

## What about Culture?

It is very important to distinguish between culture and political culture. Culture, in general, which forms out of a people's ethnicity, religion, language, etc. is more constant. Political culture, on the other hand, is more dynamic. It changes with new rulers and the introduction of new ideas. Outside political influences, like European colonialism, had an enormous impact in disrupting the traditional political culture of many non-Western countries and creating new ones to take their place. Burma's traditional political culture, centred on monarchy and Buddhism, which itself was an import from India, was transformed by the impact of British colonial rule.

Burma's decades-long relationship with authoritarianism does not mean that the country's traditional culture is hostile to democracy. On the contrary, the country's thirst for democracy and freedom is quite visible in the repeated electoral successes of the NLD and the public adulation of Burma's most famous citizen, Ms Aung San Suu Kyi. As a democracy activist, Suu Kyi is held in high regard both inside Burma and internationally. Her bravery in the face of military repression—she's been under house arrest for years multiple times and has been subjected to many violent attacks—has only added to her aura and repute. As a core element of Burma's traditional political culture, Buddhism provides a social contract theory of state as invoked by Suu Kyi in her book, *Freedom from Fear* (see note 16). Additionally, the Asian Values debate, a political ideology that became popular in the 1990s, defined common elements of society, culture and history among Southeast Asian nations, which aimed to foster a pan-Asian identity. This implied that Asians respect authority; prioritize society over self; and shun individualism and, by implication, individual political rights, in favour of collectivism. This did not hold much resonance in Burma.

The Asian Values debate promoted the idea of moral relativism as opposed to the prevailing Western notion of the universality of values and rights. Relativism highlighted the role of history and culture in the pushback against the Western understanding of human rights as an atemporal, ahistorical and aspatial concept, devoid of cultural specificities. To counter this perceived Western ideological dominance, one of Burma's former prime ministers Gen. Khin Nyint, opined about democracy in a speech he made on 30 August 2003:

> Democracy can only materialize after taking into account the historical background and objective conditions of the country concerned. It is also a truth that democratic practices differ from one country to another. There exist differences between the countries that practice democracy today and the historical background, geographical conditions as well as the culture and character of the people of our country.[17]

In the same vein, the future coup leader Gen. Min Aung Hlaing, in February 2018, made a similar culturally relativist argument:

> Each country's democracy has a different background. Myanmar's background of democracy is one thing. Thailand's democracy is different. We can only make use of good things we can apply, but we cannot say whose lessons should be applied to whom. In fact, a democracy or political system needs to be stable and not shaken. If it's stable, the people will have confidence and live happily.[18]

But traditional culture is not the same as political culture. Political culture is something that is acquired or developed through a combination of political struggles and experiences in the government. Noted Burma scholar Josef Silverstein talks about two divergent political cultures that evolved in Burma through colonial rule. In his view, colonial rule introduced modern values in Bamars, but kept the ethnic groups isolated and strengthened their traditional beliefs. This prevented dialogues and understanding, got the two to remain distant from each other, and stymied the emergence of a national political culture.

'Social order', write historians Michael and Maitrii Aung-Thwin, is 'the most important concern of the people of Myanmar throughout their history', while 'union solidarity' is 'the primary objective of the modern Burmese state'.[19] They write from what they call an 'indigenous angle of vision', wherein the authors privilege Burmese voices and Burmese agency in the analysis of their country's ups and downs, as opposed to an understanding of Burma that categorizes the country based on Western standards of strong/weak, democratic/undemocratic, prosperous/failing etc. They argue that 'the past decades in Myanmar did not turn out to be a (moral) struggle between democracy and authoritarianism, freedom and tyranny, the masses and the elite, but an (empirical) one between effective and ineffective rule, order and disorder, elites and other elites—in short, a struggle between the forces of strength and the forces of weakness'. To elaborate, this view implies that Burmese politics should not be seen from the Western prism of being necessarily or primarily a battle between the forces of good and evil, or between what is moral and immoral. Nor is it a struggle between freedom and tyranny. Rather, from the insiders' perspective, Burmese politics has historically been a contest of strength of political actors, or effective and ineffective governance, in which the desire of stability and order plays the decisive role. In this view, stability trumps democracy. This is in keeping with the cultural fabric of Burmese society, whether outsiders, especially Western analysts of Burma like it or not.

While this argument has merit, one has to keep in mind that it is far from unusual for many societies to value social order and continuity of tradition as fundamental necessities for political stability. Yet, social order does not necessarily require authoritarian rule. It can be achieved through democracy. Democratic politics can preserve social order, especially in multi-ethnic societies like India. It can have the same effect in imperfect multi-ethnic democracies like Malaysia and Singapore. And in Japan, an ethnically more homogenous but deeply conservative society, social order has not broken down but has been preserved by democracy, albeit under a dominant party system.

At the same time, authoritarian rule, especially if it produces benefits for only a select group, like the military, can lead to breakdown of social order, inviting unrest and protest, as in Indonesia under Suharto, or Thailand under military rule, or the Philippines under the Marcos dictatorship. In other words, authoritarian rule does not necessarily produce social order, and social order and democracy need not be incompatible.

As mentioned, Burma is also the place where the 'democracy versus Asian values' argument of the 1990s has been thoroughly discredited, as mentioned earlier about the lack of resonance in Burma with Asian values championing collectivism over individualism. The 'Asian values' debate started when its proponents claimed that East Asia's economic success came from a respect for authority that the proponents of Asian values saw as common to East Asian societies. Related to this was the claim that democracy was inimical to development. East Asia's 'economic miracle' happened because of authoritarian rule in key countries and territories: namely South Korea, Taiwan, Indonesia (under Suharto), and Singapore. China would soon join this group.[20] Its most famous proponent was Singapore's former Prime Minister Lee Kuan Yew. In a speech to the Philippine Business Conference on 18 November 1992, Lee said: 'The exuberance of democracy leads to undisciplined and disorderly conditions which are inimical to development.'[21] Speaking alongside Lee was his host, the Philippine President Fidel Ramos. Ramos retorted that the Philippines was under a dictatorship for decades, yet achieved little growth. Under Ramos, Philippines did quite well in terms of economic growth.[22] He privatized and deregularized several industries critical for economic development such as electricity, telecommunications, and banking oil. He reformed the taxation system and brought down external debt levels. These measures helped the Philippines be favourably compared with the other tiger economies of East Asia like Malaysia, South Korea, Taiwan, and Thailand. As Ramos put it: 'I can appreciate how brushing aside obstacles to his agenda can save a lot of time for any political leader, But this prescription fails to consider our ill-fated flirtation with authoritarianism not so long ago.'[23]

In December 1993, veteran Singapore diplomat Tommy Koh published an essay titled *The 10 Values That Undergird East Asian Strength and Success*. Of the ten, value number one reads:

> East Asians do not believe in the extreme form of individualism practiced in the West. We agree that every individual is important. However, he or she is not an isolated being, but a member of a nuclear and extended family, clan, neighborhood, community, nation and state. East Asians believe that whatever they do or say, they must keep in mind the interests of others. Unlike Western society, where an individual puts his interests above all others, in Asian society the individual tries to balance his interests with those of family and society.[24]

This is the clearest exposition of the communitarianism versus individualism strand of the Asian Values debate. By making the individual a part of groups like family, neighbourhood or nation, Koh provides an ideological justification for the claim that measures that benefit the nation are automatically in the interest of the individual. This homogenizes the needs of diverse communities and makes them subservient to the cause of the nation.

A few years after Tommy Koh's essay, on 7 June 1996, Lee Kuan Yew got himself tangled in Burma's democracy debate when he asserted that its military was the only institution capable of 'keeping the country stable and preventing civil war'. He was sceptical of Aung San Suu Kyi's ability 'to govern if ever she came to power'.[25] Lee added that she should 'remain behind a fence and be a symbol. I have visited (Burma), and I know that there is only one instrument of government, and that is the army'.[26] This led to protests at Singaporean embassies in the region, and Lee's effigies were burnt. Aung San Suu Kyi herself said: 'Mr Lee is a smart man, but he is not always right.'[27] In another restrained statement, she said, 'I accept that everybody has the right to express his opinions and beliefs freely, so I am not angry with Mr Lee Kuan Yew. But I would like Mr Lee Kuan Yew to understand that we in Burma are in need of a system whereby everyone has the right to free expression.'[28]

Is Burma's culture, overwhelmingly shaped by Buddhism, intrinsically opposed to democracy? Far from it. As noted, Buddhism provides a democratic understanding of governance. Aung San Suu Kyi understood this well and employed it for her cause of challenging military rule, when she noted in 1989:

> The Buddhist view of world history tells us that when society fell from its original state of purity into moral and social chaos a king was elected to restore peace and justice. The ruler was known by three titles: *Mahasammata*, 'because he is named ruler by the unanimous consent of the people'; *Khattiya;* 'because he has dominion over agricultural land'; and *Raja*, 'because he wins the people to affection through observance of *dhamma*' (virtue, justice, the law).

While such views may seem antiquated, Suu Kyi's words have parallels to social contract theories of the state in Europe, as expounded by Hobbes, Locke and Rousseau. Suu Kyi concludes that since the Buddhist view provides for the ruler to be chosen by popular consent and for governance to follow the law and norms of justice, the concept of elected and accountable government is 'not alien to traditional Burmese thought'.[29]

To be sure, Buddhism can also play into pro-government nationalism. As David Moe, who specializes in Buddhist nationalism and theology of reconciliation in Southeast Asia, notes, 'History tells us that Buddhist nationalists in Myanmar have imitated the militant Buddhist nationalists in Sri Lanka since British colonial rule.'[30] But as an early history of Burma published during the inter-war period, argues: 'It is incorrect to say the government as an undiluted despotism. It was that, and nothing more, at the capital and in its environs. But the king's arm was never very long or strong . . . Far away in the quiet countryside dwelt the mass of the people, a homely folk who were ruled by their elders and headmen . . . [They] had to deal out reasonable justice to folk among whom they were born and lived and died . . . The village in Burma . . . was a democracy to a very real degree, and the elders had their say in public affairs.'[31] In line with Suu Kyi's argument that democratic government was not alien to traditional Burma, this account reinforces our understanding of rural Burma experiencing democratic politics, while the monarchy was limited to urban areas.

Finally, cultural norms of respect for authority are not permanent. It depends on what the current form of governance is being compared against and how those in authority behave towards those they rule over. A Burmese youth I spoke to argued that the military did earn respect and legitimacy, for its role in the anti-colonial resistance that led to Burma's independence. But it lost it due to its subsequent oppressive role, despite the cultural deference authorities might enjoy in society:

> The Tatmadaw is often contrasted to the British of old even now due to oppression, lack of political expression, and general hypocrisy of a ruler that knows what's best for Burma but is self-serving. Japan is also [unfavourably] compared to [the military regime in Burma], but to a much lesser extent. In Burmese history, they helped liberate the colony from Britain

during the Second World War, only for the Burmese people to turn against them due to the similarities between Japanese and British attitudes towards the Burmese people. I'm sure if you read any book about British rule and the world war era in Burma, it will show a common pattern. I am sure I'm not the only one who thinks that way. There's some truth to the army being a great existence because they freed Burma. It wasn't a perfect liberation by any means, but there were a number of capable patriots seeking to run the country well. But there were many political events that came after, which turned the military into the form it is today.

What changed then? He continued:

From a cultural standpoint, the Burmese are actually fairly obedient to higher authorities. You can especially see that in the culture of family, where the younger must respect the older who are in higher standing. That being said, the military lost that respect after some brutal repressions from Ne Win's regime and onwards. Some pretty significant milestones came during Ne Win's rule. Even though the military performed a coup and installed Ne Win as leader in 1962, nobody in the country was particularly worried. They trusted the higher ups. However, a series of crackdowns especially starting in 1974 started changing that view. In 1974 Ne Win ordered shootings of rioters. They were responding to protests of students arguing with the military where UN general U Thant should be buried. The military, after the casket had been removed and stolen back and forth, decided to raid the students involved, resulting in injuries and deaths. Upon hearing the news, the general public began rioting. The crackdown was extremely brutal and news of it spread across the country despite the strong control over media. More protests and uprisings over the discontent and repression of the military continue to this day, with some notable ones being the 1988 uprising, the 2007 saffron revolution, and more.

To sum up, a cultural predisposition towards respect for authority is not permanent. It depends on how a government treats its own people. Governments that start off with high political support lose it fast and far when they start repressing political freedom and brutalizing their own people, no matter under the pretext. Burma is no exception.

## Ethnic and Racial Diversity

What about ethnic and racial diversity? One lingering image of Burma, famously articulated by J.S. Furnivall, is that of a 'plural society'. Furnivall, who became the National Planning Adviser to the Government of Burma after its independence, defined a plural society as 'consisting of several groups living side by side but separately, not united for common welfare or for any common desire for individual profit. In such a society, economic relations predominate over all other aspects of life; it is inherently unstable and, unless held together by some master force, must founder in anarchy'.[32]

This, of course, described the conditions during the colonial period, fostered in no small part by the policies of the colonial regime. But the idea lingered as a key factor behind Burma's political fragility, and consequently makes for a partial explanation for the country's slide towards authoritarian rule since it played into the hands of the military's self-image and self-legitimation as the only force that can keep the country together. As Robert Taylor, a Burma expert who has made decades-long contribution to the field of Burma Studies, notes, 'The dominant problem of Burmese politics since independence has been that of national unity. Because of the great ethnic, linguistic, and cultural heterogeneity of the population, no government has been able to meet all the demands placed upon it by various minority and tribal groups for political autonomy, economic development, and cultural independence.'[33]

'Burma,' the late Singaporean anthropologist Ananda Rajah, noted, 'has the unenviable reputation of having the largest number of ethnic insurgencies together with one of the longest-running communist insurgencies of any country in the world.'[34] What is even more notable is that the ethnic groups are themselves fractured, riddled with competition for leadership and allegiance, with different insurgent movements claiming to represent the same ethnic group.

The current population of Burma is 57,526,449.[35] Although there are some 135 indigenous ethnic groups in the country, the government recognizes eight major 'National Ethnic Races': Bamar, Chin, Kachin, Kayin (Karen), Kayah, Mon, Rakhine, and Shan.[36] In terms of percentage of the overall population, the Bamar are the majority at 68 per cent, followed by Shan at 9 per cent, Kayin (Karen) at 7 per cent, Rakhine at 4 per cent, and Mon at 2 per cent. The Tayoke/Chinese-Burmese comprise 3 per cent, Burmese Indians 2 per cent, and other groups, including the Wa, Naga, Lahu, Lisu, and Palaung, comprise 5 per cent of the total population.[37] Burma's population is predominantly Theravada Buddhist (89 per cent), the rest being Christian, Muslim, Hindu and animist.[38]

Ethnic diversity can lead to conflict and impede the development of a shared political culture conducive to democracy. Ethnic minorities residing in the outlying areas of ethnically diverse countries may develop a different political culture from those groups that live in the heartland. This has been the case with Burma. British rule not only aggravated ethnic/racial divisions but also led to differing exposure to ideas of nationhood and governance.[39] As Silverstein notes:

> The British continued the traditional separation of the Burmans and the minorities in the surrounding hill areas. In doing so, they deepened and widened the divide, not only physically, but culturally as well. By establishing indirect rule in the hill areas

the British ensured the survival of local cultures, traditions and leaders. The separation between the peoples of the two areas made it possible for the minorities to remain politically static while changes among the Burmans moved ahead. The British recruited members of the minorities for the police and the military, which aligned them with British power and, along with the spread of Christianity in the hill areas, strengthened the divide between Burmans and non-Burmans.[40]

Silverstein further notes that British colonial rule 'deprived the youth of modern education and the ability to interact with their Burmese contemporaries'.[41] The minorities in the hills did not take part in the nationalist movements during the inter-war period (1918–39), which was when the Bamar elite were most exposed to ideas of democracy and modernity.[42] This widened the gulf between the Bamar and the minorities and the basis of their lack of understanding and mistrust of the changing Bamar political culture. So, when Britain, the protector of minorities left, the latter's future prospects became riddled with doubts.[43]

To be sure, Burma is not the only country to have such diversity: Indonesia, the largest country in Southeast Asia, consists of some 1,300 ethnic groups, with 95 per cent native to the archipelago.[44] However, Burma's ethnic challenge is different. Being a mainland Southeast Asian nation, as opposed to Indonesia's maritime location and archipelagic structure, Burma is more vulnerable to cross-border movement and external support for ethnic insurgencies, making them harder to control, especially for groups like the Wa that receive direct access and support from China.

Ethnic conflicts bedevilled Burma immediately after independence. Since 1949, when the Karen National Defence Organization fought a bloody war with the Tatmadaw, numerous armed ethnic groups have carried out armed struggle against the state. According to one estimate, during a forty-year period between 1949 and 1989, over fifty ethnic political parties and militias operated in the country, from all the major ethnic groups including the Karen, Kachin, Shan, Karenni, Arakan, Chin, Mon, Kayan, Naga, Akha, Kokang, Palaung, Lahu, Wa, Mongla, and Pa-Oh. In addition, Burma also convulsed under some twenty mainly Bamar-led communist groups.[45] Periodic efforts at ceasefire and political agreements (such as during 1958, 1963, 1980, 1989, the 1990s and after 2011) have not led to long-term peace, largely due to the tension between 'the goal of a federal state on the part of most insurgent movements and the insistence by the military on a unitary state'.[46] After the partial ceasefire agreements with the Kachin, Kayah, and Shan in the 1990s, many new armed groups appeared. The largest armed group is the United Wa State Army (UWSA), commanding some 30,000 troops. While the conflicts have led to instability and disorder, they also created hundreds of thousands of refugees and internally displaced people. In 2019, some 100,000 refugees were reported to be on the Thailand side of the Thai-Burma border.[47] The estimate of Rohingya refugees in Bangladesh was close to 900,000 in 2021.[48]

The problem of ethnic diversity can be managed through political arrangements like decentralization of authority and federalism, as India and post-Suharto Indonesia have done. However, the idea of federalism has been controversial in Burma from the very beginning of its independence from British rule. A good sense of the resistance to federalism was provided by Aung San Suu Kyi in her reply to a question I asked her during a group video conference organized by the Council on Foreign Relations in November 2011. My question was:

Do you support a federal system for Burma? You said that the ethnic minority problem has to be settled politically. But we also need some institutional arrangements. And would you support, like, a Burma as a federation similar to, say, Indonesia or India?

Her reply:

> With regard to whether or not we believe in a federal system, first of all, let me say that the word 'federal' has been misused terribly in Burma. It has become a very controversial word simply because it was not understood properly or perhaps it was understood quite well or too well by some politicians, but they deliberately misused the word to get the kind of political, to create the kind of political situation they wanted. There were many—and I think there were many members of the army as well as some politicians—who equated federalism with secession. They said that federalism would mean the dissolution of the union. Of course, we know that this is not so, and so we had to try to make the people understand first what federalism means. And if they understand that federalism simply means the division of powers between the central government and the state government—governments and that this all has to be embodied in the constitution and the right of secession does not follow automatically, that also will or will not be in the constitution, and if they were to understand that, people would be much less afraid of the word 'federalism'. And then I think the people of Burma can decide what kind of system they want.[49]

Aside from this 'misunderstood' conception of federalism in Burma, a federal system does not necessarily bring about a sense of national identity that cuts across varied ethnic groups. To some degree, Burma's predicament has to do with the fact that there has been no vision of a national identity that supersedes ethnic identities. In a book completed before the February 2021 coup, Thant Myint-u, an American-born Burmese historian and the grandson of former UN Secretary-General U Thant, lamented:

The core strategy of the state since independence—of seeing Burma as a collection of peoples with the Burmese language and culture as the core—has failed, and will continue to fail . . . Race and identity have been at the heart of Burmese politics since the start of modern Burmese politics a hundred years ago. Colonialism and the immigration of millions of people from India brought an identity crisis that has not yet been resolved. Any brighter future will depend on Burma crafting a new and more inclusive identity, one not tied to race and one not based on a notion of uniting fixed ethnic categories . . . finding new sources of national identity separate from notions of ethnicity, and embarking on an aggressive agenda to end discrimination in all its forms, are elements of a conversation that has been almost entirely absent.[50]

And this remains of critical importance if Burma is to develop a long-term and stable democratic future.

# Chapter 3

## Explaining Burma II: Things
## That Might Have Been Different


Geography, and cultural (ethnic/racial) diversity, though not immutable, are not easy to alter. A country's boundaries can change with secession, war or foreign invasion. Independent Burma has never been subjected to outright invasion, although foreign interventions did occur. A more important factor has been the contestation over Burma's internal boundaries among ethnic groups and regions. But even that, while a constant source of violence and a legitimizing force for the military, has not been decisive in shaping Burma's fate as a nation. In any case, internal borders are closely tied to ethnic and racial diversity. These have been critical to Burma's fate as a nation. But they do not change much. Even if the Rohingya tragedy, which has been likened to ethnic cleansing, would have consumed their entire population, Burma's ethnic and racial diversity would not change by any consequential margin. This is because, according to the last available census reports from 2014, Burma's Muslim population declined from 3.9 per cent of the total population in 1983 to 2.3 per cent. This figure, however, does not include the 1.2 million mostly Rohingya Muslims of the Rakhine state, who are not 'enumerated' in the census and are 'officially considered a foreign population by the Central government'.[51]

Burma's fate might have been very different without a series of events that deeply influenced its trajectory since the Second World War: war, foreign intervention, foreign policy choices, and the emergence and entrenchment of a military regime. It is to these that we turn to in this chapter.

## War and Foreign Intervention

War and foreign intervention can have long-term consequences in weakening and destroying democratic development in postcolonial nations. Foreign intervention can take varied forms. One form comprises the long-term economic and political effects of wars fought on a country's soil by foreign powers. The legacy of the Second World War, when Burma was still under British colonial rule, continues to have a lingering effect on Burma's political dynamic, giving its armed forces justification to interfere in the country's political processes and ultimately seize power. Japan's invasion and occupation of Burma from 1942–45, and the subsequent war against Japan by the allied nations, caused major devastation of Burma's population, economy and infrastructure,[52] thereby robbing the post-independence government of much-needed resources for development and stabilization. D.G.E. Hall, one of the leading historians of Burma who had taught history at Rangoon University from 1921 to 1934, summed up the effects of the war in Burma in the following words:

> The Japanese occupation of Burma wrecked the country's economic system. Burma suffered more from the war than any other Asiatic country save possibly Japan herself. Many of her towns were reduced to ashes by Japanese air-raids. Her oil works, mining equipment and river transport systems were destroyed by the retreating British so as to be useless to the enemy. Allied air-raids kept her railways out of action. The Japanese systematically looted the country of machinery,

scientific apparatus and even furniture. All her normal external markets were lost. The complete stoppage of her rice export, through the failure of the Japanese to take it, led to mere subsistence farming . . . The Burmese had to comply with the very heavy demands of the Japanese for forced labour . . . [53]

Moreover, the war aggravated Burma's ethnic divisions that British colonialism, as noted in Chapter 2, had nurtured. From 1941, the British Special Operations Executive (SOE) organized guerrilla groups to destroy industries in Burma that could fall in the hands of the Japanese. The official British history of the SOE, *The SOE in the Far East* by Charles Cruickshank, a historian who served in the UK Ministry of Supply during the Second World War, notes that these guerrilla groups were mobilized 'as much on hostility to the Burmese of the plains as on loyalty to the British regime'.[54] As noted by a former diplomat and Asian security expert, Andrew Selth, 'The hill people were encouraged in their traditional racial enmity towards the Bamars and in their belief that, on the defeat of the Japanese and return of the British, they would be rewarded for their services in a particular way.'[55] After the war was over, there was an effort by Aung San, the former Governor of British Burma and father of Nobel Peace Prize winner Aung San Suu Kyi, and his followers to create a sense of national unity by praising the efforts of some ethnic groups (he singled out the Kachins and the Chins) who helped his Burmese National Army to fight the Japanese. However, this did not cut much ice, as the hill people also remembered that many Bamar people, including Aung San's comrades, had initially collaborated with the Japanese.[56]

After the Second World War, Burma suffered from another form of foreign intervention: externally supported insurgencies that were ideologically opposed to democracy and were seeking the overthrow of elected governments. The most serious of such challenges to democracy in the post-Second World War period were communist insurgencies, supported by the Soviet Union and in Southeast Asia's case, China. Southeast Asian countries, including Indonesia, Malaysia (of which Singapore was a part till 1965), Thailand and the Philippines faced foreign-supported communist insurgencies after the Second World War. The Communist Party of Burma (CPB), founded in 1939, revolted in April 1948. Some of these movements also carried out cross-border attacks. Chinese support for insurgencies in Southeast Asia did not cease until the 1970s under Deng Xiaoping, and in the case of Burma continued into the 1980s.[57] The party's propaganda machine and leadership then retreated into China, but elements of the CPB have reportedly reentered the country after the February 2021 coup. We will discuss what they are up to in the post-coup landscape in later chapters.

Burma served as the battleground not only for Britain's confrontations with Japan and the China-backed communist insurgency, but also for another unique form of foreign intervention. The Kuomintang (KMT) moved to Burma after being defeated and pushed out by the People's Liberation Army (PLA) once the Chinese Communist Party (CCP) won the civil war in 1949. The Kuomintang army is remembered as 'the first foreign invader of independent Burma'.[58] Numbering perhaps about 16,000 at its peak, and backed by the Central Intelligence Agency and the national government in Taiwan, the Kuomintang army carried out an offensive into China against PLA, thereby inviting the PLA's incursions into Burma as retaliation. KMT's presence violated Burmese sovereignty, in defiance of protests from the U Nu government against the UN. Their actions also caused a major shift in the Burmese economy and politics owing to their involvement in the cultivation and trade of opium. They occupied a sizeable part of Shan state, until their defeat in a joint operation by the PLA and Burmese armed forces in 1961, after which they retreated into Thailand and eventually evacuated into Taiwan. One major outcome of the KMT army's operation in Burma was to empower and embolden the Burmese military. In their effort to defeat the foreign army, the Burmese military took over the direct administration of Shan state, at a time when they also assumed the role of interim government between 1958 and 1960. Burma scholar David Steinberg argues that this may have encouraged a belief in the military and its political and administrative mission and capacity, which may have 'contributed both to the coup of 1962 and their belief in the military's capacity to govern the country'.[59] Robert H. Taylor, a Burma expert who once taught at the School of Oriental and African Studies (now SOAS University) in London takes a more cautious view, but still believes that the consequences of the Kuomintang army's presence in Burma had far-reaching effects on Burma's stability and democracy. He claims:

> It cannot be demonstrated that the KMT problem provided justification for the 1962 coup, but certainly the continued support provided the Shan, Karen and perhaps the Kachin rebels by the KMT, through their arms and training in the 1950's and early 1960's, was an important contributing factor. If the army had not had to contend with the KMT in the early 1950's, the insurgency problem would have persisted, if at all, on a much smaller level. The continual support of modern US weapons to the insurgents via Nationalist China increased the rebels' military power vis-a-vis the government. Being strong, the minorities felt they did not need to compromise their demands. Prime Minister Nu appeared to give in on many points to meet the demands of the minorities. The conciliatoriness on Nu's part appeared to Ne Win and the army as giving in to unreasonableness, and they intervened before Nu could conclude his efforts to restore domestic peace by granting greater regional autonomy.[60]

Thus, we can see China's interference in Burma came via two channels—as support for the CPB-led insurgency and by using the PLA to fight the KMT and their allies. The Burmese army, as a result, became more embroiled in managing internal security and began assuming a larger role in domestic politics.

## Foreign Policy: Neutralism to Isolationism

Aside from direct and indirect foreign intervention, a country's foreign policy orientation can affect its democratic development. Did Burma's foreign policy orientation, which went from non-alignment in the 1950s to isolationism from 1962, prevent the growth of democracy? To answer this, we must look back on the history of Burma's foreign policy orientation, starting with Aung San's vision for the country in the 1940s.

Aung San was a champion of pan-Asianism and regional cooperation. His vision for Burma's role in international affairs was not one of self-isolation, but that of active engagement.

'The one fact from which no nation, big or small, can escape is the increasing universal interdependence of nations. A free and independent Burma is quite ready to enter into any arrangement with other nations for common welfare and security etc.'[61]

Aung San believed that regional cooperation could compensate for Burma's weaknesses in the defence and economic spheres. In a paper titled 'Defence of Burma' dated 1945, he argued that the defence of Burma required a helping hand from neighbours.

'As an entity unto herself also, Burma must be strong in her defence and will need the helping hand of one or more of her neighbours at least—an entente of Burma, Indo-China, Thailand, Malaya, Philippines, East Indies, Yunnan, and Eastern India on this side of the Brahmaputra.'[62]

He called for the permanent establishment of a regional organization involving Burma and its neighbours, while simultaneously developing ad hoc forms of collaboration on specific issues of common concern. He saw no difficulty in co-existing peacefully with Burma's larger neighbours, India and China. He felt that Burma's destiny lay within the community of Southeast Asian and Asian nations, with whom it shared deep and historical bonds.[63]

Aung San was a staunch anti-imperialist, committed to ending British rule in Burma. His efforts were instrumental in the signing of the Aung San-Atlee Agreement in January 1947, which promised Burma full independence within one year.[64] He also helped found many political groups and institutions, including the Tatmadaw and is widely revered as the Father of the Nation. Aung San's life came to a cruel end six months before the British granted the country independence. In another unfortunate twist of fate that reinforces the notion of Burma being a tragic nation, the nine people including Aung San, who were assassinated by a small group of men impersonating soldiers on 19 July 1947, were among the most promising and experienced political leaders of Burma. Had they lived, Burma would have experienced a robust period of nation-building like that of its neighbour, India. On 4 January 1948, Burma became an independent nation, but soon got mired in an intractable civil war that began in August 1948, between the Burmese military and insurgents.

After Aung San's death, independent Burma's first Prime Minister U Nu took on the mantle of nation-building. Under U Nu , Burma pursued a policy of non-alignment. U Nu was a close ally of Indian Prime Minister Jawaharlal Nehru, himself a key architect of the Non-Aligned Movement (NAM). The seeds of NAM were planted at the 1955 Asia-Africa Conference in Bandung, Indonesia. Burma under U Nu was one of its five official sponsors, under a group known as the Conference of Southeast Asian Prime Ministers, also called the Colombo Powers. NAM originated in the aftermath of the Korean War to balance the two major power blocs of the US and the USSR. A forum of 120 countries not formally aligned with or against NATO or the

Warsaw Pact, NAM was established by postcolonial developing nations like India, Egypt, Ghana and Indonesia. This group aspired to play an influential role in mediating regional conflicts like the Indo-China War of 1962. In 1957, U Nu appointed his closest confidante and advisor, U Thant, as the Burmese Ambassador to the UN. In 1961, U Thant received a unanimous vote from the General Assembly to be appointed as the third Secretary-General of the UN, giving Burma global recognition.

U Nu was unceremoniously ousted from power by General Ne Win on 2 March 1962. A year after Burma's independence, in January 1949, Ne Win was appointed by U Nu as Chief of the Armed Forces (Tatmadaw). In the late 1950s, when the Burmese economy became stagnant and the civilian government was unable to restore order and stability, U Nu invited General Ne Win to assume leadership for a caretaker government. Ne Win's government managed to restore order, hold elections in 1960 and handed back power to the victorious U Nu. Barely two years after his electoral victory, U Nu was overthrown in what would become Burma's first period of military rule.

After seizing power, Ne Win did not cut off all links with the outside world. He continued to follow U Nu's policy of neutrality and remained active in NAM. Burma continued to seek and receive economic and military aid from major powers, including the US and Britain, aside from reparations from Japan.[65] The regime also engaged China and the Soviet Union, with Ne Win himself visiting Moscow, Washington DC as well as Beijing.

However, Ne Win also initiated Burma's eventual isolationism by refusing to join the Asian Development Bank founded in 1966. While initially active, Burma eventually withdrew from NAM in 1979, as it believed NAM was not 'non-aligned' enough.[66]

The most significant part of Ne Win's isolationism, however, had to do with Burma not joining ASEAN, which was theoretically open to all Southeast Asian nations when it was founded in 1967. In his desire not to antagonize China, which was deeply suspicious of ASEAN as a successor to SEATO and as a Western front against China, Ne Win declined membership.[67] When ASEAN eventually decided to grant Burma membership, it was amid increasing Western objections to Burma's political repression and its abysmal record of human rights abuses.[68]

Going back to our question from earlier in the chapter—Did Burma's foreign policy approach have an impact on their political development?—it can be argued that isolationism limited the exposure of an authoritarian regime to ideas of human rights and democracy that were promoted by the West. This might also explain why Burma chose to limit regional integration and cooperation by not joining ASEAN. If so, this was certainly ironic, since on this score, Burma's military had little to fear in terms of being contaminated by ideas of democracy and human rights. ASEAN was founded out of a shared disposition towards authoritarianism and was firmly opposed to Western promotion of democracy and human rights. Indeed, ASEAN itself functioned as a veritable club of authoritarian or semi-authoritarian states since its founding in 1967; its original five members included military regimes in Indonesia, the Philippines and Thailand.

Another way in which Burma's foreign policy affected their political development has to do with the country's lack of integration with the regional political economy, especially East Asia's export-led growth strategy pursued by neighbours such as Thailand, Singapore, Malaysia and Indonesia. This might have undermined the prospects for democratization in Burma. Supporting this view is a body of writing that holds that rapid economic growth fostered by foreign investment and trade relationships can lead to political change, especially by creating a 'liberalizing middle class'. Scholars have long considered democracy the result of an urban, educated and wealthy middle class. Increasing economic development is considered to engender a 'civic culture' of the middle class, as citizens become more vocal in demanding political representation and the state's accountability to its citizens. Burma's democratization did not benefit from this dynamic, however. But, as some scholars have argued, this has proven to be a bit of a myth as rapid growth and the rise of a middle class did not bring about democratic transition in Singapore, Malaysia, Thailand or Indonesia.[69]

India offers a good counterexample where the absence of a foreign investment-friendly, export-led government need not stymie a nation's democratic development. Until the early 1990s, India stayed away from globalization and regional economic integration, pursuing a socialist economic agenda that was especially hostile to multinational corporations. This period was also marked by high tariffs against foreign imports, a good deal of which still remains in place today. But Indian democracy did not suffer any long-term setback, except for an authoritarian interlude from 1975 to 1977, which had little to do with the country's economic development approach.

The counterexamples mentioned above seem to point towards the understanding that Burma's lack of democratic development and transition from military rule cannot be attributed to its foreign policy isolationism. Aung San's preference for regional cooperation and Pan-Asianism may have created an open and inclusive Burma. His anti-imperialism translated into Burma's preference for non-alignment and neutrality. U Nu's active participation in NAM did bequeath a larger international role for Burma, but his successor Ne Win championed neutrality to the extent of pulling Burma out of NAM and giving birth to a long period of international isolation. Did isolation curse Burma's democratic experiment?

I argue that all the above factors did play a role and contribute to the breakdown of Burma's democratic experiments, especially (1) the colonial legacy in creating a divided political culture between the majority and minority ethnic groups; (2) the path taken by founders in placing unity over liberal democracy and diversity and (3) foreign policy isolationism and a socialist economic policy that distrusted foreign investment and stayed away from regional and international economic cooperation projects. But these factors are not wholly unique to Burma and do not, on their own, guarantee the breakdown of democracy. In fact, as mentioned previously, there have been other Southeast Asian cases where these factors have not led to perpetual military rule. However, when these reasons operate in tandem, they can form the basis of ungovernability, as was the case with Burma. Apart from these three factors, another important reason for democracy's failure in Burma's case has to do with the self-fulfilling logic and dynamic of regime survival.

Strengthening our understanding of challenges to democracy in newly independent nations, Burma's former Prime Minister U Nu presciently noted the following:

The enemies of democracy, such as have surfaced in countries in which democracy is just putting down roots, fall into three categories:

1. Some politicians begin in the approved fashion, with victory at the polls. But later, because of either moral turpitude or incompetence (or both) on their part, public confidence is forfeited, and they find themselves facing electoral defeat. In such a situation they may delay elections or rig them. If despite their unfair practices they should still lose, these men will cling to power by suspending the people's rights and by outright seizure of the government by unlawful military means.

2. Some politicians are tools of foreign powers. They know full well that they do not command the respect of their people. They also know full well that, lacking this respect, they have little or no chance of winning votes in a free election. So they take the offensive against the democratic system and denounce all free elections. Finally they beg for assistance

from foreign governments likely to support them, and they go into rebellion against their own government.

3. Some military officers, being only human, begin to covet the power of the politicians. And since they have the weapons, they are tempted to use them as a readier and surer means of gaining political control, rather than risk defeat in free elections.[70]

While these challenges can apply to most developing nations that have experienced democratic breakdowns, Burma's case is particularly apt for the third kind: the military acquiring a taste for political power.

## The Logic of Regime Survival

U Nu's reflections fit closely with insights from political science as to why postcolonial states might suffer from internal instability in general and democratic breakdowns in particular. According to this view, most postcolonial nations suffer from two critical challenges. The first is the 'weakness' of the state.[71] Australian Mohammed Ayoob, a leading scholar of security issues in the Third World, characterizes this weakness as a problem of 'legitimacy of the state structure', reflecting the fact that postcolonial states 'have not developed the capacity to ensure the habitual identification of their inhabitants with the post-colonial structures that have emerged within colonially-dictated boundaries'.[72] Ayoob claims that citizens of newly independent nations did not develop an adequate sense of trust in postcolonial institutions that were largely remnants of colonial structures, i.e., those institutions that routinely marginalized their lives when they were colonial subjects were also the ones that impacted their lives as citizens of independent nations.

This problem of identification reflects a lack of synthesis between the postcolonial nation-state and the traditional structures of society. Udo Steinbach, a German scholar of the politics of the developing world, finds the explanation of this disjunction, or what he calls 'national fragmentation', in the political domain. According to him, 'the concept of 'nation', introduced by colonial powers or by small elites who saw in it the prerequisite for the fulfilment of their own political aspirations, materialized in a way which went against 'territorial, ethnic, religious, geographical or culto-historical traditions'.[73] This disjuncture between how the colonial powers created what eventually became the postcolonial nation and the pre-existing social structure set the stage for postcolonial nations gaining independence with low legitimacy in the eyes of the citizens.

The gap between state and nation was not bridged by the 'national movements' against colonialism, for, as pointed out by Barry Buzan, Emeritus Professor of International Relations at the London School of Economics and Political Science, the nationalist forces that drove the struggle against colonialism were 'not the positive unity of a coherent national group, but the negative one of common opposition to occupying foreigners'.[74] Rarely in the postcolonial world have states retained the loyalty and identification of the whole of society and citizen population, including those who fought against colonial domination, at the postcolonial stage. This, in turn, gives rise to a multitude of security challenges and problems for the newly independent state, manifested primarily, though not exclusively, in separatist and secessionist movements. Examples of this abound throughout the post-Second World war era like the Moro rebellion in the Philippines, the Eritrea problem in Ethiopia, the Tamil problem in Sri Lanka and the Polisario in Morocco.

The second challenge for postcolonial nations concerns not the state but the regime that presides over it. The notion of 'regime security' refers to the ability of the ruling group or elite to successfully manage and overcome problems of governance while maintaining the continuity of its authority. Thus defined, regime insecurities may or may not reflect the tendency of the regime to use political power for selfish ends or ensure its self-preservation through the use of violence. Although such practices are common in postcolonial nations, it is important to bear in mind that the postcolonial world is also replete with examples of regimes that are genuinely committed to the goal of national development and enjoy considerable mass support, but also do not escape serious challenges to the continuation of their authority because of their failure to build indigenous institutions to cope with the political consequences of modernization and development. In Western countries, the question of governance and the durability of leadership is a political rather than security issue, settled through agreed and well-defined constitutional rules and procedures, which are mediated by stable political institutions. Most postcolonial states, on the other hand, tend to exhibit a very low 'level of consensus on fundamental issues of social and political organization'.[75] Given the lack of consensus, political institutions are correspondingly weaker, and the prevailing mode of political rule is likely to enjoy a low level of legitimacy, even when the regime is committed to the long-term goal of development. A regime facing such a challenge could either resort to repression or seek legitimacy by rapidly bringing to its people the fruits of development.

Viewed in this perspective, a key political and security predicament of the postcolonial state is not just the problem of the protection of core values of the state, such as political sovereignty, territorial integrity from external threats and economic well-being, but also the problem of maintaining national cohesion and ensuring regime survival in the domestic context. Two additional realities about security in the postcolonial world are also important here.

1. Regime security trumps national well-being: A careful look at the national and international security policies of many authoritarian postcolonial states shows that regime security

considerations are not easily distinguishable from national or societal security and welfare considerations. This is because regimes or ruling elites try, and frequently succeed, in presenting their own legitimacy problems as a national and state security problem. Thus, the overall perception and agenda of state and national security may actually reflect the regime's concern with its own survival. More often than not, invoking the banner of state and national security is deemed necessary to justify the use of violence against domestic opposition factions, who question the legitimacy of their own government.

2. External challenges to internal security: Internal security considerations, related to both the state and the regime, act as a major determinant of the perception of, and response to, external challenges. In other words, a state's response to external events is often defined by its regime in terms of the latter's own perception of the potential impact of such events on its own domestic vulnerabilities. In this context, threats to regime security need not be from a purely domestic source. External events and agents could affect regime security, either by manipulating the regime's domestic opposition or by creating the image of an alternative political order. Since the legitimacy problems of a regime concern the ideological and political belief-systems of the population, external events could dominate the 'national security' agenda of a regime, even when they do not pose a direct military threat to the state. As such, regimes may define the seriousness of external threats in terms of the extent to which they project alternative political and ideological models to the ones presided over by them. As Bahgat Korany, Professor of International Relations and Political Economy at the American University in Cairo, succinctly points out in the case of the Iran-Iraq war (1980–88), the Iraqi decision to launch an attack on Iran was based not so much on

fear of revolutionary Iran's military might (which was seriously depleted by purges and desertions) or the desire to overturn a border agreement, the terms of which had been seen as a humiliation by the Iraqi regime. Rather, it was the fear that 'Iran's Shi'a dominated revolution was encouraging Iraq's Shi'a majority to revolt and topple the Sunni-dominated state elite'.[76]

Both these problems were acute in postcolonial Burma, where the military not only faced internal rebellions, but also feared the subversive impact of the West's campaign for human rights and democracy promotion. They played into the hands of the military in seizing and maintaining its hold on power. And in doing so, the Tatmadaw developed an elaborate and extremely tight system of regime maintenance that employs inducements of privileged lifestyle and harsh penalties for dissidence and defection, a system that a Burmese interviewee described to the author as the 'military hostage system'. Through its training system, provision of separate and superior living conditions, privileged access to essential services, propaganda, and the arrangement of opportunities for gaining economic benefits through corruption, the Tatmadaw has created a parallel society, a separate culture and network of identity and privilege that one would lose if they were to defect from the military.

Defecting from the regime, in both civil government and military service, implies rebelling against a system that is geared towards ensuring a separate sociocultural identity for soldiers and officers. This helps create an acute sense of dependency about the cadres' livelihood and even their physical survival. Andrew Selth, one of the most seasoned observers of the Tatmadaw, described the system as

> one in which many members of the armed forces, particularly the more senior officers, benefit financially from their rank and positions. Extra-curricular sources of income take many forms.

All officers profit directly and indirectly from their shares in the Tatmadaw's massive public companies, Myanmar Economic Holdings Ltd. (MEHL) and the Myanmar Economic Corporation (MEC). Through them, more than 130 business entities can be linked to the armed forces. Many officers also have quasi-legitimate interests in private businesses, often exercised through family members. They also benefit from a variety of unethical and illegal business arrangements. More junior officers seem to rely mainly on graft and corruption to line their pockets. Even the ORs use their military positions and access to scarce resources to make 'tea money', for example, by dabbling in the black market or by extorting payments from members of the public. As one Yangon businessman has lamented, 'Either you have green (US dollars) or real khaki green, or you can't do business and make real money in my country.'[77]

But not all the instruments of the system are black or corrupt or based on material inducements alone. This system also relies on benefits, of education, and a better life for poor people who choose to join the military, including access to essential services such as electricity and medicine.

The hostage system was based on indoctrination through a disciplinary culture that rewards obedience and loyalty over performance capacity, especially among junior officer ranks like second lieutenants. Punishment against any signs of disobedience is especially harsh during training.[78] Violators serve harsh prison sentences, while family members also face retaliation. The system creates a fair degree of separation between the soldiers and the society they are meant to protect, making it easier for them to indulge in excesses that routinely become human rights abuses.

Given this mindset, why did the military accept free elections and democratization after 2008? Because this seemed to be the right time for making limited concessions as long as its privileges were not severely compromised. Aware that it might be losing legitimacy and support, the Tatmadaw leaders, ever more concerned with regime survival, including the personal survival of the leaders, had to accept some change, but within limits and without a sense of irreversibility. As I wrote, after a visit to the country, in 2012:

> The reforms in Myanmar are being largely driven by . . . [a] sense of growing frustration with the status quo, a desire for positive change among the Myanmar elite, including sections within the armed forces to break the country's isolation and catch up with its neighbours and the world at large, and the personal image and approach of the current President [Thein Sein] . . . A real reason behind reforms could also be a calculated sense of regime security on the part of the military, which felt it could afford to step back a bit after having enacted a constitution that entrenches its hold on power for the long term.[79]

The military tried to fashion a political solution that A Melissa Crouch has aptly described as 'authoritarian constitutionalism' and 'preemptive constitution-making' by authoritarian regimes.[80] Authoritarian constitutionalism refers to 'the manipulation of the constitutional order by authoritarian rulers through constitutional means', under the assumption that there is, or was, a democratic constitutional order in the first place. Pre-emptive constitution-making inhibits the transition to liberal democracy and instead contributes to authoritarian resilience. In other words, constitution-making can pre-emptively lead from one form of authoritarian rule to another. In Burma, the 'military-state' constitutionalism can be viewed as a variation of authoritarian constitutionalism, which facilitates the co-existence of the military, civilian actors, and institutions. Three key elements of this form of authoritarian constitutionalism, argues Crouch, include the political leadership of the military, a national ideology used to the advantage of the military, and rule by a centralized administration. Through this approach, the military can control all branches of government.

The Tatmadaw has thus entrenched its role in political governance by indulging in constitution-making. This is a preventive tactic commonly used by authoritarian rulers to thwart a transition to a constitutional form of democracy, wherein militaries are legally required to protect the rights and freedoms enshrined in a constitution. However, pre-emptive constitution-making does not always succeed. Over time, the Opposition, which had been deprived of power, can see through the scheme and demand changes, either through the street or the ballot box. The defects of Burma's 2008 Constitution, like the reservation of 25 per cent seats for the military in the Parliament or the permanent ban on Aung San Suu Kyi from national leadership because of a provision obstructing a candidate with a foreign spouse assuming leadership position, were well recognized by the opponents of the Burmese military. Protestors demanded genuine constitutional reforms, and when the prospect of those demands coming to fruition increased after the 2020 election, the military swooped in and once again set the clock backwards.

# Chapter 4

## The Long Prelude

From the Thought Warriors

*I felt curious and appreciative of this significant history I got to experience. However, I have noticed that the military junta has had a strong authority in every aspect of governance even since before the coup.*

*The easiest way to figure out the future of the country is to revisit its own past. The 1962–2015 era of Myanmar is almost the exact thing that is going to happen in current Myanmar.*

\* \* \*

The seeds of Burma's February 2021 coup were planted at Burma's birth as an independent nation.

After decades of conflict, spanning 1824 to 1885, Burma had become a British colony in 1886. It was first ruled from British India, and then turned into a separate crown colony in 1937. On 4 January 1948, at 4:20 a.m., Burma got independence from British rule. This precise timing was chosen because it was the most auspicious day and moment according to Burmese astrology.[81] The political outlook for the country belied its auspicious beginnings.

## The Birth of Independent Burma

Indeed, an interesting exchange between two leaders of Burma's colonial master, Great Britain, reveals this ambivalence about Burma's future. Debating the motion on the Burma Independence Bill,[82] Prime Minister Clement Attlee expressed much hope for Burma's first Constitution:

> The production of this constitution and its adoption without dissent by the Constituent Assembly within a period of less than four months is, I think everybody will agree, a very remarkable achievement. Very few Constituent Assemblies have worked so quickly. The constitution has been described to me by experienced constitutional lawyers as being a remarkably able document. Its general principles embody the practice of Western democracies, and in particular those which obtain in the British Commonwealth . . . In fact, it is remarkable that in the constitution of the Upper House the minorities collectively have more seats than the majority race of the Burmese . . . We are all aware that the success of constitutions depends less on their actual provisions than on the way they are worked out and worked by the members. But if the spirit of co-operation that has been shown between the various communities in all these negotiations is exhibited in the future, I think that future should be bright.

On the other side, the leader of the Opposition and former Prime Minister Winston Churchill took a dramatically different view. He noted:

> Burma is an appendage of India and is likely to reproduce, though, of course, on a far smaller scale, the horrors and disasters which have overspread her great neighbour . . . There is no assurance that the power of the new Government

will be sufficient to maintain internal order, or, I might add, national independence against far larger and far more powerful neighbours. We stand on the threshold of another scene of misery and ruin, marking and illustrating the fearful retrogression of civilisation which the abandonment by Great Britain of her responsibilities in the East have brought and are bringing upon Asia and the world . . . On those grounds we shall, at the close of the Debate, move the rejection of the Bill.[83]

Churchill is, of course, a notorious defender of British imperialism and had opposed India's independence from Great Britain a few months earlier on 15 August 1947. His pro-imperialist and racist views no doubt influenced his attitude towards Burma's independence. While the situation in India was dire at the time of independence, Churchill's comments were proven wrong in India's long-term development. India was able to achieve relative stability and economic development in the medium and long term after independence, matching its former colonial master's GDP by 2020. Why did Burma fail?

A clue to this might come from a speech by Burma's most important leader, General Aung San, widely considered the Father of the Nation. His various speeches show him dismissing a number of familiar arguments against Burma's independence. In a speech to the Anglo-Burma Council on 8 December 1946, he outlined various challenges facing an independent Burma: its inability to defend itself, possible attack by neighbours, lack of financial resources and inadequate technical skills. He considered these challenges as far from insurmountable. On national defence, he argued:

'If the criterion of a nation's ability to defend itself is to be taken as a reason for the independence of that nation, then I am afraid no nation in the world deserves to be independent. As a matter of fact, only in an independent Burma shall we be able to arouse

the greatest enthusiasm on the part of the people to defend their
own country . . . ' [84]

What about the problem of national unity? Aung San was
acutely aware that Burma faced serious challenges on that score. His
vision was for an inclusive polity. As he put it:

' . . . what do we mean by national unity and what form it should
take. By national unity, we don't mean only top unity; we mean
the unity of the entire people, irrespective of race, religion, sex
and sectarian and party interests, in action and not in words for
national tasks and objectives.'[85]

Overall, Burma's leaders were optimistic about their country's
future, but not starry-eyed.

Burma's struggle for independence was led by the Anti-Fascist
People's Freedom League (AFPFL), spearheaded by Aung San.
The initial basic principles of Burma's Constitution were worked
out in February 1947 at the Conference of the Nationalities,
known as the Panglong Conference. It was convened by the Shan
and other non-Bamar groups. The Agreement of 11 February
1947 had Chin, Kachin and Shan agreeing to join the Union.
But other ethnic groups, including large groups like the Karen,
Mon and Arakanese, did not attend the Conference. The key issue
here was not democracy, but national unity. As David Williams,
founder and executive director of the Center for Constitutional
Democracy at Indiana University Bloomington, put it, 'Burma's
problems do not originate in a simple contest between democracy
and autocracy; instead, they grow from a struggle among identity
groups concerning constitutional power sharing.'[86]

Although national unity was of paramount concern, Aung San
did not think this goal could be achieved through a 'unitary state',
where all powers are concentrated with the central government.
Making a crucial distinction between such a 'unitary state', and a

'union', where the minority area will enjoy a degree of autonomy, in a speech to the AFPFL Convention on 23 May 1947, he explained:

> When we build our new Burma, shall we build it as a Union or as a Unitary State? In my opinion it will not be feasible to set up a Unitary State. We must set up a Union with properly regulated provisions to safeguard the rights of the national minorities.[87]

Some scholars have interpreted Aung San's wording, 'union', as implying a 'federal union',[88] but it is unlikely that he had in mind US-style federalism, in which the states retain significant powers, the major exceptions being control of defence, foreign affairs and monetary policy. More likely, Aung San had in mind something closer to the Indian federal system. The 1947 Burmese Constitution was influenced by the Indian Constitution, which was drafted by the Indian Constituent Assembly between 1946 and 1950, a much longer process than in Burma's case. The Indian Constitution made India a 'unitary system with federal characteristics', while the US is regarded as the opposite: a federal system with unitary characteristics.

As both Burma and India were British colonies, and Burma was administratively considered part of India by the British, Aung San thought it natural for Burma to look to the Indian Constitution for inspiration. In 1947, he invited Sir B. N. Rau, who was the Constitutional Advisor to India's Constituent Assembly. Sir Rau holds a significant place in the constitution-building projects of both India and Burma. Like Burma, independent India was trying to accommodate the needs of multiple ethnic communities who had difficult relationships—not only with each other but also with the central administration. To ensure the territorial integrity of the nascent independent nation-state, leaders believed in the creation of a strong centre, with relatively weak states, so the balance of power and authority could tilt towards the national government vis-à-vis the state governments. As such, the Indian Constitution makes the central government far more powerful, while giving the states power over matters such as education and policing. Powers over residual matters not explicitly given to the states reside with the Central government.

## The Union and Minorities

However, the lack of participation from the Karen, Mon and Arakanese in the February 1947 Panglong Conference made leaders of the ethnic minority communities apprehensive of how they might fare under a democratic system where the majority Bamars would hold decisive power. A constitution that makes for a strong centre and weak states, particularly with ethnic Bamars at the helm, could result in discrimination and aggrandizement against minority communities in the future. At the Panglong conference, Aung San dramatically proclaimed to the ethnic groups: 'If Burma receives one kyat, you will also get one kyat.' But the unity he was hoping for was proving elusive. Suspicion and distrust proved hard to shake off. In a bid to appease ethnic minorities, Aung San and other Bamar leaders agreed to grant autonomy to the minorities, especially the Chin, Kachin, and Shan who were considering the idea of a parallel, 'Frontier Areas Federation.'[89] According to the Frontier Areas Committee Enquiry Report of April 1947, the minority groups, particularly the Chin and Kachin, agreed to join the Federation of Burma, provided they could 'secede at any time'.[90]

Unfortunately, despite his desire to accommodate, Aung San never lived to see how the Constitution would work. He was assassinated on 19 July 1947, two months before the drafting of the Constitution was completed on 24 September 1947. (It came into effect on 4 January 1948, the day Burma formally gained independence.) His death also meant that his vision of Burma's unity remained unrealized. After his assassination, the leadership of the AFPFL went to U Nu.

Burma held elections to the 255-strong Constituent Assembly in April 1947. The resulting 1947 constitution created a multiparty, bicameral, parliamentary democracy. Like the Indian Constitution, it provided for fundamental rights for all citizens, and non-discrimination on the basis of birth, race, religion, and sex. Other similarities included the Preamble, fundamental rights, Directive Principles of State Policy and bicameral parliamentary democracy.[91] A notable difference was that Burma's Constitution gave its states the right to secede from the Union ten years after independence.[92] According to Chapter X of the Constitution, 'Right of Secession':

201. Save as otherwise expressly provided in this Constitution or in any Act of Parliament made under section 199, every State shall have the right to secede from the Union in accordance with the conditions hereinafter prescribed.

202. The right of secession shall not be exercised within ten years from the date on which this Constitution comes into operation.

203. (1) Any State wishing to exercise the right of secession shall have a resolution to that effect passed by its State Council. No such resolution shall be deemed to have been passed unless not less than two-thirds of the total number of members of the State Council concerned have voted in its favour. (2) The Head of the State concerned shall notify the President of any such resolution passed by the Council and shall send him a copy of such resolution certified by the Chairman of the Council by which it was passed.

204. The President shall thereupon order a plebiscite to be taken for the purpose of ascertaining the will of the people of the State concerned.

205. The President shall appoint a Plebiscite Commission consisting of an equal number of members representing the Union and the State concerned in order to supervise the plebiscite.

206. Subject to the provisions of this Chapter, all matters relating to the exercise of the right of secession shall be regulated by law.[93]

While the language of Chapter X of the Constitution seemed to allow the right of secession to 'every state', this was subject to limits and exclusions. Out of the five special areas envisaged by the Constitution, four were recognized as 'states', namely the Federated Shan States, Kachin State, Karen State, and the Karenni State. The Chins were designated as a 'Special Division'. Of these, the Kachin State and the Karen State were specifically excluded from this right of secession, while the right did not apply to the Chins who were not designated as a 'state'. Hence, only the Shan and Karenni States were permitted to exercise the right of secession after a period of ten years and subject to a plebiscite.[94]

The Indian constitutional expert B.N Rau would praise the Burmese Constitution's 'magnanimous treatment of special regions and racial groups'.[95] But the selective granting of secession rights created tension at the heart of the Burmese political order, between the aspiration for unity on the one hand, and the constitutionally provided right of autonomy and secession to certain ethnic groups and states on the other. As Robert Taylor observes, 'The first constitution of Burma tended to exacerbate the national unity problem because it defined majority-minority relations in bipolar cultural and ethnic terms. By appearing to grant rights to specific minorities and creating a quasi-federal system of ethnic states, this constitution simultaneously politicized and rigidified the institutional mechanisms of minority and Central government relations.'[96] Being accommodating to some minorities but not others made Burma's first Constitution unifying in theory but divisive in writing. It set the stage for the centre's confrontational relationship with ethnic minorities in the coming decades.

## Earliest Thinking on the Democracy Question

The desire for unity was also reflected in the administrative structure of the state, which was heavily centralized. Noted Burma scholar Mary Callahan argues that the Burmese leaders at the time of independence, including Aung San, put national unity above democracy, which concerns the granting of individual political rights to citizens. Callahan claims that Aung San and other leaders were more committed to socialism, especially the control over natural resources, than democracy. As she puts it, these leaders 'had no interest in the promotion of liberal democracy', arguing that: 'For Aung San and many of his colleagues, regaining control over Burma's wealth on behalf of the people of Burma was of paramount importance, not the array of legal provisions that protect individuals in a Western-style democracy.'[97] Callahan cites a writing by Aung San from 1941. 'What we want is a strong state administration as exemplified in Germany and Italy. There shall be only one nation, one state, one party, one leader. There shall be no parliamentary opposition, no nonsense of individualism.'[98]

It is a moot question whether Aung San's views might have changed by 1946. Democracy and unity need not be mutually exclusive. It is interesting that in her important speech on 26 August 1988, Aung San Suu Kyi cited her father's views on the importance of democracy for Burma's future, while also stressing the prior importance of national unity. 'I am participating in the struggle for freedom and democracy in the footsteps and traditions of my father,' said Suu Kyi, but

> to achieve democracy the people should be united. That is very clear. It is a very plain fact. If there is no unity of purpose we shall be unable to achieve anything at all. If the people are disunited, no ideology or form of government can bring much benefit to the country. This must be firmly fixed in the minds of the people. If there is no discipline, no system can succeed. Therefore one people should always be united and disciplined.[99]

It appears that Aung San still put unity before ideology or political system. The juxtaposition of unity and democracy implies two realities that continue to bedevil Burma. The first is that by virtue of counterposing unity against democracy, Burmese leaders ensured that the goals remain in conflict with one another and that one is preferable to the other. The second reality is that their conceptualization means unity needs to necessarily precede the successful establishment and consolidation of democracy. This means that it is likely that Burma may have a non-democratic government whose imperative is to establish unity first and foremost, before considering the task of establishing democracy. It did not take long for this likelihood to become a reality.

## 1949 Revolts, 1958 Power Plays, 1962 Military Government

Tensions came to the fore not long after independence and escalated to a degree that crippled the body politic. Revolts broke out in many ethnic areas. The various armed ethnic rebellions such as the White Band People's Volunteer Organization (PVO), Karen National Defence Organization (KNDO), and Mon National Defence Organization (MNDO), were joined by communist movements, including the Burma Communist Party (White Flag Communists) and the Communist Party of Burma (Red Flag Communists). By the spring of 1949, most of Burma's countryside and even parts of the capital city, Rangoon, were under effective insurgent control. The Karen troops in the Union army started deserting in early 1949.

In response, Prime Minister U Nu, who had assumed power after Aung San's assassination, transferred power to a temporary caretaker government in 1958, under Army chief General Ne Win. To be clear, these groups did not have the same demands. The communists wanted to topple the democratic government, while the ethnic insurgents sought autonomy and federalism.

In 1958, the AFPFL split into two factions. The 1960 general elections were won decisively by U Nu's faction, now called

Pyidaungsu ('Clean') faction, which received 57.2 per cent of the votes, as against its rival AFPFL faction. This was called the 'Stable' faction and was backed by the armed forces and received 30.7 per cent of the vote share.[100] Despite their emphatic return to power, the U Nu government could not stabilize the country. It could not secure the loyalty of minority ethnic groups that remained concerned with their autonomy and their attempts to gain a share of the country's natural resources. Summing up the challenges that U Nu faced, a trio of Burmese scholars, Maureen Aung-Thwin, Thant Myint-U and Thant Mynt-U, note,

> 'Fundamental constraints doomed U Nu's good intentions from the start: factionalism among the AFPFL and the various groups within the reigning political coalition; rebellious compatriots; the physically devastated post-war nation; and, perhaps most important, his inability to reconcile his own Buddhist aspirations with the practical needs of the modern state he led.'[101]

The country seemed ungovernable, with the writ of the government limited to areas around Rangoon. Even areas that had better transport and communication infrastructure were not under Central government control. 'The civilian government was, in many instances, unable to exercise much influence beyond Rangoon.'[102] This paved the way for Ne Win to overthrow the civilian government in 1962. Prime Minister U Nu, along with his cabinet, got arrested and was replaced by a Union Revolutionary Council of twenty-one members plus Ne Win as chairman. 'The assignment of U Thi Han, a civilian non-military member of the Union Revolutionary Council, to a Foreign Affairs portfolio is indicative of the low priority assigned to Burma's foreign affairs problems.'[103] This is further evidence of how Burma's foreign policy transformed from a period of engagement under U Nu to one of isolationism under Ne Win.

## Ne Win's Military Government

A leading member of the Union Revolutionary Council, Brigadier Thaung Dan, insisted that the Tatmadaw's seizure of power was necessary 'to rescue the Union'.[104] Analysing Ne Win's motivations for the coup, a US State Department memo from March 1962, later declassified, noted:

> General Ne Win has stated that one of his reasons for the latest coup was to check the disintegration of Burma. It would appear that General Ne Win was not only referring to the serious economic problems caused in part by the Government of U Nu but to the increasing demands of Burma ethnic minorities for a federal type government. General Ne Win has viewed skeptically U Nu's handling of the ethnic minorities' demand for a federal form of government which if approved would have made Burma proper a constituent state on a par with the other minority states within Burma. The Burmese Army feared that ... U Nu may have felt compelled to make concessions to the minorities or face the possibility of the secession of the Shan States from Burma. Also, the Burma Army was aware of Shan and Karen insurgent overtures to the Thai and Lao Governments for assistance in their independence struggle with Burma.[105]

The new regime abolished the Parliament and the federal system established under the 1947 Constitution and replaced it with a one-party state under the Burma Socialist Program Party (BSPP). Combining aspects of Buddhism and Marxism, the 'Burmese Way of Socialism' advanced a programme that included a nationalisation of agriculture, other commodities, industry and distribution system, with a view to establish a 'planned, proportional development of all the national productive forces'.[106] The nationalisation programme led to the government controlling some 15,000 private firms, which were absorbed into called State

Economic Enterprises, and the forcible expulsion of 200,000 Indian nationals who had controlled a large part of the economy. Anti-Chinese riots also ensued, as the Chinese had also been a major force in the economy.[107]

There would be no independent media. The regime blamed parliamentary democracy for the country's problems and found its goals of a socialist economy incompatible with parliamentary democracy. The new ideology, announced on 30 April 1962 by the 'Union Revolutionary Council' of the military, was pursued in a robust way. 'No purely military leadership in Southeast Asia has made such great efforts in the ideological field.'[108] At one level, it seemed like an utopia, with words such as these found in a statement made at the Defence Services Conference in 1958:

> Man's endeavour to build a society set free at last from anxieties over food, clothing and shelter, and able to enjoy life's spiritual satisfactions as well, fully convinced of the sanctity, dignity and essential goodness of life, must proceed from the premise of a faith only in a politico-economic system based on the eternal principles of justice, liberty and equality.[109]

At another level, national disunity—the major cause of the 1962 coup—increased because of 'the existence of several dissident minority parties and groups' that kept fighting government forces when the latter wanted to capture and destroy them.[110] It was not just that Burma was experiencing discontinuity in its political system, from a system of parliamentary democracy to military rule. Independent Burma's first and second leaders were vastly different from one another. Although both were socialist in their outlook,

> U Nu depended on his deep Buddhist faith to cope with the headaches of national integration and economic progress within a federalist union. In contrast, the General opted for a

xenophobic solution called 'The Burmese Way to Socialism', a highly centralized path to official autarky led by a single party and backed by a well-equipped and loyal military. Each leader aspired in his own way to rebuild a politically and economically viable Burmese socialist state without needless dependence on the outside world. Both failed.[111]

## Social Unrest, New Protests and a New Constitution for a Militarized State

Ne Win's economic policies included nationalizing private businesses and creating government monopolies for staple goods like rice and salt. He forced farmers to sell their rice to the state at fixed prices, decreasing their incentives for production, which led to nationwide shortages. Decreased rice production also affected exports and led to a foreign-exchange crisis. There was mass social unrest, with protests taking place in 1965, 1969 and 1970. As its policies failed, in 1974, the government adopted a new Constitution, ostensibly transferring power to a People's Assembly, albeit headed by Ne Win himself. Burma expert Robert Taylor argues that the new Constitution was more representative of the country than the 1947 one, which had been adopted by a constituent assembly that was dominated by the AFPFL. By contrast, the 1974 constitution was drafted by a commission with fifteen sub-commissions that had gathered views from a wider range of citizens, including in localities. This time, Burma's government did make an effort to consult a wider range of citizens. Moreover, Taylor points out that

'in contrast to the previous Constitution, which was a document sanctioning a politicians' and lawyers' government, the new one reflected the BSPP's critique of the two party system and the perceived need to have guided political participation under the

Party and Party-organized mass and class bodies catering for the people'.[112]

The new Constitution retained some of the core features of the 1947 Constitution, including a parliamentary executive system. But under the 1974 Constitution, any amendment to the basic principles and procedures would require a referendum. On surface at least, the 1974 Constitution was more 'unconditional' and more 'unchangeable' in its commitment to constitutional government.[113]

Nonetheless, it did not alter the fabric of Burma's political system. Rather, it legitimized military rule. It paved the way for a single-party system, based on East European communist frameworks. It formalized Burma as a

> unitary, centralized state, enforced with power located within the BSPP, which meant military control. Even the modest autonomy previously granted the minorities was rescinded. The periphery was without effective voice. A unicameral legislature, the Pyithu Hluttaw, was a means to legitimate military authority. A single slate of BSPP candidates for election was proposed from the center, and no choices were permitted. Although 'elected' representatives were obligated to return to their constituencies to learn the problems of their electorate, the system did not work, as fear prevented criticism of the military hierarchy and its policies and programs.[114]

As such, despite the progressive parts of the 1974 Constitution, two things became more likely for Burma's future. One was the legitimation and institutionalization of single party/military rule. As the only political party allowed to function, the BSPP governed Burma under a totalitarian military dictatorship for decades. The second involves the constant presence of anti-government protest movements throughout the country, like the 8888 Uprising against the BSPP in 1988.

## Ne Win Resigns: The 1980s

The 1980s were a fateful decade for Burma's politics. Ne Win stepped down from the Presidency in 1981, transferring power to retired general, San Yu, but retained effective control as the chairman of BSPP.[115] In 1988, there were widespread student-led protests against the government. They came to be known as the 8888 Uprising and involved hundreds of thousands of monks, children, university students and common people. The ensuing government crackdown killed thousands. The protests led to Ne Win's resignation as chairman of the BSPP. While announcing his resignation, the seventy-seven-year-old Ne Win cited his 'advanced age', and surprisingly admitted that the protests 'showed the lack of trust and confidence in the government'. He admitted to being 'indirectly responsible' for the protests. He also announced a referendum on the one-party rule. 'To find out whether the majority or the minority are behind, a referendum must be held so the people can choose between the existing one-party system or a multiparty system.'[116] Explaining the developments, Georgetown University academic, Prof. Steinberg argues that the 1988 protests were the result of 'economic incompetence, political repression, and minority disaffection'.[117]

## The Emergence of Aung San Suu Kyi

It is at this juncture that Aung San Suu Kyi emerged as the main opposition figure in Burma, starting with the April 1988 student protests, the first among the 1988 protests, taking place at the Rangoon Institute of Technology (RIT) and through her first political speech delivered on 26 August 1988. Burmese scholar Mya Maung, who was Professor of Finance at Boston College, has aptly described her as an 'accidental tourist in the political sphere'[118] due to her previous lack of political engagement.

'In the image and shadow of her legendary father, General Aung San, who was responsible for gaining Burma's independence from British rule, this young woman [aged forty-three at the time] was seen as a savior who would likewise free the oppressed people of Burma from an unjust rule.'[119]

Suu Kyi's reform efforts were bolstered by two military leaders who served with General Ne Win in the Tatmadaw but bravely spoke out against the injustices committed by the BSPP. General Tin Oo, who was forced to resign as commander-in-chief of the Tatmadaw in 1977 and became imprisoned, helped establish the National League for Demoracy (NLD) in 1988. He was joined by General Aung Gyi, serving as NLD President, and Aung San Suu Kyi, as the party's general secretary. Despite General Gyi's friendship with General Ne Win, the former was extremely critical of the Burmese Way of Socialism and emerged as a prominent Opposition leader.

From the outset, Suu Kyi was not shy about invoking her father's name and views, including General Aung San's views of democracy. In her first public speech on 26 August 1988, she cited her father's words.

We must make democracy the popular creed. We must try to build up a free Burma in accordance with such a creed. Democracy is the only ideology which is consistent with freedom. It is also an ideology that promotes and strengthens peace. It is therefore the only ideology we should aim for.[120]

Claiming that these words were the reason why she was joining the pro-democracy movement, she also argued that Burma can achieve democracy even without borrowing Western ideals and techniques,

'by turning to the words of the Buddha on the four causes of decline and decay—failure to recover that which has been lost, omission to repair that which has been damaged, disregard for the need of a reasonable economy and the elevation to leadership of men without morality or learning'

—and apply them to their situation. In other words, she said,

> when democratic rights had been lost to military dictatorship,
> sufficient efforts had not been made to regain them, moral
> and political values had been allowed to deteriorate without
> concerted attempts to save the situation, the economy had been
> badly managed, and the country had been ruled by men without
> integrity and wisdom.'[121]

In response to the 8888 Uprising, the military suspended the 1974 Constitution and dissolved existing administrative and legislative organizations. The demonstrators demanded multiparty rule and an end to single-party rule. General Ne Win resigned by July 1988. The BSPP called for elections, but protestors called for an interim government to conduct elections. After the BSPP rejected the protestors' demand, the protests became more violent and lawless. On 18 September 1988, the military re-assumed power in the country and established the State Law and Order Restoration Council (SLORC) under General Saw Maung who assumed power.[122]

> The establishment of the SLORC 'was designed to shore up
> the military as the ruler in spite of the earlier failed political and
> economic programmes by the previous military-led government.
> That military administration changed its name from SLORC in
> 1997 to the State Peace and Development Council (SPDC),
> but its top leadership remained intact. This fall from political
> and economic grace—a functioning if creaky democracy with
> a well-educated elite and an economy with the potential for
> growth and development—has been precipitous and tragic for
> its diverse peoples, who remain among the poorest in Asia.'[123]

Burma became beset with human rights abuses during the SPDC's reign. Western non-governmental organizations such as Amnesty International and Human Rights Watch catalogued and called out the military regime for its draconian behaviour that included murder, torture, rape, arbitrary executions, recruitment of child soldiers and political imprisonment.[124] Aung San Suu Kyi had a promising start with the 8888 Uprising, but SLORC's brutal defeat of the protests ended with her imprisonment.

## Suu Kyi Under House Arrest

On 20 July 1989, Aung San Suu Kyi, now the General Secretary of the NLD, was placed under house arrest for the first time (this would last until 1995).[125] Confident of their victory after brutally defeating protestors, the SLORC decided to hold elections in May 1990, in which the NLD won more than 80 per cent of the seats (392 out of the 485).[126] Refusing to acknowledge their victory, SLORC imprisoned NLD leaders; Aung San Suu Kyi was placed under house arrest and the chairman of NLD, Tin Oo was sentenced to seven years of hard labour. Some NLD leaders who retreated into Karen-majority areas on the Thai border, which was not under SLORC control, formed a government in exile, the National Coalition Government of the Union of Burma (NCGUB).[127] SLORC's intimidation forced the NLD to dismiss Aung San Suu Kyi, still under house arrest, as Secretary-General of the party, in December 1991.

Internationally, however, Burma's domestic situation was getting more attention. In 1991, Aung San Suu Kyi was awarded the Nobel Peace Prize, 'for her non-violent struggle for democracy and human rights', in the words of the Norwegian Nobel Institute. Her goal, the committee added, 'was to establish a democratic society in which the country's ethnic groups could cooperate in harmony'.[128] Burma's internal politics came under increasing international scrutiny. Between the fall of communism in the Soviet Union and the rise of liberal-democratic forces in the 1990s, international pressure mounted on the regime to respect human rights and implement democratic reforms.

A military bulletin issued on 24 April 1992 announced the SLORC Chairman General Saw Maung would take leave as his health had become 'severely impaired by the stress of work and heavy responsibilities of the State'.[129] The regime announced plans for a national convention in January 1993 to draft a new constitution.

Despite the NLD's protests, in April 1992, the SLORC moved ahead with its plans to draft a new constitution by announcing the formation of a National Convention, with a steering committee of fifteen members, out of which eight were active military officers. Meetings organized under its auspices in June and July invited the NLD and other political parties, but discussions yielded no agreement. In October 1993, the SLORC announced six basic principles for constitution-making:

1. non-disintegration of the union;
2. non-disintegration of national solidarity;
3. consolidation and perpetuation of sovereignty;
4. emergence of a genuine multi-party democratic system;
5. development of eternal principles of justice, liberty, and equality in the State; and
6. participation of the Tatmadaw [military] in the leading role of national politics of the State in [the] future.[130]

The undemocratic clauses inserted into the new Constitution included a 25 per cent reservation of seats for the military in the Upper and Lower Houses of the National Assembly and the disqualification from the Presidency of anyone married to a foreigner (the SLORC may as well have labelled this the 'Suu Kyi Condition'!). These 'reforms' were intended to prolong SLORC's control of national politics.[131]

The foreign policy isolation that began with General Ne Win's 1962 coup transformed into full-blown international condemnation during SLORC's reign. A constitution that tried to accommodate some ethnic minorities in 1947 mutated into one that accommodated only the military minority, forsaking the majority of Burma's citizens.

## New Constitution, Suu Kyi Released, Opposition Continues, Regime Consolidates

The National Convention, which was the SLORC's constitution-making exercise, held on 16 September 1993, agreed on 104 basic principles to be included in the formation of a new constitution.[132] But critics saw these principles along with the six guidelines mentioned before as an attempt by the military to craft a political system that 'would have essentially ensured a commanding role for the Burmese armed forces in the future affairs of the state'.[133] Yet, things appeared to be on the move in a positive direction when Suu Kyi was released from house arrest on 10 July 1995, along with two former NLD chairmen, Tin Oo and Kyi Maung.

Before her release, Suu Kyi had met two generals, Senior General Than Shwe and intelligence chief Khin Nyunt, in 1994. Despite the appearance of reconciliation, however, the regime did not seem sincere about the full opening up of the political system, leading Suu Kyi and NLD to boycott the National Convention in November 1995. In December 1995, the head of Burma's military intelligence, General Khin Nyunt, called Suu Kyi and NLD 'the adopted sons and daughters of colonialists' who were 'moving to cause disruption to the National Convention only for their party's interest'.[134]

In 1997, the SLORC became the SPDC. The same year, Burma was admitted to ASEAN as a full member, thirty years after ASEAN came into existence. ASEAN had taken credit for the political developments in Burma through its Constructive Engagement policy. Yet, the claim seemed questionable when Suu Kyi was again placed under house arrest for a second time, in 2000 until 2002.[135] This time though, the international pressure in her support was much more visible. A joint statement issued on 11 September 2000, by fourteen female Foreign Ministers and their equivalents, including the US Secretary of State Madeleine K. Albright, strongly condemned the regime's action. They were 'appalled' by the detention of her and other NLD members. Calling the detainees 'tireless champions for democracy in Burma', the statement described their detention was 'an affront to people throughout the world'. It called on 'the Burmese Government to stop its harassment of the democratic opposition and begin immediately a dialogue with Aung San Suu Kyi and other democratic leaders aimed at reconciliation among the Burmese people'.[136] Perhaps responding to the international pressure, including sanctions imposed by the US and the EU, which had rejected ASEAN's Constructive Engagement policy that carried no sanctions, in 2001, the Burmese government released over 200 political prisoners. The UN Special Envoy, Razali Ismail, was able to visit Rangoon and was credited with arranging secret talks between Suu Kyi and the regime. Despite the release of 200 political prisoners, over 1,000 still languished in prisons. The regime also allowed the NLD to open their offices and softened their attack on Suu Kyi.[137] In return, the NLD also appeared more conciliatory.[138]

In another example of a change that didn't actually look like a change, the SPDC's first secretary and the intelligence chief with whom Suu Kyi met prior to her release in 1995, General Khin Nyunt, was appointed as the new prime minister in August 2003. This wasn't much of a change because Khin Nyunt, along with Senior Generals Than Shwe and Maung Aye, was one of only three men who were still active in government from when SLORC first came to power in 1988. In the interim fifteen-year period between 1988 and 2003, Burma witnessed major geopolitical changes, widespread international condemnation, and numerous protests and detentions. But through all this, the military's chokehold on national politics only increased.

## Khin Nyunt's Plans for Burma's Future

In a speech on 30 August 2003, Khin Nyunt[139] outlined a seven-point 'road map' for the country. The seven points included:

1. Reconvening of the National Convention that has been adjourned since 1996.
2. After the successful holding of the National Convention, step by step implementation of the process necessary for the emergence of a genuine and disciplined democratic system.
3. Drafting of a new constitution in accordance with basic principles and detailed basic principles laid down by the National Convention.
4. Adoption of the constitution through national referendum.
5. Holding of free and fair elections for Pyithu Hluttaws [Legislative bodies] according to the new constitution.
6. Convening of Hluttaws attended by Hluttaw members in accordance with the new constitution.
7. Building a modern, developed and democratic nation by the state leaders elected by the Hluttaw; and the government and other central organs formed by the Hluttaw.[140]

The government's plan called for transforming Burma into 'one where the level of development of the country is comparable to those in the international community', creating 'a genuine multi-party democracy system', and 'a peaceful, modern and developed State', that will achieve not only 'peace and stability, progress and development but also . . . national unity spirit and Union spirit'. In his call for turning Burma into a 'genuine and disciplined democracy', Khin Nyunt dismissed that the 1988 uprisings represented a step towards democracy:

> Some unscrupulous persons distorted the undeniable historical
> fact and tried to term the unrest and demonstrations that happened
> during 1988 as a movement for democracy. However much they

try to persuade with sweet words, a careful analysis of the events of 1988 will show that people who tried to get political gain, people who were swayed by instigations and encouragement of western countries and people with leftist views who had donned the cloak of democracy united to deliberately create anarchism among the demonstrators and protestors who had grievances against the previous government. As the group who were making demonstrations and launching struggles and demands with the aim of getting political gain and the group of people who were waiting for an opportunity to loot and destroy combined to form the majority, anarchism reigned over the nation and the Union was on the verge of disintegration. The people were facing untold hardship and difficulties and the Tatmadaw which has the responsibility for national defense and security of the nation had to unavoidably assume State responsibilities.

The General claimed that political reforms that were carried out since 1988 and were to be implemented with the new Constitution were meant 'to ensure the best possible future after studying the weaknesses and strength of the democracy system that had been practiced in the past'.[141]

Yet this vision of 'a modern, developed, and democratic nation'[142] was seen as a ploy to give the military a veneer of legitimacy and to maintain their hold on power. It was labelled as 'highly controversial and arguably illegal' by the exiled Burma Lawyers' Council.[143] Aung San Suu Kyi had been released from house arrest in May 2002 after nearly two years.[144] But on 30 May 2003, her convoy was attacked by a mob sympathetic to the regime, killing four of her bodyguards. She was again arrested and taken to Insein prison in Rangoon, but later moved to house arrest. Despite its rhetoric, the regime was far from willing to give up power.

As it was achieving little success in co-opting the NLD, the military turned its attention to placating ethnic groups. A major breakthrough occurred in December 2003-January 2004, when it negotiated 'a gentlemen's agreement' and an informal ceasefire with the Karen National Union (KNU). This agreement with one of the most successful foes of the regime was a significant development in the country's long-running civil war. But like other ethnic groups, the KNU itself was divided over the merits of a negotiated approach, and negotiations to formalize the agreement made little progress, until talks were suspended to focus on the national convention that was in progress. In October 2004, when a KNU delegation arrived in Rangoon to resume talks with the regime, Prime Minister Khin Nyunt had been purged and replaced by Soe Win as the new prime minister. Thanks to the internal power struggle, Khin Nyunt's replacement rendered his negotiating approach and team of negotiators defunct.[145,146] Later, Khin Nyunt would describe himself as 'a sitting duck for all kinds of politically motivated attacks from all quarters, domestic and abroad'.[147] His purge might well have been due to his independent streak, going in defiance of the regime's wishes, including a suggestion to release Aung San Suu Kyi and Tin Oo from house arrest.[148]

The National Convention to draft a new constitution resumed in May 2004, with its membership size expanded from 702 members in 1993–96 to 1086, although the number of political parties represented was down from forty-eight to twenty-nine. The NLD, as before, boycotted the convention, while a higher number of minority delegates—from 215 in 1993–96 to 633 in 2004—participated.[149,150] In May 2004, the George W. Bush administration stated: 'Rangoon's constitutional convention has not allowed for substantive dialogue and the full participation of all political groups, including the NLD, it lacks legitimacy.'[151] According to a statement by the Inter-Parliamentary Union that 'without being preceded by the unconditional release of all political prisoners and the lifting of all restrictions on human rights and political activity', the Convention was 'designed to prolong and legitimize military rule against the will of the people as expressed in the 1990 elections'.[152]

Another five sessions of the Convention would be held with the final session, concluded on 3 September 2007, adopting the Fundamental Principles and Detailed Basic Principles. The chair of the Convention, Lieutenant-Gen. Thein Sein, the country's future President, called it 'fundamental for [the] perpetual existence of the Union of Myanmar'. The international community responded sceptically, with the UN Secretary General Kofi Annan hoping for 'opportunities in the period ahead to improve the outcome of the National Convention in ways that are more inclusive, participatory and transparent'. His offer to assist in reviewing the Constitution's principles and provisions was ignored.[153]

In November 2005, the capital of Burma was formally moved from Rangoon/Yangon to Naypyidaw. The rationale for this move was greater 'information security, defence-in-depth against possible foreign invasion, desire to get rid of the colonial past, isolating civil servants from the general public, gaining a sense of control in state-building, and the influence of traditional world views.'[154] Geographically, Naypyidaw is located closer to the Shan, Karen and Karenni states, indicating the military's need to maintain a strong presence near turbulent regions. Like its constitutional and leadership changes, the change of Burma's capital from Rangoon/ Yangon to Naypyidaw was another superficial change that belies any substantive transformations in the country's political present or future.

## The Saffron Revolution That Was Not to Be

As the National Convention was formally declared closed in 2007, Burma saw another wave of anti-government protests, this time led by monks. Called the Saffron Revolution, it triggered a brutal military crackdown. The immediate causes for the uprising were rising fuel prices and other living costs. The uprising showed that the public had not been reassured by the constitution-making process and was demanding an end to political repression and economic deprivation. The reaction from the international community was neither robust nor effective. As I wrote in one of my earlier articles, ASEAN, which had successfully demanded that Burma give up the rotating chair of the grouping for 2006, was unwilling to apply any pressure towards political reform, out of deference to its non-interference doctrine. "The international community needs to prove that while taking a moral high ground on Burma's crisis, it can also offer concrete ideas and approaches to advance the democratization and national reconciliation process beyond the current policy of sanctions and boycott."[155]

But the Saffron Revolution did have some effect, given the centrality of Buddhism to Burma's cultural life. 'The incidents of military beating and the humiliation of Buddhist monks in their robes have major consequences both for the military itself and for the population as a whole.' During the uprising, the people of Burma were able to see images of its violent suppression by the regime's troops through satellite antennas.[156] On the one hand, the increased visibility of the army's atrocities could spell another round of protests and instability on the part of the public, tied with a potential increase in military deserters, as the targeting of peaceful Buddhist monks may not be tolerable for everyone. On the other hand, the crackdown might have reinforced the military's unity and determination, not least due to a realization of the costs of losing their grip on national politics. The regime might also have been emboldened by the feeble international response against the repression.[157]

In another of history's echoes, the 2007 protests and their brutal repression led to the drafting and adoption of another constitution in 2008. In its long succession of constitution-making, the 2008 Constitution was Burma's fifth and last, as it is still in effect today.

# Chapter 5

## A False Dawn

From a Thought Warrior

*Under [the] 2008 [Constitution], Tatmadaw had already had this idea of a coup . . . a long time ago. In 2010, they puppeted Thein Sein Government as a civilian government and gave the NLD for a chance of five-year term from 2015–20. They did everything to throw down or ruin within the tenure of NLD, aiming to form a coalition government after the 2020 General Election. They already had 25 per cent seats, still needed another 25m+ 0.1 per cent to form a coalition government. That's why Min Aung Hlaing met his alliance of twenty-three parties just before the coup. Min Aung Hlaing and his alliances might have made attempts to steal votes, but unexpectedly, NLD also stole a bunch of votes to gain the status of 'NLD won the election with might and gain'. Then, under the military's scenario, the idea of coalition government has vanished, so they did a coup.*

\* \* \*

## The 2008 Constitution

Constitution-making is at the heart of Burma's political challenges. Burma's military regimes have found promises to undertake constitutional change, and long-drawn-out processes in doing so, as a way of silencing political dissent and legitimizing their rule through decades of conflict and warfare. The 1947 Constitution granted certain minority regions the right to secede from the Union of Burma but did not go far enough to provide democratic guarantees to minority communities.[158] The 1974 Constitution makes way for the BSPP as the sole political party of the nation, legitimating single-party rule. The 8888 Uprising in 1988 caused General Ne Win's surprising admission of the BSPP's excesses and demands for a national referendum about the change from a single party to a multiparty system. Once the SLORC descended on the political scene, the referendum was never held, and the 1974 Constitution was suspended. In 1992, the SLORC set up a National Convention to draft a new constitution. Disagreements about federal powers, centre-state relations with ethnic minorities and the military's intransigence derailed constitution-making until 1997 when SLORC morphed into the SPDC. In 2003, under PM General Khin Nyunt, the SPDC released a 'Seven Step Roadmap to Democracy', highlighting its genuine desire to make Burma democratic. By 2004, General Khin Nyunt was arrested, and many officers close to him got purged. The SPDC resumed the National Convention in 2005, and this brings us to Burma's fifth attempt at constitution-making and their third Constitution.

Burma's 2008 Constitution, a central part of its second democratic opening and ultimately its collapse, can be traced all the way back to the SLORC's attempt to write a new constitution after suspending the 1974 Constitution. The process was influenced not only by changing domestic politics, especially with the emergence of Aung San Suu Kyi on the political stage, but also by a global trend towards democracy and human rights after the end of the Cold War with the fall of the Berlin Wall in 1989 and the collapse of the Soviet Union in 1991. The drafting of the 2008 Constitution was finished in February 2008 and was formally adopted on 29 May 2008. Its main provisions included a presidential system with a bicameral legislature, consisting of a Hluttaw or lower house and an Amyotha Hluttaw or upper house. The Constitution divided the country into different areas. First, seven non-ethnically designated, but Bamar majority-dominated regions:

1. Sagaing
2. Taninthayi
3. Bago
4. Magway
5. Mandalay
6. Yangon
7. Ayeyarwady Regions

Second, seven ethnically designated states:

1. Kachin
2. Kayah
3. Kayin
4. Chin
5. Mon
6. Rakhine
7. Shan States

And finally, six self-administered areas:

1. Danu
2. Pa-O
3. Palaung
4. Kokang Self-Administered Zones
5. Wa Self-Administered Division in Shan State
6. Naga Self-Administered Zone in Sagaing Region

Naypyidaw (Nay Pyi Taw, or royal capital), which became the new capital city in 2005 partly to relieve the congestion in

Yangon and partly due to its central location that might allow the authorities to keep a better grip on the troublesome ethnic areas in the periphery, was designated as a union territory.

The adoption of the 2008 Constitution started on a hugely inauspicious note. On Friday, 2 May 2008, Cyclone Nargis hit the southern parts of Burma, killing about 140,000 people and causing immense devastation. Despite the catastrophe, a nationwide referendum on the Constitution went ahead,[159] inviting criticism from the NLD and international observers.[160] Official results showed that over 98 per cent of eligible voters cast their votes, with 92.48 per cent voting in favour of the Constitution.[161]

The Constitution, which is still in effect today, contained a number of provisions that gave the military significant powers, such as:

1. Representatives appointed by the military were guaranteed 25 per cent of the seats in each of the houses of the Parliament.
2. The military would have the prerogative of appointing a vice-president (one of the three such positions in the country) from its ranks (serving 'defence services personnel'), who may or may not be a member of the Parliament. (One of three would assume the position of President if elected by the Parliament, leaving the other two as vice-presidents.)
3. The military also had the monopoly over appointing the cabinet ministers for defence, border affairs, and home affairs, all of whom have to be serving military officers without any requirement for them to resign from the military. Aside from these three, the President would have the discretion to appoint other cabinet members from the ranks of military.
4. Article 59.f barred anyone with a spouse or children who is a foreign national from becoming the country's President or vice-president. This meant Aung San Suu Kyi would be

ineligible for becoming President since her late husband
and two children were British citizens.

5. The military would be free from civilian oversight and
was empowered to suspend civilian rule when a state of
emergency was declared.

Perhaps most important in preserving the military's control
over the country was the provision (under Article 436) that any
constitutional amendment would require 'more than 75 per cent
of all the representatives' of the Parliament. Since the military
was guaranteed 75 per cent of the seats, this provision gave a de
facto veto to the military over constitutional amendments. Any
amendment that challenges the interests and privileges of the
Tatmadaw, as mentioned above, would be exceedingly difficult, if
not impossible, and would require overwhelming support from the
civilian members and some support from within the military.

In retrospect, and in more recent events, the overwhelming
victory of the NLD and the disastrous performance of the military-
backed Union Solidarity and Development Party (USDP), in
the November 2020 elections, did create a realistic chance for a
constitutional amendment, since it would need the defection of
a relatively few military or pro-military representatives. Such
an amendment, which would scrap the military's privileges and
prerogatives, as the NLD had made no secret of wishing, acted as
a trigger for the military takeover. Finally, the 2008 Constitution
ensured that parliaments and governments of the constituent
states/regions enjoyed little authority to administer themselves.
There was no vision for a truly federal system, which the ethnic
minorities had long desired and the military had strongly and
brutally opposed.

By falling short of the democratic aspirations of the NLD
and the federal aspirations of the ethnic minorities, the 2008
Constitution satisfied the military, despite the concessions it had to
make.[162] This 'militarized constitution-making', as Burma scholar

Nyi Nyi Kyaw puts it, ensured the continued participation, and even dominance, of the military in key parts of the government, relegating the civilian political forces 'to a status from where they may never constitutionally depose the military'. The Constitution also did not provide for a meaningful system of power-sharing and resource allocation with the ethnic minorities.[163] Being 'made by and for the benefit of the military and the majority [Bamar]', the 2008 Constitution, Kyaw adds, 'not only cost it nationwide legitimacy, but also ultimately undermine[d] its endurance'.[164] Constitution-making is a legitimizing endeavour and the end-product is meant to bequeath political legitimacy to the executive. However, Burma's 2008 Constitution was the end-product of a non-inclusive process that carried the seed of its own demise.

While the NLD harboured, sometimes with little show of patience, the goal of amending the Constitution, it was aware that it was neither going to be an easy process nor come without major consequences. As an American Burma specialist David Steinberg noted, from the junta's point of view, the 2010 elections were 'designed to wipe out the 1990 election results which the NLD swept'.[165] There was no possibility that the military would renegotiate the 2008 Constitution.

In 2010, the government announced new election laws, and the NLD ultimately decided to boycott the election. The military-backed USDP claimed a resounding victory.[166] The NLD lost its status as a legal entity in the Parliament, although it continued as a political force. Aung San Suu Kyi was released from yet another house arrest after the election and stated that the party would continue to be involved and will 'use various means to carry out [its] political activities outside the Parliament.'[167]

The military claimed the election as the country's official transition from military rule to civilian democracy. U Thein Sein, a former general and member of SPDC (erstwhile SLORC) and chair of the 'Convening Commission of the National Convention' drafted a new constitution with the rest of the committee, and former prime minister Than Shwe was now sworn in as president on 31 March 2011.

As head of a new, quasi-civilian government, Thein Sein initiated several political reforms. He invited ethnic armed groups in November 2011 to a peace talk, released prominent political dissidents, and granted permission for the NLD to re-register and contest in the April 2012 by-elections. He also deregulated Burma's previously censored media and allowed peaceful demonstrations to occur, albeit under tight conditions, where organizers need to get prior permission from the authorities or risk a year-long imprisonment for unpermitted protests. Thein Sein also permitted the right to strike and the formation of labour unions.[168] As a result, Thein Sein, who was previously strongly condemned for his authoritarianism, was praised as a champion of change, democratization and liberalization.[169]

The NLD, having boycotted the 2010 elections, decided to contest the by-elections of 2012 for forty-eight vacant seats, winning forty-three of the forty-four seats it contested. Among those who got elected was Aung San Suu Kyi, who now officially became the leader of the Opposition in Parliament. Suu Kyi was optimistic, saying: 'We hope that this is the beginning of the new era where there will be more emphasis on the role of the people in the everyday politics of the country.' She also emphasized the importance of the people enthusiastically participating in the democratic process.[170]

The USDP party General Secretary, U Htay Oo, attributed the NLD's big win to 'the popularity of the party leader Daw Aung San Suu Kyi' and contended that 'voting was based on what people think they know, rather than [on whether they] . . . love or hate the USDP party'.[171] Nay Zin Latt, a political advisor to President Thein Sein, saw the NLD victory as an opportunity to 'liven the relatively new Parliament's proceedings and improve the quality of its debates'.[172]

This atmosphere of hope and optimism was shadowed, as dark clouds were gathering over the Rakhine state, where the military's response to the communal clashes between the Buddhists and Muslim Rohingyas was turning increasingly violent against the latter.[173] As violence continued throughout 2012 and 2013, and human rights agencies expressed growing concerns, the Rohingyas were castigated as illegal immigrants and troublemakers. Former PM General Khin Nyunt, when he served as the first Secretary-General of the SPDC, stated in a letter to the UN that the Rohingyas 'are not originally from Myanmar but have illegally migrated to Myanmar because of population pressures in their own country . . . They are racially, ethnically, culturally different from the other national races in our country.'[174] It would appear that this view had not changed in the post-2011 period. The view persisted of the Rohingyas being outsiders, which lent urgency to the notion that deportation was an effective solution to the 'Rohingya issue'.

## National Ceasefire Agreement

While the Rohingyas were being dealt with in increasingly brutal ways, the new government moved to address and improve its relations with Burma's other ethnic groups that were officially recognized. In August 2011, the government announced a peace plan that called for state- and regional-level ceasefire agreements before allowing Ethnic Armed Organizations (EAO) to move without carrying weapons. The Central government promised to engage the ethnic groups in political dialogue and promote educational, health, and communication infrastructure in their areas. This was to be followed by a nationwide ceasefire agreement in Parliament, represented by different ethnic nationalities and political parties.[175]

Beginning in November 2013 at the EAO Conference in Kachin State, sixteen EAOs established a Nationwide Ceasefire Coordination Team (NCCT) to negotiate a Nationwide Ceasefire Agreement (NCA).[176] At this conference, the basic principles for drafting a NCA were established. The NCCT then met with the government negotiation team, and the Union Peace-making Work Committee (UPWC), and agreed to work on a single draft for the agreement.[177] By March 2015, the NCCT and UPWC agreed to a final draft and sought approval from the highest authorities on both sides. On 15 October 2015, eight EAOs repudiated the EAOs Summit Meeting decisions and agreed to sign the NCA. While seven EAOs refused to sign, six were not allowed to sign.[178] The NCA provided for two main outcomes, both of which remain incomplete and contested: a process of Union-level and sub-national political dialogue, and a joint ceasefire monitoring mechanism.

The EAOs that agreed to sign the agreement played an important role in ceasefire monitoring. However, what remains problematic is the present and future status of the governance regimes and service delivery systems that were developed by each EAO over the past several decades. The mechanism for handling the relationship between EAO and government service delivery is inadequate. For those citizens living in conflict-affected areas, the EAOs and non-state actors are the only available regulatory authorities and source of assistance. They provide the face of local governance, while the state of Burma and its armed forces are often experienced by citizens as violent and predatory.[179]

## 2015 Elections

In November 2015, the NLD, led by Aung San Suu Kyi, won a landslide victory in the general elections.[180] It won 86 per cent of the total seats in the Parliament that were contested, excluding the 25 per cent reserved for the military. In March 2016, U Htin Kyaw was sworn in as Burma's first civilian President in half a century, and a new office of the State Counsellor was created for Aung San Suu Kyi, given the ban on her holding presidential office under the 2008 Constitution.

While the NLD could not directly challenge the military's virtual bloc over changing the constitutional provisions that barred Suu Kyi from becoming president,[181] it tried to secure more power for her as state counsellor, a position she apparently conceived for herself. This raised her status and placed her just beneath the President and above the two vice-presidents. Additionally, Suu Kyi also became the foreign minister, giving her international visibility and status. But while she seemed to be content with these arrangements, they were not sufficient to overcome the lingering unhappiness among NLD cadres about playing second fiddle to the armed forces as rulers of the nation. The 2008 Constitution preserved key privileges for the military that would extend the idea of a 'disciplined democracy' that it helped build.[182] It was unlikely that the civilian government would challenge the military's overall control of national security or defy the Tatmadaw over key political issues, like the idea of a federal Burma. The subservient position of the civilian government vis-à-vis the military remained unresolved, feeding into continued ethnic tensions and conflicts, ultimately contributing to the collapse of Burma's democratic experiment.

## The Rohingya Crisis Deepens

In August 2017, clashes broke out in Rakhine State after a militant group, Arakan Rohingya Salvation Army (ARSA), claimed responsibility for attacks on police and army posts.[183] As a result, the government declared ARSA a terrorist organization and the military mounted a brutal campaign against the group, destroying hundreds of Rohingya villages and forcing hundreds of thousands of Rohingya to flee to Bangladesh in the process.[184] At least 6,700 Rohingya were killed in the first month of the conflict,[185] and a later report by the UN Human Rights Council found that the military had deliberately also targeted civilians.[186] The conflict would be described as ethnic cleansing by UN Secretary-General Antonio Guterres.[187] A UN report claimed the Burmese military had 'genocidal intent' against the Rohingya, citing the patterns of abuse by the military against Rohingya civilians and the climate of impunity created for security forces that followed the atrocities committed.[188] Zeid Ra'ad Al Hussein, who became the UN High Commissioner for Human Rights in 2014, called the crackdown in Rakhine State a 'textbook case of ethnic cleansing'.[189]

The crisis in the Rakhine state attracted much international attention. But some of its consequences were domestic. In a national address from the capital city of Naypyidaw on 19 September 2017,[190] Suu Kyi addressed the military crackdown against the Rohingyas for the first time. She noted: 'We condemn all human rights violations and unlawful violence', adding 'we feel deeply for the suffering of all the people caught up in the conflict.' 'The security forces,' she further noted, 'have been instructed to adhere strictly to the code of conduct in carrying out security operations, to exercise all due restraint, and to take full measures to avoid collateral damage and the harming of innocent civilians.' However, her words at best were perceived as disingenuous and at worst as an attempt to cover for the military, especially when she said, '[W]e want to find out why this exodus [of Rohingyas] is happening.' As Azeem Ibrahim, author of a 2017 book titled *The Rohingyas: Inside Myanmar's Hidden Genocide*, noted '[E]ither she doesn't know or is simply trying to deceive. Both are very bad.'[191] The fact that the UN, along with numerous national and international rights groups as well as the government of Burma, had issued reports detailing the causes behind the conflict, did not help her credibility. Her comments drew widespread international criticism. Amnesty International described the speech as a 'mix of untruths and victim-blaming'.[192] Her decision to go to the International Court of Justice at Hague in 2019 to defend Burma against accusations of genocide further diminished her international standing.[193] In a statement she made at the court, she did not even use the word 'Rohingya', adhering to her government's stance that no such ethnic group exists.[194]

The Rohingya crisis and the ensuing genocide, while not directly contributing to the February 2021 coup, supplement our understanding of the Tatmadaw's impunity. Since Burma's founding, the military has had free rein to govern the country as it saw fit. This involved seat reservations in the Parliament, constitutional guarantees, inflated budgets, crackdowns in the name of national security, holding and cancelling elections arbitrarily: in short, the military held Burma hostage and extorted from the country. Viewed along this line, the February 2021 coup resembles other previous acts of military aggrandizement. As such, the Rohingya crisis may not have caused the coup, but the conflict and crackdown of 2017 gave the military ample opportunity to reaffirm its own self-image as the protector and defender of the country's security. At the same time, while Suu Kyi's words may have found some domestic support, they also created the perception, not only on the part of the ethnic minorities but also the anti-military population at large, that she had gone too far in appeasing the military. As a Thought Warrior puts it, the coup happened because:

> The military couldn't get enough of stealing the country's resources and the failed strategy of the civilian government NLD a.k.a. Daw Aung San Suu Kyi. She could have done way better instead of putting all the blame on the ethnic armed organizations and defending the military. She even did it at the international court with the genocide case. I wouldn't deny the fact that the country was much developed and was offered many international aids and projects during the civilian government period, but it was too stupid of her to always reconcile with the military, which was obviously useless. And last but not least, the people's ignorance of the country's politics.

However, apart from ethnic conflict, there were also other catalysts that would likely have contributed to the coup: namely, the economic interests of the Burmese military, a power struggle between General Min Aung Hlaing and Aung San Suu Kyi, and the General's personal ambition to remain in power.

## The Economic Interests of the Military

The military's economic interests and privileges that affected their incentives in regime survival in Burma are already discussed in Chapter 3. But some further elaboration might be useful here, as threats to those interests, or the fear of losing them, may have been a major contributing factor to the 2021 coup. In 2018, the Independent International Fact-Finding Mission on Myanmar identified five areas of alternative revenues for the Tatmadaw:

1. Business conglomerates
2. Interests in active conflicts in Kachin and Shan states
3. Infrastructure projects in Rakhine
4. Donations given to support 'clearance operations' against the Rohingya in August 2017,
5. Joint ventures and other relationships with foreign companies (in China, Singapore, and Russia), and
6. Arms transfers and sales from companies with ties to the Tatmadaw.[195]

The International Crisis Group similarly concluded that such economic considerations lay behind the military's, especially at the leadership level, determination to keep the levers of power in its hands.[196] Sean Turnell, economic advisor to Aung San Suu Kyi who was imprisoned by the military after the coup, says Burma's emergence as a major exporter of natural gas has benefited senior generals.[197] Using publicly available information on gas revenues, a non-governmental organization called 'Publish What You Pay' outlined in a 2021 Policy Brief that international oil and gas companies such as Chevron and the French energy giant, Total, continue to send revenue to the state-owned Myanmar Oil and Gas Enterprise (MOGE) and to the military. Despite suspending some gas-divided payments, 90 per cent of the money still continues to flow into the Tatmadaw's coffers.[198]

The military also earned substantial revenues from the narcotics trade. Part of the notorious 'Golden Triangle' with Thailand and Laos, Burma was at one point second only to Afghanistan in producing illicit drugs in the world.[199] Around 2015, Burma was the world's second-largest grower of opium poppies, the main ingredient of heroin, much of it centred on the Shan State, with the Kachin State being a distant second.[200] The Shan state also accounts for the world's largest meth trade.[201] Burma's drug trade had been rising both before and after the country's political opening. The military had long benefitted from the drug trade in a variety of ways, especially by taxing and extracting protection money from farmers, drug traders and delivery men. In the Shan State, the epicentre of opium poppy seed cultivation in Burma, army units use such means to 'live off the land,' often under the direction of the central military authorities. Revenue from the drug trade is also a way of recruiting militias for fighting insurgents and protecting infrastructure such as dams, oil and gas pipelines, and seizing land from farmers for plantations.[202]

Prior to the coup, certain policies of the civilian government had threatened the military's income from illicit economic activities. In 2019, the General Administrative Department (GAD) was brought under civilian control, a sign of the military's weakening grip on government administration and patronage, which was a key component of its ability to accumulate and protect its wealth.[203] Additionally, the military's revenue from the jade-mining industry was threatened by reforms to the Myanmar Gemstones Law, which aimed to improve labour conditions and safety in the industry.[204] To be clear, such measures were not enough to break the military's income. The Tatmadaw remained 'a well-endowed institution'.[205] This is because the Burmese military has long nurtured 'crony capitalism', an economic system in which individuals and firms with political connections and influence are given unfair advantages. Two military-run conglomerates, Myanmar Economic Corporation (MEC) and Myanmar Economic Holdings Limited (MEHL), act as key sources of wealth, with stakes in diverse economic sectors ranging 'from banking and mining to tobacco and tourism. MEHL also operates the military's pension fund. Aung Pyae Sone, the son of coup leader Gen Min Aung Hliang, owns several companies, including a beach resort, and has a majority stake in national telecoms carrier Mytel.'[206] The NLD government, as such, knew the limits of how far it could go in pushing the military out of its businesses and sources of revenue.[207] Moreover, given the military's role in the country's economy and politics, it also benefited from economic growth since 2011, allowing it to exist as an isolated 'state within a state' with massive access to resources.

## The Elusive Economic Take-off

Burma's economic performance under the Thein Sein and NLD governments, despite the slow pace of economic reforms, was creditable until the 2020 COVID-19 outbreak. According to the World Bank,[208] after a low 3.3 per cent growth in 2015, in the four years between 2016 and 2019 (all under the NLD government), Burma's annual GDP growth rate averaged over 6 per cent, the highest being 10.5 per cent in 2016. It fell to 3.2 per cent in 2020. But combined with respectable growth rates achieved during the Thein Sein period—7.5 per cent in 2011, 6.5 per cent in 2012, 7.9 per cent in 2013, 8.2 per cent in 2014—Burma's economic performance during the period of opening was, by conventional measures, good, if not spectacular.

Net flows of Foreign Direct Investment (FDI) grew from USD 2.52 billion in 2011 to 4.8 billion in 2017 but fell to 1.83 billion in 2020.[209] Burma's per capita income in current US dollars rose from 460.9 in 2008 to 1061.3 in 2011 to 1467.5 in 2020.[210] Indeed, the World Bank in January 2020 reported that Burma's economy remained 'stable', and 'continue[d] to show resilience despite the global slowdown and domestic uncertainties'.[211]

Aid from the European Union, Japan, the US and multilateral agencies poured in, making Burma one of the world's largest recipients of foreign aid. According to an Asia Foundation Report issued in February 2018, Burma had jumped to the seventh place globally as a recipient of foreign aid, from seventy-ninth place in 2010. Between 2011 and 2015, it has received a commitment of USD13.7 billion in aid.[212]

To be clear, Burma, according to World Bank categories in 2018, remained a lower middle-income country, along with Cambodia, Laos, and Vietnam, and ranked 147 out of 189 countries in the 2019 Human Development Index.[213] Corruption remained a major challenge, although Burma had improved its ranking in Transparency International's Corruption Perception Index, rising from 157th place in 2013 to 136th out of 176 countries in 2016.[214] The surge of foreign investment and economic growth slowed down, as Suu Kyi's government struggled to implement further reforms, and the military's suspected genocide of Rohingya drew international backlash. But Burma's share of the population living below the national poverty line halved, between 2005 to 2017, from 48.2 per cent to 24.8 per cent. It remained acute in rural areas, however, where much of the population lives.[215] While some of these performance improvements occurred during the military regime, we should be cognizant of the fact that Burma was making progress by shedding its isolationist stance and opening up to the world.

The political effects of a country's economic performance often come from expectations about the future, rather than the actual performance indicators. There was little doubt that for all its challenges, Burma was full of hope and enthusiasm about its economic future under democratic rule, especially among its youth. This optimism existed despite the immense effects of the COVID-19 pandemic in causing widespread misery and lowering growth. Hence if the question was 'did economic failure of the 2011–2020 period contribute to the coup?', the answer would be a firm NO. Any suggestion that the gap between expectations and reality in the economic performance of the NLD government could have been a significant factor that led to the February 2021 coup, does not cut much ice. The situation in 2020 was very different to that in 1962, when General Ne Win, removed the democratic government in Burma to establish what he called the 'Burmese Way to Socialism', with the nationalization of businesses and government monopolies. Similarly, General Saw Maung seized power in 1988 to establish the 'Burmese Way to Capitalism,' which was supposed to be an 'open market controlled by a hard state'.[216] In 2010, the military-backed Union Solidarity and Development Party initiated market reforms that did not sustain.[217] This time it was electoral irregularities that moved the Tatmadaw to seize power, which rather exacerbated the economic crisis in Burma.

Despite all its limitations and failures, the period of democratic opening had net positive results for the country. In the words of a *Thought Warrior*:

> *In the past people in Burma had not seen any stable democratic government even in the 1950s under U Nu. That gave justification to army rule. But the army failed to promote economic growth and lost respect and support. Then the period of 2011–21 was both more democratic and also economically open and dynamic, despite problems. During these ten years, people thought Burma could have both democracy and development. Are they willing to sacrifice both of these now under the return of military rule? I think resistance to army rule will grow.*

# Chapter 6

## The Return of History

From the Thought Warriors:

*Here we go again.*

*The reason [for the coup] is clear: they are power-mad people so it's not very surprising that they will steal every single thing out of the whole country and exploit these things for themselves.*

*I think it's a long-term plan of the juntas. They wanted to conquer the country . . . every second and there's no wonder they made the coup.*

*[The military was] afraid of losing their seats in the Parliament because they have to be in control of the country to keep making themselves richer and richer. They look up to countries like Russia and China. They want to be in control of everything and develop the country like leaders of those countries so that citizens feel grateful to them. Citizens have been hating and belittling them for so long that they want to be acknowledged that they can do better. They aren't capable, but they think they can. It seems like Min Aung Hlaing (MAH) wants to become a historical figure after death.*

\* \* \*

There was hope and optimism in the air. Burma was rising, growing, opening, and transforming. It seemed like after decades of darkness, democracy and development were attainable goals. But alas, an election cast a dark shadow over Burma's future.

## A Fateful Election

The military coup in Myanmar happened on the very day, 1 February 2021, when the newly elected Parliament was to meet after the 8 November 2020 general elections. It was neither sudden nor unexpected. The most immediate cause was the general election itself.

The 2020 elections saw ninety-seven political parties contesting for 315 seats in the Lower House, 161 in the Upper House, 612 in state and regional Parliaments and twenty-nine ethnic affairs ministry seats.[218]

The voting turnout reported in the media was high, with an estimated 70 per cent of the thirty-seven million eligible voters in Burma casting their vote.[219] While generally regarded as free and fair, the election was not without blemishes. For example, the Union Election Commission disenfranchised nearly 73 per cent of Rakhine voters, and the Rohingyas were already an unenumerated group, stripped of their voting rights from 2015.[220] International observers noted the cancellation of voting in fifteen districts (nine in Rakhine state and six in Shan state) in the Lower House/People's Assembly and seven districts (all in Rakhine state) in the Upper House/National Assembly.[221] While not totally free or fair, the elections were generally free from violence. The major exception to this was in the Rakhine state where Burmese troops battled ethnic insurgents of the Arakan Army (AA).

The Carter Centre, a non-governmental nonprofit organization founded by former US President Jimmy Carter that looks into election-monitoring and democratic institution-building in many countries, issued a 'Preliminary Statement' on 10 November 2020 about the Burma election. The statement noted:[222]

Although important aspects of the electoral process were impacted by restrictions imposed to combat the pandemic, the Carter Center's international election observation mission found that voters were enthusiastic and able to freely express their will at the polls and choose their elected representatives . . . Following a sometimes contentious pre-election period, election day itself occurred without significant incidents or major irregularities being reported by mission observers. In polling stations visited by Carter Center observers, election procedures were widely adhered to, with the conduct of voting assessed positively in ninety-four per cent of polling stations visited. In polling stations where counting was observed, the process was conducted according to procedures and in the presence of party agents. Tabulation proceeded smoothly in tabulation centers observed by the mission, although access for mission observers was limited or denied in three cases.

The Carter Center did register some concerns about the 'quality of democracy' in Burma:

. . . the quality of democracy in Myanmar continues to be undermined by serious deficiencies in the legal framework, including the reserved seats for military appointees, highlighting the need for reform to bring the country in line with international obligations. Ongoing conflict in many areas of the country and the exclusion of more than two million people from the electoral process because of violence or discrimination further undermine the democratic character of the election process.

Another observer group, the Asian Network for Free Elections (ANFREL), which had stationed observers at 400 polling stations, did note 'irregularities' due to the COVID-19 pandemic and ongoing conflicts. This made the election not as free and fair as the 2015 general elections. ANFREL noted that 'despite the raging Covid-19 pandemic, 27.5 million people voted thanks to the hard work of polling staff and election or health officials; their voices cannot be silenced'. Overall, the report stated, the 2020 vote was 'by and large, representative of the will of the people of Myanmar'.[223] Apart from the large voter turnout, the results also allowed for a marginally enhanced representation of women in the legislature. Suu Kyi managed to retain her popularity, even among ethnic minority voters, contradicting the predictions made by political commentators. After decades of political instability, the Burmese were keen on achieving political stability, and the success of the NLD ensured continuity in leadership and a semblance of political stability.

One major concern of international election observers was the disenfranchisement of the Rohingya population. Thomas Andrews, the UN Human Rights Council's Special Rapporteur, stated, 'Even before a single vote was cast, the upcoming election in Myanmar would fail to meet the standard of free, fair, credible and transparent election that reflected the will of the people.' Andrews continues to say that 'the results of an election could not accurately reflect the will of the people, when the right to vote was denied because of a person's race, ethnicity, or religion'. Andrews saw no evidence that the Burmese government was willing or prepared to 'facilitate the right to vote for hundreds of thousands of voting-age Rohingya located in Rakhine state or in refugee camps in Bangladesh'.[224] A similar concern was also expressed by the EU. While recognizing the high turnout for the polls in the face of the COVID-19 pandemic, the EU spokesperson called for the full inclusion of all ethnic, religious, and minority groups of the country, including the Rohingyas.[225] But the EU itself received criticism for promoting the mVoter 2020 app, developed under the EU-funded STEP Democracy Project. The app was developed to support the electoral process, but the EU unintentionally implicated itself in the exacerbation of religious tensions and discrimination against Rohingya minorities.[226, 227] The app included information about candidates' race and religion, as well as those of family members, which resulted in the disqualification of several Rohingya candidates. While some EU representatives advocated for the removal of all controversial information and denied knowing about the inclusion of such information beforehand, others praised the app for its capacity to provide information about prospective candidates despite the controversy.[228]

Aside from rising Rohingya exclusion, the Carter Centre raised other concerns with the election, on the legal framework with issues about reserved military seats, UEC appointment procedures, and candidate requirements, on election administration including the lack of transparency, management of advance out-of-constituency voting, and unclear procedures, as well as with voter registration. The Center did not find any issues at the polling stations visited but media outlets reported that voters were missing from voter rolls for the ethnic affairs minister races in Mandalay and Yangon.[229] Additional concerns included candidate registration such as citizenship requirements and privacy violations; the lack of female participation where, for instance, only 16 per cent of candidates were women or no women were serving as UEC commissioners; campaign environment including censorship; inconsistent enforcement of COVID-19 restrictions; the death and candidate abductions that were previously mentioned; social media as a platform for disinformation and hate speech directed at ethnic and religious minorities or women; and election observation wherein some observers faced additional reporting requirements on deployment plans that reduced their ability to ensure transparency.[230]

Overall, the election of 2021, though flawed, was largely legitimate.[231] In all, this was a fateful election: it promised continuity and political stability for many. But for some, like the Rohingyas and other ethnic minorities, the election results were a repudiation of their concerns and democratic aspirations. It bestowed a large mandate to the NLD, but for others, it was business-as-usual with the continuation of discrimination and disenfranchisement.

## Winners and Losers

Ultimately, the November 2020 elections emphatically returned the NLD to power. Of the total 498 seats in the Parliament (both houses combined, excluding the 25 per cent reserved for the military), the NLD won a total of 396 seats. In the lower house, with a total of 330 seats, the NLD won 258, while in the upper house, with 168 seats, it secured 138 seats. The USDP, the military-backed ruling party since 2011, managed to get only twenty-six seats in the lower house and seven in the upper house, or thirty-three seats in total in the entire national Parliament. In the 2015 elections, the NLD had won a total of 390 seats (255 and 135 seats in the lower and upper houses, respectively), while the USDP got thirty and eleven, respectively, for a total of forty-one.[232]

This tilted the balance of power in the Parliament. To form a government, a party needs to win half of the total seats in the Parliament (both houses), and NLD had scored well above that. But what was more striking was the narrower gap between the NLD and the USDP in the national Parliament. Taking into account the 25 per cent seats (166) reserved for the military, the NLD accounted for about 62 per cent of the total 642 seats in the national Parliament (including the military seats), while the USDP's total accounted for about 5 per cent; USDP plus the seats reserved for the military was under 31 per cent.[233] The NLD itself was shy of the votes it needed to amend the Constitution, but for the military, the lower number of seats won by the USDP was cause for concern.

The NLD's sweeping victory is attributable also to the 'first past the post' electoral system and the ongoing COVID-19 pandemic. But the most important factor was Suu Kyi's popularity, and the perception of the NLD as the best hope for bringing about the end of military dominance in Burmese politics.[234] The NLD has been heavily criticized worldwide, but it continues to remain popular in Burma, as it is viewed as the only effective bulwark against military rule. Despite her controversial statements between 2017–19 that seemed to lend support to the military's heavy-handed responses to the Rohingya crisis—which were received well domestically— Aung San Suu Kyi is still considered to be someone who can stand up to the military, as attested by her record of house arrests. She also used the coronavirus crisis to her advantage, as her everyday media appearance exhorting people to take precautionary measures reinforced her popular image as 'mother Suu'.[235]

## Dark Hints

But even before the polls concluded, rift and suspicion had surfaced between the NLD and the military. On 3 November 2020, Sr Gen. Min Aung Hlaing stated that the civilian government was making *'unacceptable mistakes'* in the run-up to the general election of 8 November, in a rare interview with a local media outlet:

> [T]here is no problem for normal mistakes. But some are unacceptable mistakes. They have a lot of time to do corrections . . . [there were] widespread violation of the laws and procedures of the pre-voting process . . . and [the Tatmadaw had] told the election commission we want a free and fair election . . . I said in an interview with media in 2015 . . . that we would accept the result by the election committee as long as it was free and fair. However, for now, we are in a situation where we need to be cautious.[236]

His comments were noted by the US State Department, and in a 2 February 2021 press briefing, the department said, 'Burmese military alleged that . . . there was fraud in the voting process that took place in November. According to local and international observers, there were no widespread provable fraud allegations; they're just allegations.'[237]

Interestingly, closer to the polling day, while the NLD was expected to win the polls, it was not expected to repeat its 2015 electoral performance. Among the reasons was its failure to reach out to ethnic groups.[238] The Tatmadaw might have calculated that the elections would result in a hung Parliament. It seems to have expected better results by the military-backed USDP. This, along with an alliance of ethnic political parties—Karen, Kachin, Kayah, Mon and Chin—they thought would prevent a sweeping NLD victory.[239] However, it turned out to be a miscalculation.

After casting his vote in the Zeyar Thiri township near the capital, Naypyidaw, Sr Gen. Min Aung Hlaing seemed positive, accepting the result of the election, whatever they might be:

> I will have to accept the people's wish and the results that come with it. There's no denying it . . . We need to think about the public's feelings and concerns and aim to console them . . . This is very important for me. To ease the pain of citizens and what they're feeling. It's a must.[240]

Although it is impossible to be sure, perhaps at that moment he was still feeling confident for USDP and the overall prospects for the army's hold on power. At least there was no sense that the military might challenge the results openly. Thus, when asked about how he voted, Gen. Min Aung Hlaing replied that he voted for the party that 'prioritizes nationalism, religion, and education. And the party that prioritizes our three main national causes. I voted for a party that would work well with us. I completely believe it's a group of people that can create a better future.'[241] In any case, there was no sign of major grievances about electoral irregularities at this point. At least the military did nothing we know of to disrupt the polls and the counting of votes.

But when the result became known, the USDP came out with accusations of electoral fraud and irregularities. To quote USDP spokesperson Win Win Aung, '[w]e reject the election because it was unfair. We call on the election commission to hold a new, disciplined election in cooperation with the military as soon as possible.'[242] The party demanded a re-poll 'in order to have an election that is free, fair, unbiased and free from unfair campaigning'.[243]

The Tatmadaw's attitude towards the election outcome was also foreshadowed by its views on the Rakhine situation. Soon after the election, on 12 November 2020, Gen. Min Aung Hlaing assured the United League of Arakan/Arakan Army (ULA/AA)—the ULA is an Arakanese political organization based in Kachin state with the AA as its armed wing—that he would support by-elections in the Rakhine state before the end of 2020. The ULA/AA had demanded:

'In most of the townships in Arakan, however, elections were cancelled. As a result, the people of those constituencies were disenfranchised. They lost their representation. Their voices cannot be heard, and the rights of the citizens and of the indigenous ethnic groups and their basic democratic rights cannot be defended through their elected representatives. Our organization sincerely desires that by-elections be held in those constituencies in order that the people do not lose their rights. To that end, we have extended our unilateral ceasefire effective from 11th November through to 31 December 2020. Myanmar Army should cooperate with the NLD government to hold by-elections as soon as possible by halting ongoing offensives in Arakan and declaring a comprehensive ceasefire embracing the whole nation.'[244]

In response, the Tatmadaw commander's office issued a statement. Reminding that the Tatmadaw had 'ceased its operations till the end of November 2020 for the successful holding of the 2020 multiparty democracy general election of the Republic of the Union of Myanmar,'[245] it stated:

> Tatmadaw has already expressed its serious stance on the freeness and fairness of the multiparty general election and on enabling all the eligible voters to cast votes at the respective constituencies. Hence, the Tatmadaw welcomes the statement of ULA/AA and assures utmost coordinated efforts to hold a by-election in the areas where the election has not been held.[246]

On 26 January 2021, the Tatmadaw spokesperson Brig. Gen. Zaw Min Tun, when questioned by the media if he could rule out possibilities of a coup, said, 'We can't. The military will act in line with all laws, including the Constitution.' He also added, 'I am neither saying the military will seize state power, nor that it won't.'[247] While addressing the cadets of the National Defence College on 27 January, 2021, Gen. Min Aung Hlaing said ominously, '[The] Constitution is the mother law. We have to follow the Constitution. If the law is not respected or followed, we must abolish it. Even if it is the Constitution, we must abolish it. In the time of the Revolutionary Council, the 1947 Constitution was abolished.'[248] He also said, '[T]he 2008 Constitution is effective. I'd like to note that it is a very important basic factor in politics. No one should be negligent [of this].'[249] The reference to the Constitution by the Tatmadaw Chief was in the context of Constitutional Article 20 (f), which states that the 'Defence Services is (sic) mainly responsible for safeguarding the Constitution'.[250]

Two days after this speech, on 29 January 2021, the first tanks and armoured vehicles started patrolling the streets of Burma's major towns. At first, it seemed that there might be ground for a mutual understanding between the NLD and the military. Talks between the two reportedly took place over the issue of voter fraud. But these failed. On 1 February, the military carried out a coup preventing the newly elected legislators from taking their oath of office in Parliament. Gen. Min Aung Hlaing declared a one-year state of emergency, while NLD leaders including Aung San Suu Kyi were placed in detention.

## What the Constitution Says

While Gen. Min Aung Hlaing referred to the Constitution to justify his action, the coup was constitutionally illegal. Article 40 of the 2008 Myanmar Constitution has three parts:[251]

40. (a) If there arises a state of emergency characterized by inability to perform executive functions in accord with the provisions of the Constitution in a Region or a State or a Self-Administered Area, the President is empowered to exercise executive power in that Region, State or Self-Administered Area and, if necessary in doing so, the President is empowered to exercise legislative powers concerning that Region, State or Self-Administered Area in accord with the provisions of this Constitution.

(b) If there arises or there is sufficient reason to arise a state of emergency endangering life and property of the people in a Region, State or Self-Administered Area, the Defence Services has the right, in accord with the provisions of this Constitution, to prevent that danger and provide protection.

(c) If there arises a state of emergency that could cause disintegration of the Union, disintegration of national solidarity and loss of sovereign power or attempts therefore [To this author, the wording 'therefore' implies 'thereof'] by wrongful forcible means such as insurgency or violence, the Commander-in-Chief of the Defence Services has the right to take over and exercise State sovereign power in accord with the provisions of this Constitution.

None of the three sections justifies the coup. Clause 40(a) vests the authority to assume executive and legislative powers of the union with the *President* (who is a civilian), not the military leader. It is the President who must determine the need for an emergency and do so only if and when the executive is no longer able to perform its functions. Article 40(b) allows the armed forces to act only if there is a development 'endangering life and property of the people'. The key word here should be 'the people' and their well-being, not the privilege of the military. Even then, the action called for is to 'prevent the danger and provide protection', not to take over the whole country. A coup was not what the 2008 Constitutional drafter had in mind when they wrote down Article 40.

Another relevant article of the 2008 Constitution on handling an emergency situation is Article 417. It reads:[252]

> If there arises or if there is sufficient reason for a state of emergency to arise that may disintegrate the Union or disintegrate national solidarity or that may cause the loss of sovereignty, due to acts or attempts to take over the sovereignty of the Union by insurgency, violence and wrongful forcible means, the President may, after coordinating with the National Defence and Security Council, promulgate an ordinance and declare a state of emergency. In the said ordinance, it shall be stated that the area where the state of emergency is in operation is the entire Nation and the specified duration is one year from the day of promulgation.

The provisions of Article 417 are identical to that of Article 40, except that it clearly and exclusively vests the power of declaring an emergency in the office of the President. The President may coordinate with the National Defence and Security Council, which includes the commander of the armed forces, but the latter cannot declare an emergency on their own. There was no such consultation and coordination before the Tatmadaw launched its coup on 1 February 2021.

In other words, both Articles 40 and 417 set the benchmark of a military takeover to be very high, specifying disintegration of the Union, of national solidarity or loss of sovereignty, as justification. Yet, no such developments had taken place; the elections were mostly peaceful, there was no prospect of a loss of Burma's sovereignty, and no sign of any impending disintegration of the nation. Nor was there any new insurgency or escalation of existing ethnic tensions.

The violence that engulfed Burma came after and as a direct result of the coup. Without the coup, there would have been no threat to Burma's sovereignty, integration and people's life and property. These were the consequences, not the causes of the coup.

## What Then Led to the Coup?

As noted in Chapter 1, in announcing its takeover of the government on 1 February 2021, the military had claimed fraud in the November 2020 national elections. But this claim has been debunked by independent analysts. An Australian Burma expert, Melissa Crouch, dismissed the military's claims of electoral fraud as 'hollow', further noting, 'The military has jumped to the powers the Commander in Chief is given under a state of emergency without going through the legitimate process to get there. The actions of 1 February 2021 are best understood as a coup, not a constitutional state of emergency.'[253]

Why the military seized power on 1 February 2021 was one of the main questions I had asked my Thought Warriors. They gave a variety of answers. Here are a few:

> *Due to the greed of a group of people that has been unjustly holding on power since a long time ago.*
>
> *They did the coup because they had already calculated that there's no loss for them. Some say, only MAH and a few people around him knew about the coup before 1 Feb. MAH might want the power*

*in his hand like Ne Win (announcing his government as caretaker government could be a clue.) When the idea of coalition government vanished, they planned a coup because there's no loss for them and NLD leaders prompting for negotiations with SAC was a point. Military might have guessed that the NLD is so weak in terms of politics and revolutions.*

*I can't think of any comprehensible reasons why the military brought out a coup. This unintelligent action only puts more problems on them. However, this military coup, the people of Myanmar altogether (especially Burmese ethnics) come to realize how authoritative, repressive and atrocious this blatant military junta is.*

*Weak and wrong strategy of the civilian government and the negligence of the urban people in county's politics.*

*For the sake of a small group of people, they not only monopolized their opposing party but also ruined the future of the citizens. They humiliate our rights by imposing frauds on state leaders and sending every person who opposes them to prison. Moreover, they are mercilessly killing everyone who opposes them, which is a similar act of genocide.*

It is noteworthy that some of my respondents blamed the breakdown of Burma's democracy on Aung San Suu Kyi. As a non-activist student put it, Suu Kyi went too far in appeasing the military: 'When Daw Suu went to ICJ to defend and cover for the military [it] was a wrong move.' A teenager's view was simpler and blunter: 'Daw Suu couldn't handle the past situations well.'

A host of other factors also contributed to the coup.[254] The crushing defeat of the Tatmadaw-backed USDP in the 2020 election would have strengthened the fear of an impending political shift, including NLD-initiated amendments to the Constitution denying the military its privileges, like the guaranteed 25 per cent quota in parliamentary seats.[255] Looking at the circumstances leading to the coup, it may be difficult for one to escape the conclusion that the coup was the direct result of the military's fear of loss of privilege after a disastrous election performance, and

General Min's personal stakes in staying in control. As Georgetown University academic David Steinberg notes:

> The first coup in 1958 was intentionally transitory, while the second in 1962 was for perpetual control. The third coup in 1988 brought an end to what had become a failed people's revolution. This present coup incited a revolution, the outcome of which remains in doubt. But with the military's effective control over its 'interests', the coup seemed unnecessary. The Tatmadaw's humiliating election defeat that denied the presidency to its aspirant—coup leader and Senior General Min Aung Hlaing— may be responsible.[256]

General Min Aung Hlaing's impending retirement deserves special consideration in looking for reasons behind the coup. Approaching the mandatory retirement age of sixty-five in July 2021 (he was appointed as commander-in-chief in 2011), the general was described as 'ambitious but cornered'. According to a senior diplomat based in Yangon, '[T]here was no path for [Min Aung Hlaing] to assume a leadership role in this government through the means that the Constitution provided.'[257] After seizing power, the military regime abolished the retirement age of sixty-five in May 2021.[258] For Gen. Min, retirement not only meant loss of privilege, but also carried the fear of prosecution. There had been calls for a trial of those responsible for war crimes against the Rohingya. Reports circulating before the 2020 elections suggested that Gen. Min Aung Hlaing was being offered the Presidency, and that he and other officers and their family were seeking immunity from prosecution after retirement. These possibilities might have come true had the military-backed USDP fared better in the elections and was in a position to negotiate with the NLD. The fact that Gen. Min Aung Hlaing was expecting a high political office was clear from an interview he gave to a Russian magazine in June 2020 when he had stated: 'The first priority is to successfully hold the 2020 elections. Then, if there is trust, we might also have to consider how we could participate in politics.'[259]

Apart from the circumstances that seemed to compel Gen. Min Aung Hlaing to take over power, his personality also seemed to be conducive to using force to get his way. Nicholas Coppel, a former Australian ambassador to Burma, who had met him on several occasions said, '[T]he senior general is not a listener—he talks and others listen.' To Coppel, the general seemed isolated, and his 'management style [was] conducive to ignorance and arrogance'.[260] An article in *Washington Post* cited former foreign officials calling him as 'controlling, egotistical and ambitious, unwilling to go quietly into retirement as scheduled later this year'.[261] These traits indicate intransigence—a refusal to change his views about the USDP's poor electoral performance. His rigidity ensured that he was used to getting his own way, making the coup seem inevitable.

His increasingly strained relationship with Aung San Suu Kyi also played a role in the coup. Their relationship outwardly had seemed cooperative. The two held regular meetings, although there was never much trust.[262] Both were strong, highly egoistic personalities. Aung San Suu Kyi herself has been criticized for being controlling and developing a 'personality cult' of her own, demanding 'loyalty and obedience', from followers.[263] Western diplomats who met Gen. Min Aung Hlaing observed that he 'distrusted and disliked Suu Kyi intensely' and had 'never reconciled to civilian rule led by her from the very beginning.'[264] The relationship between the two seemed to have deteriorated as NLD seemed increasingly impatient to amend the Constitution to cut back the military's political and administrative privileges and especially after Suu Kyi's failed effort to defend the military at the 2019 proceedings on war crimes and crimes against humanity at the International Court of Justice in the Hague.[265] The clash of two obstinate leaders, refusing to negotiate and compromise, seems to have doomed Burma's elections, making the coup more likely.

## The Aftermath

In the immediate aftermath of the coup, the military regime tried to give the impression that its takeover was temporary and that its intention was to return Burma to 'democracy'. In a speech on 1 August 2021, Gen. Min Aung Hlaing announced 'We will accomplish the provisions of the state of emergency by August 2023.' This timeline was itself problematic, since under Article 417, as noted earlier, the duration of an emergency was set at one year, but Gen. Min Aung Hlaing's speech set the timeline to be two years. In the same speech, the coup leader made another promise: 'I guarantee the establishment of a union based on democracy and federalism.'[266] In his desire to avoid prosecution and remain politically relevant, statements about implementing democracy after violently overpowering the government seem hypocritical and cynical.

The military's statements implied that it was digging in for the long haul. In November 2021, Gen. Min Aung Hlaing noted: 'Politically, we are facing various kinds of criticism and restrictions,' He added, 'Now is the time our people must be working together to ensure development and stability of the country.' The junta promised to carry on with vaccination against COVID-19 and pursue an export-oriented economic development approach.[267]

The impression one gets from these statements and promises was that the newly formed State Administration Council (SAC) regime would seek to establish 'performance legitimacy', giving governance a civilian image and normalizing the military's dominant role in the country's politics, akin to the political fabric of the Thein Sein era during 2010–15. The goal was to recreate the 'business-friendly but military-controlled state',[268] a model that had been seriously threatened by the NLD's political dominance in the past two election cycles.

Despite assurances from the regime to restore normalcy and move on with economic development, the coup plunged the country into a deep and protracted political crisis. After the military set up the SAC, the forces ousted by the coup set up the National Unity Government (NUG) on 16 April 2021, which was made up of ousted lawmakers and government officials. The country drew closer to a civil war when the NUG announced an armed wing called the People's Defence Force (PDF) in May 2021. The PDF signalled a radical shift from civilian protests and civil disobedience movements that were adopted by those who opposed the coup called the 'Spring Revolution'.[269] The PDF also marked the NLD's departure from their policy of non-violence, which existed during their previous opposition to military rule during 1988–2011.

In announcing the shift on 7 September 2021, the NUG's acting President Duwa Lashi La called for a 'revolt against the rule of military terrorists'. The NUG itself declared a state of emergency until 'the resumption of civilian rule in the country'.[270] The people's defence militias carried out attacks throughout Burma while facing the regime's 'heavy-handed, indiscriminate retaliation'.[271]

This bloody struggle marked a turning point in Burma's history. Until then, the military had mainly fought the militias of the ethnic minorities in ethnic minority areas. Now, it was fighting the ethnic majority as well. Burma was now staring at the face of a full-scale civil war. This was the very spectre of national disintegration that the military had used to justify the coup, and it was brought closer to reality by the actions of the military itself.

## State Administration Council (SAC)

In the coup's immediate aftermath, on 2 February 2021, the military formed the SAC led by Gen. Min. The SAC acted like Burma's provisional government with Gen. Min Aung Hlaing becoming the thirteenth prime minister of Burma. The SAC began with nine military members and ten civilian members. The larger number of civilian members was an attempt by the military to secure legitimacy and deny that it was a military regime. The civilian members were those who had enjoyed good relations with the military and the USDP and were drawn from each of Burma's main official national races, namely Kachin, Karen, Karenni, Chin, Mon, Bamar, Arakan and Shan, reflecting an 'ethnic balancing' approach. It was also an attempt to win over ethnic parties who had done poorly against the NLD in the election, even in their home states, especially in Shan, Mon and Kayah states.[272] The formation of the SAC was followed by the establishment of a provisional government on 1 August 2021 comprising twenty-eight ministers. The government's composition suggested 'an aspiration to achieve performance legitimacy for the regime'.[273] Out of the twenty-eight, five were active-duty military officers, while thirteen had military backgrounds. Eight were from the 2011–16 USDP government, while six had served with the NLD government of 2016–21. Several ministers were also a part of the 1988–2011 SLORC/SPDC governments.

The active-duty officers in the list of Union ministers included General Mya Htun Oo, Admiral Tin Aung San, and Lieutenant General Soe Htut, who also served concurrently on the SAC. The fact that the first two, General Mya Htun Oo and Admiral Tin Aung San, gave up their positions of Joint Chief of Staff of the Army, Navy, and Air Force and Commander-in-Chief of the Navy, respectively, which are the third- and the fourth-highest positions in the Tatmadaw, further suggest an attempt by the regime to create some distance between the military high command and the new government. The inclusion of some ousted NLD government ministers, vested with portfolios such as Health and Foreign Economic Relations, was meant to create a sense of national unity and continuity. But despite the appearance of civilianization, the new council of ministers was de facto dominated by the military, with only nine of its members being 'true civilians'.[274]

By November 2021, the military's relentless crackdown on protestors had claimed more than 1,200 lives.[275] The number would rise of course. By the time of the coup's first anniversary, the Assistance Association for Political Prisoners (AAPP) put the number of people killed by the military crackdown at 1,503, while another report, by the independent group, Armed Conflict Location and Event Data (ACLED) project, put the number of killed at a much higher level: 12,000.[276] Reported reprisals against the PDF included the torture and killing of 40 civilians in July 2021 in Sagaing, an Opposition stronghold.[277] Counterattacks and assassinations by the resistance militias killed hundreds of troops and suspected informants. There are also reports of defections from the military ranks numbering in the hundreds.

The 2020 elections changed Burma's fate. The country was developing at a good pace and opening itself to the world. Election results called for a continuation of the NLD's policies. But it seems like when Burma does well, the Tatmadaw feels ill. In the name of restoring democracy and security, Burma's military reversed the country's progress and set the clock backwards. So, what now?

# Chapter 7

## The Resistance

From the Thought Warriors:

*NUG obviously is not a perfect revolutionary government. However, it is the only government with a clear mandate. Thus, we have to go on with it while we criticize their defects. We hope that they (NUG) listen to our critique and adapt to our advice.*

*I don't believe in NUG . . . They have no intention of suffering with us, the citizens.*

*I only recognize NUG as the legitimate government. They have full domestic power, yet no control over the territory. EAOs are the saviours of this revolution. The compromise between EAOs and NUG will impact positively the future of our country in moving towards federalism.*

*I hope both NUG and EAOs will support the people of Myanmar.*

\* \* \*

## The National Unity Government (NUG)

Attempts to create a parallel government in Burma to resist the military regime began almost immediately after the 1 February 2021 coup. It moved swiftly, reflecting the depth of frustration and anger not only of the elected members of parliament who were prevented from taking office, but also of the people at large who were expecting a new NLD-led government to assume office. This marked the rebirth of Burma's democratic opposition movement.

On 5 February 2021, a 'Committee Representing Pyidaungsu Hluttaw (CRPH)', the Burmese parliament, was formed, drawing its members from the representatives elected in the 2020 election. A month later, the CRPH announced the establishment of an interim government with four acting ministers covering:

1. Foreign affairs
2. Union Government and President's Office
3. Labour, immigration, population, education, health and sports
4. Planning, finance and industry, commerce, and investment and foreign economic relations

On 10 March 2021, Mahn Win Khaing Than, the former speaker of the Amyotha Hluttaw, the upper house of parliament, was named acting vice-president. This was followed by the release of the Federal Democracy Charter on 31 March 2021. A day later, the CRPH dissolved the 2008 Constitution that the military had engineered to give itself a privileged position in the country. As its name implied, the charter envisaged a federal system and a federal army. The roadmap the charter provided included the provisions for a National Unity Government (NUG) and a National Unity Consultative Council (NUCC), which would serve as a consultative platform for the CRPH. The Charter included space for political parties, ethnic groups as well as the civil disobedience movement (CDM), and civil society organizations (CSOs).[278]

The NUG officially came into existence on 16 April 2021. It comprised a twenty-six member cabinet made up of the ousted President Win Myint and State Counsellor Aung San Suu Kyi. Two others in the top leadership position were Acting Vice

President Mahn Win Khaing Than, who now became prime minister, and Duwa Lashi La, who assumed the role first of NUG's acting vice-president, and later Acting President when President Win Myint got imprisoned. The NUG proclaimed itself as the 'only and legitimate Government of the Republic of the Union of Myanmar' and listed its goals as the 'eradication of dictatorship, abolishment of the 2008 Constitution and building of Federal Democracy Union'.[279] In May 2021, in another dramatic but expected turn, after seeing civilian protests and the resistance being crushed by the military, the NUG officially took to armed struggle by announcing the creation of a 'People's Defence Force'. In September 2021, the NUG declared a 'people's defensive war' on the military.[280] The NUG Acting President exhorted PDFs and EAOs to 'target the military and their support pillars to take control of their regions', while also calling upon 'all levels of local administrators to stop working immediately.'[281]

The NUG also swiftly took to the international stage. They got a significant boost when Burma's UN ambassador, Kyaw Moe Tun, after being fired by the military regime in February for opposing the coup, announced his intention not to leave his post, even as the military regime sought to displace him with its own ambassador.[282] The UN Credentials Committee reached a compromise with Russia and China, to allow him to remain in the post as long as he did not speak at the high-level meeting that was to be held later in the month.[283] The NUG established offices in Washington DC and Prague, and accepted the jurisdiction of the International Criminal Court with respect to all crimes in Burma since 2002.[284] This was significant, since the 2015 NLD government, led by Suu Kyi herself, had not only refused to accede to the ICC under the Rome Statute but also rejected any prosecutions under the auspices of the court, in deference to the Burmese military, over the latter's atrocities against the Rohingyas in 2017. With this shift, the ICC could investigate not only crimes against the Rohingyas in the Rakhine

State, but also any crimes committed in ethnic conflicts in Burma dating back to 2002. Moreover, the shift would authorize the court to prosecute the Burmese military for crimes committed during the coup and its continued repression of the opposition. These killings were not covered under the old ICC case as they concerned only the Rohingyas.

The NUG, however, faces challenges to its legitimacy on the domestic front. One of the most important challenges concerns the deep-rooted internal divisions between long-time members of the NLD and other NUG cabinet members.[285] Aung San Suu Kyi, the NLD supremo, is a divisive figure within the more diverse cabinet drawn from many different constituencies including its powerful but disparate ethnic armed groups. Part of the reason the EAO representatives resent Aung San Suu Kyi is rooted in the memories of her actions when she was in power before, when she supported military campaigns against ethnic groups and defended the Tatmadaw at the ICC. Some CDM supporters suspect that when she gets out of prison and gets back in power, she might dismiss all the work done by the NUG until then and that this will undermine the democracy movement. Although they sympathize with her struggles and sacrifices for democracy, they believe that she has now become a symbol of the past. As a CDM supporter, alias Ma Ei Ei, puts it, 'Things have moved very quickly. Daw Suu would face a huge public backlash if she walks out tomorrow and calls the Tatmadaw "my father's army".'[286]

Originally formed by an eclectic assortment of community and ethnic leaders, the NUG remains dominated by NLD loyalists. Activists in the field do not see the senior leaders of NUG acting as members of a truly revolutionary government, but as politicians focused on making statements. In addition to the comments from the Thought Warriors mentioned at the outset of this chapter, one CDM activist said:

*So far, the NUG still lacks essential requirements. There are people who actually work with passion while there are also black sheep of the family. Whether they like it or not, NUG has to accept that they are still incomplete. It is better not to ignore what is really happening on ground and give false hope to people who are suffering from the coup.*

Another Thought Warrior put it even more bluntly:

*[I] don't want to support the NUG since they are not a real revolutionary government. All they are doing is for them to get authority. The thing I hate about the NUG the most is that they try to deceive and clown us by giving false hopes. They look down on the military when they are the one with no absolute control over anything except the people. I would support EAOs more than the NUG.*

At the same time, the NUG has managed to create and sustain just about enough pressure to deny the Junta's State Administrative Council (SAC) domestic political legitimacy, control and international recognition. The NUG-led people's defensive war against the junta has been likened to a 'second struggle for independence'. Senior NUG leaders focus on delegitimizing the military by reminding people of its history of coups and repressions. For example, on the occasion of Burma's 74th annual Independence Day commemoration, NUG Acting President Duwa Lashi La reminded people that Burma's freedom from colonial rule did not mean freedom for its people, thanks to the military dictatorship. 'As long as the owners of the sovereignty of the country lose their rights, we cannot say the country has achieved its independence.'[287]

The NUG's military arm, the PDF, has been more active on the ground, not only fighting the military and its civilian supporters, but also taking administrative control of some areas. For example, in January 2022, the PDF, in Pinlebu Township, Sagaing Region, assembled a civilian administration in its area of control, claiming to take over, through a People's Administration Committee, the security and health affairs of civilians in the area.[288] As a PDF spokesperson said, 'We started providing health services in our villages for the first time. The NUG (National Unity Government) provided the medicine. We explained to villagers why we have to bear arms and told them not to be afraid of us because we're trying to protect them from the Burma Army (BA).'[289]

However, one key challenge to Burma's resistance movement remains. The coup has not erased the historical mistrust and animosities among Burma's ethnic groups. Reintegrating Burma's ethnic minorities with the Union has been an enduring challenge since prior to the country's independence.

## Ethnic Armed Organizations (EAOs)

Shortly after the November 2020 elections, the NLD came out with a memorandum entitled 'The Issue of Unity and Myanmar's Future' signed by Vice Chair Zaw Myint Maung. The memorandum was meant to be the first step in the NLD's reconciliation process with the ethnic groups. Addressed to forty-eight ethnic groups, the memorandum expressed NLD's desire to form a national unity government:

> The aims of the ethnic parties align with those of the NLD, and our party will focus on the wishes and desires of ethnic people in the future . . . We hope that the ethnic political parties will eagerly cooperate and work with us on the matter of a democratic federal union.[290]

The NLD vouched that it would form a government that would put unity at the forefront. A leader of the NLD, U Myo

Nyunt, said that while nothing has been finalized, it would definitely not be NLD taking all the control.[291] He added, 'NLD was willing to consider including nominees of the ethnic parties to be part of the government.'[292] The NLD also pledged that its 'first move after the election [was] to work effectively for ethnic affairs and ending the civil war'.[293] But these promises were not entirely convincing to the ethnic groups. As put by Mann Aung Pyae Soe, the vice-chairman of the Karen National Democratic Party (KNDP), 'The NLD had broken many promises in the past.' The vice-chair of the Shan Nationalities League for Democracy (SNLD) Sai Nyunt Lwin shared this skepticism about the NLD's reliability. 'Maybe they had this way of thinking before the election. But since they've won about eighty-five per cent of seats, I don't think they'll hold themselves to it.'[294]

During the election campaigns, the NLD upset the sentiments of some ethnic parties by calling on voters to 'support that party which can form the government instead of supporting ethnic parties'. But the ethnic parties were willing to give the NLD a new lease of life.[295] As Mann Aung Pyae Soe of the Karen National Development Party (KNDP) put it, 'We welcome this invitation if they are really genuine about delivering on their promises this time. Otherwise, if this announcement is just a symbolic gesture to please the ethnic minorities, we won't accept it.'[296] The General Secretary of the SNLD, Sai Leik, added, 'The NLD should take the work of establishing a federal union more seriously.'[297]

Table 7.1 summarizes the immediate response of various EAOs in Burma to the coup. But these responses are fluid and subject to change depending on the situation on the ground as well as debates within the EAOs, which are sometimes divided as much against themselves as against other ethnic groups.

## Table 7.1

| Name of EAO | Size[298] | NCA Signatory? | Immediate post-coup reaction (subject to change later) |
|---|---|---|---|
| Arakan Army (AA) | 30,000[299] | No (member of Brotherhood Alliance[300]) | Denounced coup, threatened to end unilateral 2019 ceasefire |
| All Burma Student's Democratic Front (ABSDF) | 400+ | Yes | Denounced coup, would not engage with the military[301] |
| Arakan Liberation Party/Army (ALP/ALA) | 60–100 (2000 party members) | Yes | Denounced coup, would not engage with the military but sent officials to Armed Forces Day event |
| Chin National Front (CNF) | 200+ | Yes | Denounced coup, would not engage with military |
| Democratic Karen Buddhist Army: Brigade 5 | 1500+ | Yes | Denounced coup, would not engage with military |
| Kachin Independence Organization/ Army (KIO/KIA) | 10,000–12,000 | No | Denounced coup/escalated violence against military forces |

| Karen National Union (KNU)/KNLA | 5000+ | Yes | Denounced coup and violated NCA, would not engage with military/ KNU. Declared the NCA to be void (on 3 Sept 2021)[302] |
|---|---|---|---|
| Karen National Defence Organization (KNDO) | Unknown | No | Denounced coup/ violated NCA |
| KNU/KNLA Peace Council | 200+ | Yes | Denounced coup, would not engage with military but sent officials to Armed Forces Day event |
| Lahu Democratic Union | <100 | Yes | Denounced coup, would not engage with military |
| Myanmar Nationalities Democratic Alliance Army (MNDAA) | 2000+ | No (member of Brotherhood Alliance) | Denounced coup, threatened to end unilateral 2019 ceasefire |
| Mon National Liberation Army (MNLA) | 3000–5000 | Yes | Denounced coup, would not engage with military |
| National Democratic Alliance Army (NDAA) | 4000+ | No | Unclear/ Ambivalent |

| Pa-O National Liberation Army (PNLO) | 400+ | Yes | Unclear/ Ambivalent |
|---|---|---|---|
| Restoration Council of Shan State/Shan State Army-South (SSA-S) | 8000+ | Yes | Denounced military force against protestors[303] but no clashes with Tatmadaw, fighting SSA-N instead[304] |
| Shan State Progress Party/ Shan State Army-North (SSA-N) | 8000+ | No | Denounced military force against protestors but no clashes yet with Tatmadaw, have been fighting SSA-S instead |
| Ta'ang National Liberation Army (TNLA) | 6000+ | No (member of Brotherhood Alliance) | Denounced coup, threatened to end unilateral 2019 ceasefire |
| United Wa State Army (UWSA) | 30,000 (reserve 30,000) | No | Largely silent on coup |

The military also launched its own effort to woo the ethnic minority political parties and the EAOs. Prior to the release of the 2020 election results, Sr Gen. Min Aung Hlaing announced the formation of a Peace Talks Committee of the Tatmadaw to discuss terms for a nationwide ceasefire with the EAOs. On 17 November 2020, he met with the representatives of the United Wa State Army, the largest of the ethnic militias, to persuade them to sign the 2015 ceasefire agreement. The Tatmadaw also tried to convince ethnic minority political parties of its unsubstantiated claims of election fraud committed by the NLD and the Union Election Commission. However, these efforts bore little result.[305]

The junta made similar overtures to ethnic groups shortly after it set up the SAC, again with similar results. After this, ten ethnic armed groups that were part of a floundering Nationwide Ceasefire Agreement (NCA) announced that they no longer wanted to negotiate with the military and would support efforts to oust it.[306] In a statement, they declared, 'We support the Civil Disobedience Movement (CDM) and public protests against the military coup and military dictatorship, and we are going to find ways to support these movements and protests.'[307]

## A Complex Web

Given that the NUG and PDFs are novel entities, and militias with the organization and combat experience to take on the Tatmadaw are found only in ethnic groups, the participation of the ethnic militias is critical to the success of armed resistance against the military regime. But there are major differences in circumstances, motivation, goals, strategy and military capabilities between ethnic groups as well as within them.[308] There are also longstanding rivalries over conflicting territorial and political aims among the EAOs themselves. As such, despite their desire to support one another against the Tatmadaw, the EAOs' contrasting political objectives set the limit to inter-ethnic cooperation.[309]

Of all the EAOs in Burma, ten signed the Nationwide Ceasefire Agreement (NCA) negotiated by the Thein Sein government in 2015.[310] The NCA provided principles, including the goal of creating 'a union based on the principles of democracy and federalism', as well as political dialogue and a code of conduct for the Tatmadaw and EAOs.[311] In 2016, during the first NLD government, the ten signatories to the NCA instituted the Peace Process Steering Team (PPST). The four EAOs that had not signed the NCA, namely, the Arakan Army (AA), the Kachin Independence Army (KIA), the Myanmar National Democratic Alliance Army (MNDAA) and the Ta'ang National Liberation Army (TNLA), formed the Northern Alliance, a coalition in 2016. In April 2017, the Northern Alliance along with three non-NCA signatories, the United Wa State Army (UWSA), the National Democratic Alliance Army (NDAA) and the Shan State Army-North (SSA-N), formed the Federal Political Negotiation and Consultative Committee (FPNCC). The seven members of the FPNCC make up 70 per cent of the troop strength of all EAOs in the country.[312]

While limited in its effect, the result was an overall decrease in active military engagements between them and the military in the country. The major exceptions were the AA, TNLA and the MNDAA, although some fighting did continue in Kachin, Rakhine and northern Shan areas.

In response to the coup, some EAOs openly confronted the military, some opposed the coup but did not actively challenge the military, and some chose to remain silent.[313] The coup not only put an end to the negotiations for a formal peace agreement, but also called into question the continuing relevance of the NCA and the bilateral ceasefire agreements between the Tatmadaw and the ethnic groups. Objecting to the coup, the PPST suspended its political dialogue with the Tatmadaw. At the same time, PDF units and other militia groups sprung up in several ethnic areas to resist the military, launching attacks on local military and police bases to kill soldiers and capture weapons.[314] Attacks were carried out by the KIA in Kachin state and by the SSA-N and other militias in Shan State. In the Karen area (Kayin State), the forces of the Karen National Union claimed to have killed 267 soldiers of the Tatmadaw.[315] Armies of the Karens and Kachins have also carried out ambushes against soldiers, given sanctuary to deposed legislators, protesters, workers, and victims of military repression, seized Tatmadaw bases, facilities and trained PDFs and other resistance elements.

New militia groups emerged in the Bamar majority areas— both rural groups carrying out ambushes against military personnel, and urban underground networks targeting junta facilities and officials. Many of the new groups identified or merged with the PDF after the NUG announced their creation in May 2021, but they have not lent themselves to NUG control. The relatively less powerful militias of the Karenni National Progressive Party (KNPP)/Karenni Army, and the Chin National Front (CNF)/ Chin National Army, both of which signed bilateral ceasefires in 2012, have waged a more open conflict.

The Northern Shan State has been relatively peaceful, despite being the scene of the heaviest fighting in the decade before the coup. The Wa and Mongla (National Democratic Alliance Army) have not carried out any attacks, due to their de facto autonomy and relative distance from Burma's political heartland. The UWSA has not opposed the coup. Its spokesperson, U Nyi Rang, pointed out, 'We have longstanding good relations [with the military].'[316] The UWSA's posture might be due to its close ties with China and a desire to maintain the status quo. Their goal is to expand their authority deeper into Burma, and profit by extending Chinese influence on the Thai border.[317] Similarly, the Restoration Council of Shan State[318] maintains strong ties with China. As with the Wa, they want to guard their resources, including the drugs trade.

Some EAO leaders maintain ties with the Tatmadaw. KNU Chair Saw Mutu Sae Poe, who keeps close contact with Sr Gen.

Min, insists that political problems can only be solved through negotiation. But three Karen brigades and the Democratic Benevolent Army, which includes Karen deserters from the Border Guard Force, are fighting the Tatmadaw and the KNU is training young activists and military deserters.[319]

Among other groups, the KNLA and the KIA, who had borne the brunt of Tatmadaw attacks over the last two decades, even as the former signed the NCA, were the first to condemn the military coup, and launch attacks to regain their previously controlled areas. The KNLA ambushed key Tatmadaw positions in late March, killing scores of soldiers. Aiming to stifle the Tatmadaw's influence in their area, the Kachin are vying to strengthen the leadership of NUG and PDFs.[320] Besides shooting down a Tatmadaw helicopter, the KIA also seized ten military outposts including the strategic hilltop Alaw Bum.

In September 2021, KNU leaders declared that the Nation-wide Ceasefire Agreement (NCA), signed between the government and ethnic armed groups, is now invalid owing to the military coup. KNU leader Naw Zipporah Sein asserted that the NCA was designed by the military to compel 'ethnic revolutionary groups' to give up arms but after the coup, the military 'unfairly arrested protesters, politicians, and journalists and committed extrajudicial killings. So we can assume that the NCA is null and void'.[321] Naw Zipporah Sein also committed that the KNU Concerned Group (CG) would help NUG in administrative, military and diplomatic issues as its objectives align with NUG's vision for equality and self-determination for ethnic groups and a federal union.[322] However, the overall assessment has been that the NUG has failed to convince ethnic minorities that they will not be exploited after the fight is over and democracy restored, due to the NLD's overwhelming majority.[323]

The MNDAA operating in the eastern Shan State also did not oppose the coup. Its representatives attended the meetings by the junta's peace negotiating team that explained the reasons for the coup and urged the groups not to side with anti-regime resistance forces.[324] The MNDAA refrained from resorting to open combat to regain control of the Kokang area it lost in 2009. Other EAOs such as the Wa and the Arakan National Party (ANP) in the Rakhine State were keen on preventing political crises and disturbance in other parts of Burma from spilling over into their areas.[325] The ANP refused to dignify the NUG's plea for joining its armed resistance, and even provided a member to the SAC.[326] The AA, the main militia in the Rakhine States that had fought the Tatmadaw particularly hard till an unofficial ceasefire before the November 2020 elections, stayed out of any armed campaign against the new military regime, allegedly on the grounds that this might harm their political objectives. The AA would later fight the Tatmadaw in November 2021.

While the UWSA and the MNDAA as well as the SSA-N refrained from hostility towards the Tatmadaw, they also refused to negotiate with the military regime.[327] Some EAOs collaborated with the newly formed PDFs and ethnic-based militias. In mid-May 2021, the Karenni Army and PDFs in Kayah State attacked several Tatmadaw soldiers, while the Mindat region witnessed repeated clashes between the nascent Chinland Defence Force and the Tatmadaw. Some militias, also aligned with the Tatmadaw against their own ethnic community for business opportunities. For example, Chit Thu's Karen Border Guard Forces (BGF) were helping the Tatmadaw in their fight against the KNLA, in return for business opportunities.[328]

Overall, while the EAOs wanted the Bamar majority to implement their pledge of forming a federal union, they remained sceptical about the NLD-dominated NUG's vision of federalism, which was fiercely opposed by the Tatmadaw. The struggle over Burma's political future essentially pitted one Bamar majority group against another: the Tatmadaw versus the NLD-dominated NUG. Most of the EAOs, including Burma's three most powerful EAOs—the KIO, UWSA, and AA—were watching the struggle carefully and waiting for a window of opportunity to pursue their own long-held political aspirations.[329]

Thus, the prospects for a federal army to unite the EAOs against the military regime seem remote. The idea of a federal army was conceived during the previous military regime in February 2011 with the formation of the now-defunct United Nationalities Federal Council (UNFC) comprising fourteen EAOs. The UNFC became one of the strongest EAO coalitions in the history of ethnic armed resistance in Burma. For a Federal Army to become feasible, the KIA and/or the KNU, which are both powerful, needed to join hands to arm and sustain the NUG-led People's Defence Force. But the two needed to overcome a history of bitter animosity between them, which looked unlikely.

Since the NUG's declaration of armed struggle, there has been an upsurge in military confrontation between the military and the EAOs. In many places, the EAOs are defending people in rural areas. In one of the rural towns, the Tatmadaw was cautioned that if the military attacked the people, the EAO would incinerate the Tatmadaw's bases and the town's police station constructed on the fringes of the forest areas.[330] This was not a paper threat, as in some areas in Kachin and Shan states, EAOs did attack military and police outposts in response to the latter's atrocities on civilian populations.[331]

Though the Tatmadaw declared a five-month 'goodwill' ceasefire with all EAOs in the country from 1 October 2021 till the end of February 2022, the military media incriminated some EAOs of 'terrorism'. In the Tatmadaw-controlled newspaper Myanma Alin, the article 'Extremist Terrorism Must Fail' made imputations that the KNU, KIA, CNF, TNLA, KNPP and the Restoration Council of Shan State (RCSS) were exploiting the turbulent political climate in the country.[332] It specifically alleged that the EAOs gave military training to the PDFs, had associations with the illicit drug trade and received funds from foreign organizations.[333]

On 1 January 2022, the Committee for Shan State Unity (CSSU) released a five-point statement emphasizing its commitment to ensuring harmonious co-existence between its

ethnic groups and among union citizens countrywide to enable
the establishment of the aspired federal democratic union.[334]
Sai Leik, the CSSU General Secretary, stated that the CSSU
Secretariat approved drafts of federal principles based on equality.
Moreover, the Shan State Constitution is all set to be presented to
EAOs, political parties, and civil society organizations in the state:

> 'We will negotiate extensively to find solution and if we do
> this, we hope the federalism-based constitution will be able to
> establish unity among us. The CSSU outline for unity comes
> in three stages—Shan/Tai unity, unity among ethnic groups
> within Shan State, and unity of all ethnic nationalities within
> the whole union or country.'

Hopes for Burma's political future as a federal democracy
rest with the attitude of the EAOs. Interestingly, many CDM
members expressed more confidence in the EAOs than in the
militarily inexperienced NUG and the ethnically Bamar PDFs
aligned with it. In response to the question, *what is your opinion on
the NUG and EAOs?*', one Thought Warrior bluntly replied: '*I trust
EAOs but not NUG.*' Another said: '*NUG sucks. I don't call it either
an interim government or revolutionary government. They're just a
group of people, lobbying the masses.*'

At the same time, the differences within EAOs remain
a major factor in the mind of pro-democracy groups. For a
Thought Warrior:

> *EAOs is a broad topic. For example, I'm from Karenni state. To talk
> about EAOs in Karenni state, I must include at least four parts,
> KNPP, KNLP, KNPLF and the rest. Let's just say, ethnic politics
> is complicated.*

The NUG's call for war against the military is not supported
by some of the CDM activists. Some prefer non-violent means
not because they oppose war, but because an armed struggle is

premature. Here are the words of another Thought Warrior, who claimed to have 'much interest in political matters':

> *I cherish humanitarianism . . . I would appreciate witnessing the political evolution of my own nation. But I don't believe the current remaining civil politicians would successfully vanquish the military rule. For NUG, I don't appreciate everything they do. I don't concur with NUG waging war using others' lives against full-fledged armed terrorists, while rebel forces are still far from being fully armed and even insulting other small rebel groups who have been fighting before the establishment of NUG.'*

At the same time, the EAOs are not necessarily trusted to rise above their ethnic interests and goals. But they get appreciation for their past struggles and military competence relative to the Bamar-dominated PDFs. The EAOs, one Thought Warrior reflected:

> *will, for sure, always prioritize their ethnic communities over anything else whether they join us or not. In fact, we have to thank them for forgiving us even though we did not help them in the past. Moreover, they accepted deserters and also gave Burmese youths military training.*

The appeal of EAOs has increased as they are seen as the only hope for militarily taking on the Tatmadaw. As KNU foreign affairs officer Pado Saw Tawney explained, the people of Burma are coming to terms with the idea that nobody is going to come to their rescue.

> The people understand that . . . they cannot rely on international assistance or mediation, as the [global community] has done nothing, even after more than a thousand people have been killed for no reason. They have clearly realized they must fend for themselves.[335]

The recognition of the importance of EAOs to the struggle for democratic federalism in Burma has led to condemnation by sections of Bamar people who criticize the EAOs. Thus, one Thought Warrior could not

> believe urban people, to be exact Bamar ethnic people, are swearing at EAOs for not coming to the cities and attacking the military for them. This is how stupid and selfish the Bamar people are. No wonder some ethnicities hate us. As a Bamar myself, we got so many privileges that we neglected the difficulties of other ethnic groups. For the NUG, I am so disappointed with what they have done and are doing. Sometimes I wonder if they are even sane. All they are good at is talking nonsense [expletive] on social media stating as they do them to motivate people. I get that people need to be positive but giving false hope like we are winning 80 per cent or we will get the victory this month is not how they, the politicians that numerous citizens look up to, should motivate. This is just wrong. They should provide us with the [expletive] actions. A lot of people donate to the NUG, but I don't because I don't believe them. I would rather donate directly to the needed places than give my precious money to NUG.

While the NUG may be made up of remnants of the NLD that carried the people's mandate in the November 2020 elections, their wishy-washy behaviour towards the EAOs has affected their public perception and increased people's ire towards them. As the Thought Warriors have stated, Burma's federal democratic future is only possible if the EAOs are included as equal participants in the negotiation process. Without their involvement, what are Burma's prospects?

## Prospects

Despite their differences in responding to the coup, there is some evidence that the EAOs and the Bamar majority have tried to bury the hatchet for their shared interest in a federal future of Burma. One consequence of this is the formation of the National Unity Consultative Council (NUCC), a comprehensive, inclusive platform with the distinct aim of unifying divergent forces in support of the federal democracy objective.[336] The NUCC consists of the CRPH, the NUG, ethnic political parties and EAOs, CDM groups, and other CSOs.

The NUCC's ambition for a 'federal democratic union' that prioritizes federalism differs from the NLD's 'democratic federal union' vision, which emphasizes democracy. The NUCC's emergence also signals support for a more inclusive and consensus-based approach, which encourages the spirit of discourse and consultations among democratic forces. No single entity or individual enjoys a monopoly over the NUCC.[337] At its public launch on 16 November 2021, NUCC representatives reaffirmed that the body would reach decisions by consensus among its twenty-eight participant organizations and that it would adopt the principle of 'collective leadership'.[338]

At the same time, though presenting an unprecedented challenge to the Tatmadaw, the collaboration between EAOs and PDF units is less concrete on the ground.[339] While the Tatmadaw is a common enemy, the EAOs' divergent objectives and legacies, of past mistrust of the Bamar-dominated NLD, persist.[340] Previous inter-ethnic alliances were short lived.[341] There is a concern among the EAOs about the PDFs becoming a powerful military force in the short term to compete with them militarily.[342] Another issue is over the structure of a federal arrangement: how many states would be included and how will the NUG divide areas where multiple ethnic groups live, like in Shan State? There are also numerous local inter-ethnic conflicts over control of land, resources, and constituencies during the elections[343]. How will those local conflicts get resolved? So, Burma's future prospects throw up more questions than answers, miring the consultation process in more uncertainty.

# Chapter 8

## Déjà Vu ASEAN

*Note: The Thought Warrior had little to say about ASEAN and its role in resolving the crisis in Burma after the coup. Does ASEAN matter to them? It does not seem to.*

\* \* \*

The previous chapters have mainly dealt with the domestic developments in Burma leading to the coup and the events unfolding in its immediate aftermath. We now turn to the response of the outside countries, starting with Burma's neighbours in the Association of Southeast Asian Nations (ASEAN) in this chapter, followed by the response of the international community in Chapter 9.

### ASEAN: The Past as Prologue[344]

February 2021 returned Burma to the forefront of political challenges faced by the ASEAN. Burma had joined ASEAN as a full member in 1997. After its 2010 elections, Burma had been viewed as an asset rather than a headache. Its domestic political troubles had been largely forgotten, as ASEAN members and business interests moved to develop economic ties with Burma and celebrated its turn as ASEAN Chair in 2014.

To elaborate with some historical background, Burma did not join ASEAN when it was formed in 1967. Theoretically, the door was open to Burma (as well as to Cambodia) to gain membership in ASEAN. It was pursuing a policy of isolationism, and while ASEAN professed to stay away from great power rivalry, the military regime in Burma, facing major domestic challenges, saw ASEAN as a pro-Western grouping that might invite outside pressure or intervention for political reform and change.

Until 2011, ASEAN's policy on Burma evolved through three stages. The first was its policy of 'Constructive Engagement', which lasted from 1988 to 1998. During this phase, ASEAN's approach was governed by strict adherence to its non-interference doctrine. Under this policy, ASEAN not only shied away from criticizing Burma's military regime but it also opposed international pressure and sanctions on the country. Yet, much of the so-called 'Constructive Engagement' was economic dealings by individual ASEAN members with the government in Burma. Political persuasion and dialogue to promote political change were hardly evident, at least in the open sphere. Despite Western objection, ASEAN went ahead and admitted Burma in 1997. It cited growing Chinese influence over Burma as the main rationale for allowing admission.

The second phase of ASEAN's approach to Burma came after the Asian Financial Crisis in 1997. The crisis led to a gradual but important shift in ASEAN's overall non-interference doctrine, not just in relation to Burma, but to ASEAN's overall approach to regional problem solving. A major advocate of the shift was the then Thai Foreign Minister Surin Pitsuwan, who would later become the secretary-general of ASEAN. Surin coined the term 'Flexible Engagement' (partly borrowed from Malaysian Deputy Prime Minister Anwar Ibrahim's idea of 'Constructive Intervention', before he was ousted from power). Flexible engagement, however, did not imply sanctions or any significant pressure on Burma's regime. Rather it was mainly about soft talking with the military regime to undertake political reform and liberalization. Hence, ASEAN after some initial hesitation, did start to talk with Burma on the issue of political reform. In 2000, on the margins of the APEC summit, the Sultan of Brunei convened a meeting of ASEAN heads of government and proposed that ASEAN, when it meets in Singapore the following week, should discuss the Burma issue. On the sidelines of the 4th ASEAN Informal Summit in Singapore on 25 November 2000, Singapore Prime Minister Goh Chok Tong set aside thirty minutes during which Burma's President was asked to give a progress report on his country's political situation.

The release of Aung San Suu Kyi in September 2001 led Surin to claim that ASEAN's policy towards Burma had been successful. He insisted that 'everyone has tried to disown it [his idea of flexible engagement], but it has survived'.[345] But she was re-arrested in June 2003. Responding to her arrest, then ASEAN secretary-general Ong Keng Yong said ASEAN could not ask for her release because 'you cannot go in and tell your family member you cannot do this, you cannot do that'.[346]

While ASEAN members defended their Constructive Engagement policy, Suu Kyi herself dismissed its merits. As she put it:

> The question is for whom has it been constructive? Was it constructive for the forces of democracy? Was it constructive for the Burmese people in general? Was it constructive for a limited business community? Or was it constructive for SLORC?[347]

On 16 June 2003, ASEAN foreign ministers pressed Yangon to release Suu Kyi. In July 2003, Malaysian leader Mahathir Mohammed warned that Burma could face expulsion from ASEAN if Suu Kyi was not released soon. But other ASEAN members were not persuaded about expelling Burma. Thus, in June 2004, Indonesian Foreign Minister Hassan Wirayuda stated that it was not ASEAN's 'approach to apply sanctions in order to get results, but to continue to talk with them as part of the ASEAN family'.[348]

In 2005, ASEAN faced an important test of its Burma policy when the issue of its chairmanship for 2006 came up. It was Burma's turn to be the chair. Some ASEAN hands argued that allowing Yangon to chair ASEAN in 2006 may help to spur political reform in the country. But in the end, ASEAN succumbed to international outcry, and Burma did not become the ASEAN Chair.

In September 2005, Malaysia's Deputy Prime Minister Najib Razak conceded that 'the policy of constructive engagement has shown some dividends but not as much as we had hoped'.[349]

Nevertheless, ASEAN would not change its policy fundamentally. 'I think we have to continue to pursue this and hopefully things get better . . . We're still trying,' said Malaysia's Najib. However, in March 2006, Singapore's Foreign Minister George Yeo, stated, 'We will have to distance ourselves a bit [from Burma] if it is not possible for them to engage us in a way which we find necessary to defend them internationally.'[350] At this point, some ASEAN members were beginning to realize Burma's dwindling trust in the regional organization and that its efforts to reform Burma were having little impact.

ASEAN's response to the uprising against the Burmese military junta by Buddhist monks in August-September 2007 (the Saffron Uprising) was more radical in tone. A statement issued by the grouping's Foreign Ministers at the UN headquarters in New York 'expressed their revulsion . . . over reports that the demonstrations in Myanmar are being suppressed by violent force and that there has been a number of fatalities'.[351] It 'strongly urged Myanmar to exercise utmost restraint and seek a political solution'. Moreover, the Foreign Ministers 'called upon Myanmar to resume its efforts at national reconciliation with all parties concerned, and work towards a peaceful transition to democracy'.[352] However, there was no threat of sanctions or call for the suspension of Burma from ASEAN membership.

The third phase in ASEAN's policy towards Burma was triggered by a natural calamity, a devastating cyclone named Nargis that struck the Irrawaddy Delta and southern Yangon district on 2 and 3 May 2008. The Burmese government initially refused to accept international aid because of the potential impact a large-scale foreign presence might have on its domestic political situation.[353] In response, some Western countries, notably France, called for forcible 'humanitarian' intervention. ASEAN rejected this call. As George Yeo, who was then the chair of ASEAN Standing Committee, put it, 'It doesn't make sense for us to work on the basis of forcing aid on Myanmar because that would bring unnecessary complications and will lead to more suffering for the Myanmar people.'

In the end, ASEAN offered to act as a conduit for international aid, an offer that was acceptable to both Burma and the international community. A key role in shaping this policy and carrying it out was played by the newly anointed ASEAN Secretary-General Surin Pitsuwan, who saw a chance to put his 'flexible engagement' doctrine to practice. As he would later put it, during the operation, ASEAN was 'baptized—not by fire, but by a cyclone'.[354]

Why did ASEAN shift its policy towards Burma from what critics saw as willful indifference under the policy of 'constructive engagement' to voicing concerns and talking to the regime about the need for political reforms? There are three main reasons behind ASEAN's shift: the Burma policy was costing ASEAN dearly in terms of its international image; frustration with the slow pace of reform in Burma and growing Chinese influence in the country despite its membership in ASEAN.[355] A fourth factor could be the attitude of the new democratic government in Indonesia after Suharto's downfall in 1998, which supported political reform in Burma and was not shy to talk openly about it.

Overall, ASEAN should take some, but not much, credit for the reforms in Burma that occurred in the first decade of the 21st century. Since the early 2000s, after realizing the failure and image costs of its Constructive Engagement policy, ASEAN gradually came to encourage Burma to step up reform, albeit within a confine of its persisting, if slowly easing, non-interference principle. In ASEAN, Burma had a framework for defining and pursuing its foreign policy, which is an alternative to dependence on China. But while one should not dismiss ASEAN's role in shaping Burma's *foreign policy choices*, it is hard to prove that ASEAN alone or mainly had a major impact in shaping Burma's *domestic developments*.

A highlight of Burma's role in ASEAN after the 2010 election and the advent of the Thein Sein government in 2011 was its assumption of ASEAN's chair in 2014, which had been deferred in 2006. It was a successful effort; Burma's officials worked hard to be an enthusiastic and capable host of ASEAN and related meetings, which were attended by the US President Barrack Obama. Burma no longer seemed to be a burden for ASEAN and ASEAN provided a much-needed window for Burma to rejoin the international community, through diplomacy, trade and investment. There was little further interest or pressure from ASEAN on Burma's domestic political affairs, with the notable exception of the killings of Rohingyas when ASEAN was once again torn over whether or how much to pressure the Government of Burma. Malaysia, under the Najib Rajak government, strongly and openly condemned the Burmese government, accusing it of genocide, although its reaction was motivated by a desire to enhance its credentials in the Muslim world and to divert attention from its domestic political troubles. ASEAN countries maintained their diplomatic and economic ties with Burma and backed the Burmese government's official position. The ASEAN Summit on 20–23 June 2019, did not mention the term 'Rohingya' as wished for by Burma, but 'stressed the importance of and expressed our continued support for Myanmar's commitment to ensure safety and security for all communities in [the] Rakhine State'.[356] ASEAN backed the repatriation of Rohingya refugees in Bangladesh, although how this could be done without the willingness of the refugees themselves to return, as they were afraid of persecution or killings, was not clear. ASEAN's handling of the Rohingya crisis made it politically easier for Burma to accept humanitarian aid from ASEAN members. It might have made Burma more willing to the repatriation of Rohingya refugees. At the same time, it could have increased the Burmese government's defiance of the wider international community, including Aung San Suu Kyi's defiant but unsuccessful appearance before the International Court of Justice in December 2019.[357]

In the meantime, economic links between Burma and ASEAN members continued to flourish. In 2019, Thailand, Singapore, Malaysia and Indonesia were among the five top exporters to Burma, after China, the top exporter.[358] And in 2020, five ASEAN members: Singapore (the top overall foreign investor), Thailand. Malaysia, Brunei and Vietnam ranked among the top ten foreign investor countries (officially approved investment) in Burma, while China was the second largest investor.[359]

## A Rerun of 'Constructive Engagement'?

The reactions of ASEAN states to the February 2021 coup in Burma has varied among members. While urging the junta to refrain from violence and release political detainees, for the most part, ASEAN's collective response has been conditioned by the sensitivity of sovereignty and non-interference in one another's internal affairs. This is notwithstanding the fact that, the coup and overturning of democracy is a clear violation of its Charter, which seeks to create 'a just, democratic and harmonious environment' in the region (Article 1.4), and commits the grouping 'to strengthen democracy, enhance good governance and the rule of law, and to promote and protect human rights and fundamental freedoms'.[360] But individual ASEAN countries have used stronger language and called for more intrusive action. On the whole, though, ASEAN as a group has been more impatient with the military regime in Burma than with the military regime that came into power in Thailand as a result of the 2014 coup carried out by General Prayut Chan-o-cha. Unlike its response to the Thai coup, ASEAN's response to the 2021 coup in Burma has some concrete initiatives, including appointing a Special Envoy to negotiate on behalf of the group and diplomatic initiatives leading to the 'Five-Point Consensus', as will be discussed later in this chapter.

Brunei held the ASEAN chair of 2021, when the coup took place. It responded with similar statements about the need for dialogue, reconciliation, and 'return to normalcy', albeit with a special reference to the ASEAN Charter:

> [W]e recall the purposes and the principles enshrined in the ASEAN Charter, including, the adherence to the principles of democracy, the rule of law and good governance, respect for and protection of human rights and fundamental freedoms.[361]

Brunei would also be tasked to appoint ASEAN's special envoy for Burma, which would go to its second foreign minister, Erywan Yusof. But Yusof, despite his best efforts, would achieve very little due to a lack of cooperation from the military regime. He cancelled his visit to Burma in October 2021 when the military regime rejected his request for a meeting with Aung San Suu Kyi and other leaders, which he believed was consistent with the Five-Point Consensus.

Indonesia, ASEAN's largest member nation and widely regarded as the informal political leader of ASEAN, initially responded to the coup with a touch of cautious ambivalence. Foreign Minister Retno Marsudi urged for the cessation of violence by 'both the sides' (the military as well as the protestors) and reached out for a peaceful solution. To some observers, it seemed she was asking ASEAN not to do anything that might seriously strain ties with Burma.[362] However, with the violent retaliation by the Tatmadaw against the protestors, including the use of live ammunition, Jakarta came out with strong statements. On 19 March 2021, President Joko Widodo, in a virtual address, stated: 'Indonesia urges that the use of violence in Myanmar be stopped immediately so that there are no more victims.' 'The safety and welfare of the people,' he added, 'must be the top priority. Indonesia also urges dialogue, that reconciliation is carried out immediately to restore democracy, to restore peace, and to restore stability in Myanmar'.[363]

Later, in October 2021, during the ministerial meeting of the ASEAN, Indonesian Foreign Minister Retno Marsudi would ask that 'ASEAN should not act like "business as usual".'[364] She also warned other members of the group not to turn a blind eye to the deteriorating situation in Burma and called for preventing the participation of Burma at summits at the political level unless democracy is restored through an inclusive process.[365] This would be the most stringent diplomatic action by ASEAN against the Burmese military regime.

Malaysia has been more vocal in condemning the coup and the military regime in Burma. In March 2021, then Malaysian Prime Minister Muhyiddin Yasin stated: 'The military leadership in Myanmar is strongly urged to change its course and choose a path towards peaceful solution.'[366] The coup and the political unrest that ensued were not only a step backwards in Burma's democratic transition, but also a threat to the security and stability of the entire region.[367]

Singapore responded with the same type of statements emphasizing the need for peace and reconciliation to get Burma back on the road to democratic transition.[368] Singapore also opposed 'widespread sanctions' against the military regime. Since sanctions were not favoured by any other ASEAN member anyway, this was directed at the Western nations, the US, Australia, and the EU, which would impose sanctions on the Burmese regime.[369] As Singapore's Foreign Minister Vivian Balakrishnan put it, 'If you look over the past seventy years, the military authorities in Myanmar, frankly, do not respond to economic sanctions, do not respond to moral opprobrium.'[370] Singapore asked that the response to Burma should respect the principles of 'consensus and non-interference in the internal affairs of ASEAN Member States'.[371] Singapore would like outside powers to facilitate 'inclusive dialogue' in Burma and to 'engage' rather than isolate the military rulers in Burma.[372] Balakrishnan noted that though Singapore would not accept Gen. Min Aung Hlaing's government as legitimate, it did recognize that the 2008 Constitution of Burma provided a 'special role for the military as an institution in the body politic'.[373] Singapore Prime Minister Lee Hsien Loong would call the use of lethal force against civilian protestors as 'just not acceptable', while Balakrishnan called it a 'national shame'.[374] But while the situation in Burma was 'tragic', Lee said, it was not irreversible: '[S]ense can still eventually prevail. It may take quite a long time, but it can happen. It has happened before.'[375]

Thailand, whose current prime minister was a coup-maker and whose government had not fully moved past its image as a creature of the military, would say: 'It's their own business, it's their internal affair.'[376] 'We are supportive of the democratic process in Myanmar but what is most important today is to maintain good relations because it impacts the people, the economy, border trade, particularly now.'[377] Thailand has more immediate stakes in the Burmese domestic strife, as Burma shares its second-longest border with Thailand, at over 2,000 km. Thailand has been the recipient of millions of refugees from Burma in the past. For Thai Prime Minister Prayut Chan-o-Cha, himself a former general and coup-maker, this was not a call, but a constraint on action:

> It is not that we don't care about humanitarian problems—a life is a life. But we cannot do anything we want, because we have common borders [with Myanmar] and we rely on each other for many things . . . [though] we have kept telling them to reduce [violence].[378]

Bangkok had established close contacts with the Burmese military. As Thailand's former ambassador to Burma, Kobsak Chutikul, put it, 'The two militaries think alike as comrades-in-arms, and they can understand each other well,' alluding also that there was no need for face-to-face meetings between the leaders of the two countries who are supposed to have established 'back-channel' exchanges.[379] If Burma was isolated, Sihasak Phuangketkeow, the former permanent secretary of Thailand's Ministry of Foreign Affairs, said, 'We will be missing a very important member of the ASEAN family [but] there's only so much that we can help with Myanmar unless Myanmar decides to help itself first.'[380]

Vietnam, which chaired ASEAN in 2020, would support diplomatic efforts made in accordance with the ASEAN Charter to promote dialogue with the protection of civilians in Burma being the primary objective.[381] Other ASEAN members also seemed to have taken a back seat, although the Philippine Foreign Minister Teodoro Locsin said ASEAN has to act. 'Because passivity is complicity; and silence gives consent.'[382] Cambodia, which would succeed Brunei as ASEAN Chair (for 2022), would not interfere 'on the internal affairs of any country at all'.[383]

To sum up, the response of ASEAN members to the 2021 coup in Burma was neither uniform nor cohesive. Malaysia, Singapore and Indonesia turned out to be the most vocal critics of the military regime, while Thailand, Cambodia and Vietnam, led by authoritarian regimes, seemed to accept, if not condone the coup. These divisions were themselves a setback for ASEAN's credibility and effectiveness in responding to the coup.

## Much Ado: The Five-Point Consensus

The highlight of ASEAN's response to the Burma coup was the convening of a Special Summit, which came after a virtual meeting of foreign ministers called by Indonesia on 2 March 2021, and this proved inadequate. The ASEAN effort was elevated to the summit level, with the controversial decision to invite the head of the junta, Sr Gen. Min Aung Hlaing, to attend the summit in Jakarta. The underlying rationale for holding the summit and inviting the senior general was the hope the Burma would agree to give space to ASEAN representatives—The Special Envoy of the Chair, or its institutions, ASEAN Secretariate—to 'help the country return to normalcy'. Malaysia, however, made it clear that this did 'not construe a recognition or otherwise of the State Administration Council (SAC)', and it still looked to 'an immediate end to violence, unconditional and immediate release of political detainees, and resumption of an inclusive dialogue involving all concerned parties for a political transition and peaceful settlement of the ongoing crisis in the interest of Myanmar and her people'.[384]

The special summit was held on 24 April 2021 and produced a 'Five-Point Consensus':

- There shall be immediate cessation of violence in Myanmar and all parties shall exercise utmost restraint.
- Constructive dialogue among all parties concerned shall commence to seek a peaceful solution in the interests of the people.
- A special envoy of the ASEAN Chair shall facilitate mediation of the dialogue process, with the assistance of the Secretary-General of ASEAN.
- ASEAN shall provide humanitarian assistance through the AHA Centre. [ASEAN Coordinating Centre for Humanitarian Assistance]
- The special envoy and delegation shall visit Myanmar to meet with all parties concerned.[385]

The summit ended with a fair amount of hope in ASEAN circles that breakthrough had been achieved. Malaysian Prime Minister Muhyiddin Yassin enthused, 'Our proposals would be accepted, the general [Gen. Min Aung Hlaing] in his response did not reject (them). This is very encouraging progress.'[386] The senior general, the Malaysian Prime Minister said, had told his ASEAN counterparts that the violence was being caused by the 'other side', but 'we [ASEAN] hope that he will find a way to stop it'. This was the reward for ASEAN leaders refraining from throwing accusations at the senior general, because 'we don't care who's causing it, we just stressed that the violence must stop'.[387]

There were people who doubted whether the expectations contained in the five points would be fulfilled and were concerned that the military regime would not use the summit to its political advantage. For example, appearing on Al Jazeera TV just as the Five-Point Consensus was announced, I argued that the Special Summit would give legitimacy to the coup and its leaders, and it would have been preferable for ASEAN to send a special envoy to Burma to meet with all the parties, including NLD, before inviting Gen. Min Aung Hlaing to meet with all the ASEAN leaders.[388]

Indeed, it would not take long before it became clear that the Burmese regime had no intention of implementing the measures in the consensus. In fact, by July 2021, Singapore officially acknowledged that the military rulers in Burma have been 'slow and a little disappointing' in implementing the Five-Point Consensus despite the best efforts of the ASEAN.[389] ASEAN had not been as effective as it was expected to be, but 'this is a difficult situation'.[390]

Among other things, the military regime would refuse access to the ASEAN Special Envoy to visit and meet with the detained leaders in Burma. Barely two weeks after the April 2021 special summit with Gen. Ming Aung Hlaing, Major Htet San, a spokesman for the regime, bluntly remarked, 'Right now, we are prioritizing the security and stability of the country,' adding, 'Only after we achieve a certain level of security and stability, we will cooperate regarding that envoy.'[391] Later, the regime would agree to allow a visit by the Special Envoy but without access to detained political leaders. Sr Gen. Min Aung Hlaing would insist that some things were 'non-negotiable' and that the 'envoy could not be allowed to meet with Suu Kyi because she faces criminal charges'.[392] At the same time, the junta leader accused other ASEAN member states of not doing enough to quell the violence in Burma from 'terrorism, robbery and killings', a reference to the armed resistance put up by anti-coup PDFs and ethnic militias.

> We are still dealing with this, right up to now, but no one has put serious obstructions in the way of their violence. We were asked to solve it and we are the ones clearing up the problem. I want to say that ASEAN needs to do something about it.[393]

Meanwhile, the military regime continued the violence 'against the Tatmadaw's political opponents and civilians', as the Singapore government noted in January 2022.[394]

As mentioned above, by October 2021, the Burmese regime made it clear that it would not be implementing the consensus. ASEAN's attitude hardened. This was not surprising, since ASEAN's special summit move was looking premature and ineffectual in hindsight. And Malaysia stressed that given the situation, the principle of non-interference cannot be used 'as a shield to avoid issues being addressed',[395] and it's time to 'think about moving away from this principle and embrace 'non-indifference'.[396]

As such, also in October 2021, ASEAN decided to exclude the participation of Burma in the upcoming ASEAN summit. As the spokesperson of Singapore's Foreign Ministry put it, the decision was 'difficult but necessary . . . to uphold ASEAN's credibility'.[397] Echoing this view, the Philippines President Rodrigo Duterte told the ASEAN summit:

The lack of progress in Myanmar has put ASEAN's credibility
into question . . . How we respond collectively will either affirm
ASEAN's relevance or reveal our impotence. It is up to us to
prove that ASEAN is not just a 'talk shop'.[398]

When Burma's leader was excluded (Burma was invited to
send a 'non-political representative', which the regime turned
down) from attending the October 2021 meeting in Brunei, it
was for the first time in ASEAN's history, a summit that is the
highest decision-making body of the group was held without the
participation of all the members.[399] This was a severe blow to
the junta's legitimacy and set an important precedent for other
ASEAN members, such as Thailand, with its history of coups and
military dictatorships.[400]

Burma's military regime responded to its exclusion by accusing
ASEAN of giving in to 'foreign intervention'. The exclusion of
Burma's leader was a violation of ASEAN's Charter. Hence:
'Myanmar will not be in a position to accept any outcome of the
discussions and decisions which are ultra vires and contrary to the
provisions, objectives and cherished principles of the ASEAN
Charter.'[401]

Waiting in the wings to succeed Brunei as the chair of the
ASEAN, Cambodia was getting frustrated with ASEAN's lack
of progress in dealing with the Burma situation. In November
2021, Prime Minister Hun Sen expressed these sentiments,
admittedly mixed:

Now we are in the situation of ASEAN-minus-one. That is
not because of ASEAN but because of Myanmar itself. [T]he
military regime had abandoned its rights with a boycott.[402]

But as ASEAN Chair, Cambodia would try to break
ASEAN's informal consensus of not involving junta leader
Min Aung Hlaing in ASEAN meetings. He would like to have
the junta leader attend ASEAN meetings held in Cambodia

during its year as Chair. It seemed likely that Cambodia may once again 'disrupt' ASEAN unity,[403] as it had done in 2012 during its previous Chairmanship, when it blocked a consensus on the South China Sea in deference to China, its biggest benefactor. Then, ASEAN ended a foreign ministers' meeting for the first time in its history without a joint communique. But soon, Hun Sen realized that the military regime would not give much ground. In January 2022, Hun Sen himself visited Burma, allegedly to persuade the senior general to implement the Five Point Consensus. Later that month, a statement on Hun Sen's Facebook page read that he 'had invited HE (His Excellency) Min Aung Hlaing to attend the ASEAN summit if there was progress in the implementation of the five points agreed unanimously.'[404] But in February 2022, the Burmese regime once again turned down the request of the new ASEAN Envoy, Cambodia's foreign minister, Prak Sokhonn, to engage with what it called, 'unlawful associations and terrorist groups' that were 'perpetrating violence' in Burma. While the Special Envoy was able to visit Burma on 21 March 2022, he was not allowed to meet with the detained former President Win Myint and State Councillor Aung San Suu Kyi.

There has been no serious talk about suspending Burma from ASEAN membership. In October 2021, Brunei's Sultan Hassanal Bolkiah insisted, 'Myanmar is an integral part of the ASEAN family, and their membership has not been questioned.' 'ASEAN,' he added, 'will always be there for Myanmar, and we have continued to offer help through the implementation of the Five-Point Consensus.'[405]

But with the consensus seemingly moribund, if not dead in the water, pressure may grow on ASEAN, both from outside and from members like Malaysia, to suspend Burma, especially if the military escalates its violence against civilians and continues to thwart ASEAN's diplomatic efforts.

## Whither ASEAN?

Overall, the 2021 coup, the first military takeover of Burma after it joined the grouping in 1997, unravelled ASEAN's decades of efforts to create political stability in the country. ASEAN was facing damage to its reputation that failure to address the crisis would cause, and by having a failed state in its midst. There is also the related problem of Burma's representation in ASEAN meetings. While the Five-Point Consensus of April 2021 would remain a useful benchmark and initial roadmap for diplomacy with Burma's military regime, after a year, ASEAN had little to show for its diplomatic overtures and efforts.

ASEAN could not achieve much beyond condemnation and statements urging the junta to cease violence, release political prisoners, and restore democracy. ASEAN's approach was stymied by its policy of non-interference and also a lack of coherence among the individual members of the group, reflecting domestic interests, especially the hesitancy of authoritarian member regimes as in Thailand and Cambodia to create a precedence that might one day be used against them.

Yet, despite ASEAN's limitations in dealing with the coup and its aftermath, it remained important to the international community's response to the coup. As will be discussed in the next chapter, Western countries had their own problems in responding to the coup, beyond their strong words of condemnation and imposition of sanctions on the Burmese military regime. The US would be distracted by its chaotic withdrawal from Afghanistan and then, along with EU preoccupied with the outbreak of the Russia-Ukraine war. China would play a more active diplomatic role, but the international community in general still hoped for ASEAN to have a key diplomatic role in finding a way forward, which has remained elusive and disappointing to date.

# Chapter 9

## Worlds Apart

From the Thought Warriors:

*With . . . the slow action from the international community, this is going to take long.*

*We will gain international legitimacy, and have control over territories of the country to make sure we gain our people's power back.*

[Overall, there was little from the Thought Warriors about the 'international community's' role in Burma's crisis. Most of the comments focused on domestic forces and their interactions.]

\* \* \*

As we have seen in the previous chapter, when it comes to Burma, there is no 'international community'. The coup has amplified the divisions among the major powers over human rights, democracy and sanctions. Actions by those who have been sympathetic to the pro-democracy forces, such as the US and European Union, have been high on rhetoric but short of consequential steps in tune with the expectations and demands of those who are resisting and seeking to reverse the coup. China, perhaps the single most important power in shaping Burma's political future, and the Western countries have taken different approaches, which have undercut international solidarity. Sanctions imposed by Western countries targeting the military are highly unlikely to bring the junta to compromise to the extent that meets the demands of the opposition parties and the people in general. Moreover, the sanctions have not been supported by any concrete plan about how to resolve the crisis. The US, after the chaotic withdrawal from Afghanistan, now, along with Europe, is now seriously distracted by the Russia-Ukraine conflict. When it comes to the future of Burma, now as before, 'does the international community really care?'[406] Keeping these in mind, this chapter examines how the US and other prominent members of the international community, especially China, India, Australia, and international organizations have responded to the coup.

## United States

Immediately in the aftermath of the coup, US President Joe Biden issued a strong condemnation of Burma's new military regime. As he put it:

> [T]he military's seizure of power, the detention of Aung San Suu Kyi and other civilian officials, and the declaration of a national state of emergency are a direct assault on the country's transition to democracy and the rule of law . . . the people of Burma have been steadily working to establish elections, civilian governance, and the peaceful transfer of power. That progress should be respected.[407]

Biden urged other countries to come together to pressure the military to relinquish power and restore democracy.[408] His message was reinforced by the US Secretary of State, Antony J. Blinken:

> [T]he United States expresses grave concern and alarm regarding reports that the Burmese military has detained multiple civilian

government leaders, including State Counsellor Aung San Suu Kyi, and civil society leaders. We call on Burmese military leaders to release all government officials and civil society leaders and respect the will of the people of Burma as expressed in democratic elections on 8 November. The United States stands with the people of Burma in their aspirations for democracy, freedom, peace, and development. The military must reverse these actions immediately.[409]

US officials would repeat their demand for the release of all political detainees and the restoration of the democratically elected government to power,[410] and asked that those responsible for overturning Burma's democratic transition be held accountable.[411] At a special briefing on 2 February 2021, the State Department noted,

> 'A democratic, civilian-led government has always been Burma's best opportunity to address the problems the country faces— weak democratic institutions, inter-communal conflict and strife, an underdeveloped and closed-off economy, and a long history of human rights abuses committed by the military'.[412]

Addressing the issue of sanctions, the State Department noted that while the coup has 'triggered certain restrictions in foreign assistance to the Government of Burma', it would 'undertake a broader review of our assistance' and to 'continue with programs that benefit the people of Burma directly, including humanitarian assistance and democracy support programs that benefit civil society'.[413] On 11 February 2021, the US Department of the Treasury[414] designated ten individuals and three entities connected to the military apparatus responsible for the coup. The sanctions list included Sr. Gen. Min Aung Hlaing, the Commander-in-chief of the Burmese military, Deputy General Soe Win, first vice-president, and a number of other senior military officials along with four members of the State Administration Council (SAC). Three commercial entities—Myanmar Ruby Enterprise, Myanmar Imperial Jade Co. Ltd, and Cancri (Gems and Jewellery) Co. Ltd,[415] all of which have direct ties with the military, were also the target of sanctions by the US. Subsequently, the sanctions list was expanded to include two additional SAC members.[416] Importantly, the sanctions did not target the economy of the country so as not to add to the plight of the Burmese people.[417] Washington also initiated steps 'to prevent the generals from improperly having access to the \$1 billion in Burmese government funds held in the United States'.[418] To legally allow such measures, President Biden declared a 'state of emergency' invoking the International Emergency Economic Powers Act, the National Emergencies Act, among other US government laws, describing the situation in Burma, as 'an unusual and extraordinary threat to the national security and foreign policy of the United States'.[419]

Washington also demanded that the regime stop all violence against protestors and civilians.[420] But this had little effect, as the military significantly escalated violence against civilian protestors.[421] In response, Washington imposed additional sanctions on the regime apart from the ones they had already enforced. Just like before, the US approach to these additional sanctions, as stated by Blinken, would still be to 'specifically target those who led the coup, the economic interests of the military, and the funding streams supporting the Burmese military's brutal repression', but would not be 'directed at the people of Burma'.[422] On 10 March 2021, the US reinforced its targeted sanctions by designating two children of commander-in-chief Min Aung Hlaing, along with the six companies they control.[423] This was followed by the designation of two army units 'responsible for or complicit in actions or policies that prohibit, limit, or penalize the exercise of freedom of expression or assembly by people in Burma'.[424] Additionally, Lieutenant General Aung Soe, a Bureau of Special Operations commander was targeted, followed by sanctions against two military holding companies, Myanmar Economic Holdings Public Company Limited (MEHL) and Myanmar Economic Corporation Limited (MEC).[425] Action against the two companies, as a Treasury Department official put it, meant 'targeting the Burmese military's control of significant segments of the Burmese economy, which is a vital financial lifeline for the military junta'.[426]

## Australia

Australia's interest in Burma flows from its general policy of playing a more active engagement in shaping the overall political and diplomatic environment of Southeast Asia and Indo-Pacific regions. While, like the US, not a member of ASEAN, Australia has been openly supportive of ASEAN's role in organizing economic and political cooperation in these regions. Australia's reaction to the coup was similar to that of the US, with its then Foreign Minister Marise Payne issuing a statement on 1 February 2021:

> call on the military to respect the rule of law, to resolve disputes through lawful mechanisms and to release immediately all civilian leaders and others who have been detained unlawfully . . . We strongly support the peaceful reconvening of the National Assembly, consistent with the results of the November 2020 general election.[427]

Canberra urged the military regime to engage in dialogue to open the way for a return to civilian rule and restoration of democratic setup, as the potential impact of these events on humanitarian crises is very much disproportionate on the most vulnerable sections of Burmese society. Australia also restated that its relations with the people of Burma have been 'longstanding and steadfast', for which Canberra will continue to urge the junta to 'exercise restraint and refrain from violence against civilians'.[428]

Australia also imposed sanctions, including an arms embargo on Burma and targeted sanctions on a number of individuals linked to the coup, suspended its bilateral Defence Cooperation Programme with Burma (involving English language training), and redirected its development assistance programme to cater to the 'needs of the most vulnerable and poor including the Rohingyas and other ethnic minorities'.[429]

Australia also joined a host of other countries, including Canada, Germany, Greece, Italy, Japan, Denmark, Netherlands, New Zealand, South Korea, the United Kingdom and the US, in condemning the use of force against protestors. Echoing similar language from Western nations, it has urged the military regime to 'cease violence and work to restore respect and credibility with the people of Myanmar that it has lost through its actions'.[430]

In a similar vein, Canberra strongly endorsed ASEAN's role in Burma and the efforts by ASEAN's Special Envoy on Burma to deal with the Burma crisis as well as the UN's initiatives involving human rights of the people of Burma, especially calling for 'full, safe and unhindered humanitarian access to all people in need, and for the full protection, safety and security of humanitarian and medical personnel'.[431] To this end, it called on the international community to 'suspend all operational support to the military, and to cease the transfer of arms, materiel, dual-use equipment, and technical assistance to the military and its representatives'. At the same time, it would 'encourage the international community to work together to prevent future atrocities in Myanmar, including by supporting justice and accountability for those responsible for atrocities'.[432]

## The European Union (EU)

The EU's approach was similar to those of other Western nations, bluntly condemning the coup, urging the junta to 'immediately and unconditionally, release those arrested and exercise maximum restraint, restore telecommunications, and respect human rights, freedom of expression, fundamental freedoms and the rule of law'. Affirming that the EU stands with the people of Burma, it urged the junta to ensure the safety of the 'citizens of both Myanmar and of its [EU] Member States', and issued the threat that it 'will consider all options at its disposal to ensure that democracy prevails'.[433] It also condemned the violence and bloodshed against unarmed protestors and promised that the EU stands ready to adopt restrictive measures.[434] The main goal of the EU's response to Burma was to demonstrate 'EU's unity and determination in condemning the brutal actions of the military junta and aims at effecting change in the junta's leadership [and] sends a clear message to the military leadership: continuing the current path will only bring further suffering and will never grant any legitimacy'.[435]

On 22 March 2021, the EU sanctioned eleven individuals linked to the coup in Burma, including Commander-in-Chief Min Aung Hlaing. The measures included a travel ban and assets freeze and required EU citizens and companies not to make 'funds available to the listed individuals and entities'.[436] In a subsequent decision, the European Union expanded its targets to include

> 'natural and legal persons, entities, and bodies whose activities undermine democracy and the rule of law in Myanmar/Burma, as well as legal persons, entities and bodies owned or controlled by the Myanmar Armed Forces [Tatmadaw], or generating revenue for, providing support to or benefitting from the Myanmar Armed Forces [Tatmadaw] and thus contributing to, or benefiting from, activities undermining democracy and the rule of law or serious human rights violations in Myanmar/Burma'.[437]

These measures also include an arms embargo and ban on the export of dual-use equipment for monitoring communications that can be used for internal repression by the military and border guard police.[438] The sanctions kept expanding further to include new individuals and enterprises controlled by the military.[439] Like the US too, the EU claimed that its sanctions were targeted at the military and would not hurt the ordinary people of Burma.

Like other major powers, the EU has also supported the initiatives of ASEAN and its Special Envoy, in finding a peaceful solution to the current crisis in Burma.[440] The EU also stressed that 'a meaningful political dialogue must include all relevant stakeholders, including the Committee Representing the Pyidaungsu Hluttaw (CRPH), the National Unity Government (NUG), ethnic groups, political parties and other pro-democracy forces committed to working towards a peaceful resolution of the current crisis'.[441]

The response of the Western countries—the US, EU members, and Australia—to the coup has been similar, featuring strong language of condemnation and backed by sanctions. This sets them apart from the response of the Asian powers, China, India and Japan, which have been more accommodating, refraining from sanctions and maintaining regular diplomatic contacts with the military regime. This is not surprising. In the past too, when Burma was under outright military rule, the Asian powers were more engaging with the regime than the Western nations. This is only partly due to greater Western concerns for human rights and democracy; a more important factor has to do with the fact that the Asian powers, like ASEAN, have a more vested economic and political interest in Burma and are prepared to deal with any regime that effectively controls the country notwithstanding its ideological colour or political system. This divergence becomes clear from a brief look at the responses of China, India and Japan to the 2021 coup.

## China

China is perhaps the most important among the Asian powers, or any external power, in shaping Burma's political destiny in the aftermath of the February 2021 coup. Burma occupies a significant place in China's strategic framework aimed at enhancing its power and influence in Asia. This is due to several reasons: geographic closeness, deep and longstanding economic ties, including its investments in Burma's energy and resource sectors, Burma's role in China's Belt and Road Initiative (BRI), as well as China's strategic interests in using Burma to gain access to the Indian Ocean to counter India and the US.[442] These factors, and China's position as a permanent member of the UN Security Council, where it can block or dilute action directed at the military regime, also give China more leverage in shaping Burma's political destiny.

Predictably, China's response to the coup was in marked contrast to that of the US. China described Burma as a friendly neighbour—'pauk-phaw'—brothers connected by the same mountains and rivers; a community with a shared future through thick and thin.[443] Beijing expressed the hope that 'all parties in Myanmar will properly handle their differences under the constitutional and legal framework and maintain political and social stability'.[444] China also hoped that, while contemplating any action against the military rulers, the international community should consider political and social stability, peace, and reconciliation.[445] China did not condemn the leaders of Tatmadaw responsible for the coup. On the issue of the imprisonment of Burma's civilian leadership, including Aung San Suu Kyi, the Chinese ambassador to Myanmar Chen Hai would only make milder references:

The National League for Democracy, chaired by Daw Aung San Suu Kyi, maintains good relations with China and commits to jointly building a China-Myanmar community with a shared future, the China-Myanmar Economic Corridor (CMEC), and other practical cooperation with the Chinese side. We keep an eye on the situation of Daw Aung San Suu Kyi and others.[446]

Claiming that Beijing would play a constructive role in promoting peace and dialogue among the parties in dispute in Burma, China called for and supported mediation efforts by ASEAN and the United Nations. In Foreign Ministry Spokesperson Wang Wenbin's words, 'China will maintain close communication with ASEAN and support its mediation efforts while reaching out to all parties in Myanmar in its own way, so as to secure an early 'soft landing' for the situation in Myanmar'.[447] Subsequently, China supported the ASEAN's appointment of Erywan bin Pehin Yusof of Brunei as Special Envoy on Myanmar Affairs expressing the hope that 'the Special Envoy will live up to the common expectation of ASEAN countries and apply the effective ASEAN Way' to assist with the settlement of the issues faced by Myanmar. 'China will continue to play its constructive role in the process.'[448] China also supported the UN Secretary General's Special Envoy, Christine Schraner Burgener, expecting her to 'play a constructive role and continue her mediation efforts', and hoping that she will 'keep the communication channels with all parties in Myanmar open, [and] make extensive engagements. China will continue to be in contact with all parties in Myanmar to make its efforts for the de-escalation of the situation in Myanmar.'[449] Beijing refuted reports about Chinese aircraft supplying weapons for the Burmese military, calling them routine cargo flights carrying seafood and agricultural products, and technical help to build an internet firewall to regulate the flow of news in and out of the country.[450]

In keeping with its official 'non-interference' doctrine, China has and continues to regard the coup as Burma's internal affairs. Beijing's reactions to the military regime's suppression of protests in Burma have been quite ambivalent. As Chinese Foreign Ministry official spokesperson Zhao Lijian asserted, 'No matter how the situation evolves, China will not waver in its commitment to advancing China-Myanmar relations, and will not change the course of promoting friendship and cooperation.'[451] The same attitude was evident in Beijing's response to the killing of more than 100 civilian protesters in March 2021. Expressing serious concern about the violence and bloodshed, Ambassador Zhang Jun, Permanent Representative of China to the United Nations called upon all parties to 'exercise restraint to prevent the situation from exacerbating and getting out of control'. The same statement called upon 'the international community' to base its response to the military attacks 'on the adherence to the basic norm of non-interference in internal affairs' so as to 'create an enabling environment for domestic political reconciliation in Myanmar, instead of overstepping its responsibility or imposing pressure'.[452]

Beijing also played down acts of vandalism, looting, and arson against Chinese companies in Burma, calling them 'egregious', and leaving the responsibility to protect its citizens and property to the military rulers in Burma.[453] The Chinese Foreign Ministry would go only as far as reminding that the economic ties between the two are for 'mutual benefit' that 'boost Myanmar's economic and social development and delivers benefits to the local people'. Hence the 'lawless vandalizing, looting and arson attacks stood at odds with the interests of Myanmar and its people' and that 'the people of Myanmar [should] voice their appeal in a lawful manner, refuse to be instigated or taken advantage of, and avoid undermining China-Myanmar friendship and cooperation'.[454]

This does not mean that the international isolation of Burma after the coup has opened significant new space for China to increase its influence in the country.[455] The Burmese military maintains a deep distrust of China due to its support for cross-border ethnic insurgencies. Relations between the two countries had improved during the NLD government due to Aung San Suu Kyi's efforts. Although she did not revive the Myitsone dam and hydroelectric power project that was suspended by former President Thein Sein in 2011, Suu Kyi did agree to the China-Myanmar Economic Corridor, which is part of China's Belt and Road Initiative, linking Kyaukphyu in Burma and Kunming in China. If the military regime continues to get isolated and militarily pressured by the resistance movement in Burma, it is likely to turn more and more to China for more direct assistance, support, revival and strengthening of big infrastructure projects.[456] This would be helped by the fact that Beijing not only refused to impose any sanctions against the military regime but opposed multilateral sanctions or measures against the regime. On the contrary, China blocked sanctions or even simple condemnations proposed by the UN.[457] At the same time, China has continued its economic dealings with Burma to maintain the substantial border trade and supply of vaccines.[458] It has continued to work with Burma on the BRI projects, such as the development of a special economic zone and deep-sea port in the conflict-ridden Rakhine State. Beijing is also continuing to use the Asian Infrastructure Investment Bank, in which it has substantial stakes, to fund projects in Burma.[459] And Beijing has lobbied, albeit unsuccessfully thus far, to include Burma's military government in its meetings with ASEAN.

## India

Although India's economic ties with Burma are less extensive than China's, India shares both land and sea borders with Burma, and views the latter as an important ally in combating terrorism and insurgency, particularly in India's northeast, where Burma has been helping India on border security matters.[460] As part of India's 'Act East' (formerly 'Look East') and 'Neighbourhood First', policies, and with an eye to balancing Chinese influence in Burma, India had stepped up its own trade, development aid and security relations with Burma. India is also concerned about refugee flows into its northeast regions as a result of the coup and the military conflict between the Tatmadaw and resistance forces. Hence, it is not surprising that while India expressed the usual platitudes, urging the military regime to exercise restraint in dealing with the protestors and hoping for a peaceful resolution of the crisis,[461] New Delhi's response to the coup has been cautious and ambivalent, and has not precluded continued dealings with the military regime.

As the only country that shares a common border with both Burma and Bangladesh, India is also concerned about the outflow of Rohingya refugees to Bangladesh from the Rakhine State, as well as their influx into the northeastern border states of India, including Mizoram, Manipur and Nagaland. This would undermine India's efforts, through humanitarian assistance to Bangladesh to help Dhaka to maintain million-plus refugees in the country and to assist both countries for the speedy return and rehabilitation of the refugees in Burma.[462]

India supported the ASEAN's diplomacy in the post-coup Burma, including the ASEAN Summit in April 2021 that led to the 'Five-Point Consensus'[463] Yet, India's response to the crisis in Burma is described as low-key, even as the developments in Burma pose serious security and policy challenges to India.[464] Like China, India is more likely to use persuasion than condemnation and sanctions against the military regime to bring about any change in Burma, using the excuse of non-interference, but acting out of its strategic and economic interests in the country.[465]

## Japan

On 1 February, using somewhat softer language than his American and Australian counterparts, Japanese Foreign Minister Motegi Toshimitsu, stated,

> Japan has grave concern over the situation in Myanmar . . . where the process of democratization is being undermined . . . Japan once again strongly urges the Myanmar military to swiftly restore Myanmar's democratic political system.[466]

'Japan', noted the foreign minister, 'has strongly endorsed a democratization process in Myanmar and provided aid to support those developments, and we deeply regret actions that reverse the process . . . We'll be urging the military to reinstate a democratic political system as soon as possible'.[467] Interestingly, Japan's official condemnations of the coup have not come from the prime minister.

This reflects a longstanding Japanese policy dilemma to balance its traditional good relationship, backed by trade and development assistance, against the fear that an isolated Burma under military rule would tilt towards China.[468] Japan has not been shy to invoke Chinese influence to frame its approach to the coup. As a Japanese defence official remarked, 'If we do not approach this well, Myanmar could grow further away from politically free democratic nations and join the league of China . . . which would pose a risk to the security of the region.'[469]

While Japan supported the declared policy of the G-7 countries, of which it is a member, to reconsider their economic and diplomatic ties with Burma, it also indicated that its preferred approach would be to refrain from providing any new development assistance, rather than impose any tough sanctions against the regime.[470] In the past, too, Tokyo has been reluctant to sanction Burma's military leaders in line with the US and other Western countries, a stance that was especially evident in the Rohingya crisis.[471] Japan provided humanitarian assistance, which is uncontroversial, to Burma, such as an emergency aid of USD 5.8 million to be spent through the United Nations High Commissioner for Refugees (UNHCR), the World Food Programme (WFP), and the United Nations Children's Fund (UNICEF).[472] Like other powers, Japan, too, supports ASEAN's role in the Burma situation. It also urged the G-7 and G-20 to be engaged in finding a solution to the crisis, especially in dealing with the humanitarian and human rights situation there.

To reiterate a point made earlier, while Japan and India are closer to the US strategically, when it comes to Burma, their positions diverge from that of the US and Western nations.

Their economic interests in Burma are deeper than those of the West. An added motivation for India and Japan in engaging, rather than isolating, the military regime in Burma is their strategic competition with China for influence in the country and in the Southeast Asia region. India and Japan are both aware that by joining the hardline Western policy against the military regime, they would open the door to increased Chinese influence in Burma. In this respect, they also reflect the concerns of ASEAN, which fears that the total isolation of Burma would lead the regime to turn to China for greater support and give China more influence in the country and the region. These competitive calculations among the three Asian powers as well as different concerns of Asian countries and the West are a major obstacle to a united front against Burma's military regime, which also undercuts the possibility of an immediate diplomatic solution that will reverse Burma's military coup and restore democracy. These factors also undercut the role of the UN in Burma, which is discussed in the following section.

## United Nations

From the beginning, UN called upon the military leaders of Burma to respect the verdict of the November 2020 elections, reverse the military coup, free the detained leaders and other civilians and restore democracy. UN Secretary-General António Guterres promised that the 'United Nations will do everything it can to unite the international community and create conditions and explore all possible areas to put pressure on the junta to reverse course immediately'. Reacting to the widespread violence in Burma, the UN Secretary-General expressed deep concern stating, 'Reports of continued violence, intimidation, and harassment by security personnel are unacceptable.'[473] He urged the member states to use their respective influences on the military rulers in Burma to refrain from human rights and fundamental rights violations.

The secretary-general urged ASEAN 'to swiftly follow through on its own commitments', while urging the international community to support regional efforts and respond to the increased humanitarian needs.[474]

On 10 March 2021, the President of the UN Security Council issued a statement on 'The situation in Myanmar'. The statement expressed

> deep concern at developments in Myanmar following the declaration of the state of emergency imposed by the military on 1 February and the arbitrary detention of members of the Government, including State Counsellor Aung San Suu Kyi and President Win Myint and others. The Security Council reiterates its call for their immediate release.'

It then read:

> The Security Council strongly condemns the violence against peaceful protestors, including against women, youth and children. It expresses deep concern at restrictions on medical personnel, civil society, labour union members, journalists and media workers, and calls for the immediate release of all those detained arbitrarily. The Council calls for the military to exercise utmost restraint and emphasizes that it is following the situation closely.[475]

It is significant that the Security Council Statement did not condemn the coup itself. Rather it condemns the violence that resulted from the coup. Even then, it did not single out the Burmese military as perpetrators of that violence. Rather it called on the 'military to exercise utmost restraint'.

As might be expected, the UN Security Council's response was influenced by the position of China and Russia, two of its five permanent members (P5) with veto power, who were opposed to condemning the regime and imposing sanctions on it. While the Council called for an end to the military's violence against civilians, for the release of detained members of the government, including Aung San Suu Kyi and President Win Myint, and providing humanitarian assistance, this was to be done through 'constructive dialogue and reconciliation'.[476]

Following the Security Council, the UN General Assembly, which can only issue non-binding resolutions, met on 18 June 2021 to vote on a draft resolution, also entitled 'The situation in Myanmar', introduced by Liechtenstein. As with the Security Council statement, the General Assembly resolution did not 'condemn' the coup itself, but the use of 'lethal force and violence'. In other words, the General Assembly was

> *Strongly condemning* (emphasis original) the use of lethal force and violence, which has led to injuries and fatalities in many cases, against peaceful demonstrators, as well as members of civil society, women, youth, children and others, expressing deep concern at restrictions on medical personnel, civil society, labour union members, journalists and media workers, and people who protect and promote human rights, and calling for the immediate release of all those detained arbitrarily

The resolution asked:

> the Myanmar armed forces to respect the will of the people as freely expressed by the results of the general election of 8 November 2020, to end the state of emergency, to respect all human rights of all the people of Myanmar and to allow the sustained democratic transition of Myanmar, including the opening of the democratically elected parliament and by working towards bringing all national institutions, including the armed forces, under a fully inclusive civilian Government that is representative of the will of the people.[477]

The resolution also noted the investigation by the ICC into 'alleged crimes within the Court's jurisdiction in the situation in Bangladesh and Myanmar', a reference to the atrocities against the Rohingya by the Burmese military. One aspect of the resolution was to call upon member states to 'prevent the flow of arms into Myanmar', one that would have little effect. Indeed, in February 2022, UN Special Rapporteur for Human Rights in Burma, Tom Andrews, accused China, Russia and Serbia, for supplying weapons to the Burmese regime since the coup, including fighter aircraft, armoured vehicles, artillery and rockets.[478]

The resolution was adopted by a vote of 119–1, with thirty-six abstentions. The only negative vote was cast by Belarus, a staunch Russian ally, whose representative objected to what he described as a 'rushed' and 'closed' process.[479]

It should be noted that UN officials have been less reticent in condemning the junta in stronger and unambiguous language. This was made more prominent in a statement from the UN Secretary-General's office on 19 March 2021: 'The Secretary-General strongly condemns the continuing brutal violence by the military in Myanmar. The killing of peaceful demonstrators and arbitrary arrests, including of journalists, is utterly unacceptable . . . A firm, unified international response is urgently needed.'[480] In December 2021, when Aung San Suu Kyi was sentenced to two years (reduced from four) in prison for provoking political dissent and breaching COVID-19 pandemic restrictions, UN High Commissioner for Human Rights Michelle Bachelet said:

> The conviction of the State Counsellor following a sham trial in secretive proceedings before a military-controlled court is nothing but politically motivated. It is not only about arbitrary denial of her freedom: it closes yet another door to political dialogue. The military is attempting to instrumentalize the courts to remove all political opposition, but these cases cannot provide a legal veneer to the illegitimacy of the coup and military rule.[481]

But there has been no consequential action from the UN's main bodies against the military regime. A Security Council statement issued by rotating Council President Vassily A. Nebenzia of the Russian Federation on 2 February 2020 repeated previous positions. It expressed 'deep concern' about the state of emergency, called for the release of Suu Kyi and Win Myint, and other political detainees, a cessation of violence that can apply to both the military and resistance forces, including attacks on infrastructure, expressed support for Burma's 'democratic transition', respect for human rights, provision of humanitarian access to Burmese people, support for ASEAN's role, and 'their strong commitment to the sovereignty, political independence, territorial integrity and unity' of the country.[482]

Arguably, the UN's response to the coup in Burma has made little difference in finding a solution to the political crisis in Burma. This was expected or inevitable given the UN's past record on democratic breakdowns and the lack of unity among the Security Council's permanent members. That discord is now exacerbated by the Ukraine-Russia conflict, which has completely overshadowed the Burma situation. For their part, the Western nations have relied mainly on sanctions. Yet as Scot Marciel, former US ambassador to Burma (2016–20) commented,

> I don't think sanctions alone solve the problem. It's an international effort not to accept or give legitimacy to the military junta that's important. There needs to be continued diplomatic efforts to work together to create strong pressure on the Tatmadaw to recognize that it's not going to win and to look for a way out.[483]

To sum up, the position and response of the UN to the 2021 coup in Burma reflect the differing interests among its members, especially the P5 members of the Security Council, where China and Russia have taken a much more conciliatory approach than the Western members, US, France and the UK, towards the military regime. This is neither new nor exceptional to Burma but can be seen in previous conflicts such as Syria, Libya and Afghanistan. But such existing intra-P5 discords over international crises have been aggravated more recently by the war over Ukraine in which Russia is a direct party and which has weakened the UN as an institution in managing international peace and security issues. As a result, not only has international attention to the Burma situation declined, but so has the much needed diplomatic unity among the major players in world politics to bring about a solution to Burma's plight severely eroded.

# Chapter 10

## Despair and Hope

From the Thought Warriors:

*Right now, the future of everyone in the country, regardless of age, is destroyed. Due to inflation and the rise of basic commodity prices, lives of ordinary people become harder and harder. All developing processes of the country were halted by the coup. Thus, even when the coup is over, state leaders have to rebuild all the processes and work from the start. What an absurd act of selfishness.*

*On the positive side, many privileged people have come to realize the hardships of underprivileged minorities, and it has brought citizens who stand up against the military closer. Many young people who were used to ignoring politics are keeping themselves up to date with politics now. Some people have realized that idolizing and worshipping a person is bad.*

*Optimistically, this happened for good. If not, this country might be covered by imitations of democracy, which we call nemocracy under NLD. Now, many people have become politically open-minded.*

\* \* \*

What lies ahead for Burma? The coup has robbed the country of a decade of progress towards democracy and development, no matter however flawed. The country has all the makings of a full-scale civil war. Burma is, of course, no stranger to armed insurgencies, but for the first time, the military is not just fighting the militias of ethnic groups, but that of the majority ethnic groups: the Bamar.

The coup has produced economic collapse and an acute humanitarian crisis, both of which have been magnified by the COVID-19 pandemic. The future is bleak, although there may be some silver linings which would require a combination of the situation on the ground, political compromise among the parties in the civil war, and high-minded international support to lead to a positive future for the tragic nation.

Yet not all is lost, at least in the minds of Burma's youth. Asked about the consequences of the coup for the country's future, both long and short term, I got two types of responses, sometimes by the same person: negative and pessimistic, and positive and optimistic. The pessimistic ones focused on economic impact with some preparing for a long-drawn civil war, and others expressing distrust of the NUG or any alternative political institutions emerging to ensure long-term stability. Here is what a Thought Warrior felt when asked about the impact of the coup:

> Degeneration of the country's economy, dreams and future of youths being ruined, restrained human rights, civil wars, all these things are ordinary for a country under military control. It is pointless to mourn over these things. What I want to see is how the revolutionary government takes back the position. Last time, it was a fraud. People were misled by the rhetoric of politicians. I also do not have trust in the revolutionary [online] government. NUG that it can bring freedom back to people of Myanmar. Something might change when a miracle happens: like the People's Defence Forces triumph over the military, which is unlikely to happen. If not, it will just be a repetition of its old self. Unnecessary deaths, displaced people, war-torn villages and towns are the costs of this repetitive incident.

## Economic and Humanitarian Crisis

Burma's economic outlook was worsening even before the coup and the pandemic, with rising concern among foreign investors due to the slow pace of reforms, the absence of a coherent economic strategy and the danger of instability.[484] But the political turmoil following the coup and the COVID-19 pandemic have erased the impressive economic growth that Burma enjoyed over the past decades. The effects of the pandemic and the political tsunami have been all around. Households have been hit hard by massive job and labour income losses, the decline in remittances, and a rise in the prices of basic commodities.[485] Estimates of job losses run into between one to 1.2 million, especially impacting women.[486] Businesses have been wrecked by disruptions to the banking system, devaluation of the currency, and hence rising costs of imports, cash shortages and logistics problems.[487] This has affected not only agricultural production, Burma's core sector accounting for a third of its GDP and employing over 70 per cent of its workforce,[488] but also industries. The once vibrant garment industry has also experienced a 20 per cent decline in jobs. Several foreign companies have halted operations or pulled out of the country, although Chinese investors have continued operations (notably the Kyaukphyu power plant project in the Rakhine State).[489]

In July 2021, the World Bank laid out a grim picture of Burma's economy, predicting 18 per cent contraction of the GDP in the 2021 Fiscal Year (Oct. 2020-Sep. 2021). At that level, following the low growth in the previous fiscal year, the economy would be 30 per cent smaller than what it would have been had there been no pandemic and no military coup. The number of people living below the poverty line could double.[490] That would mean close to half the population would be in poverty.[491] Out of Burma's fifteen states and regions, fourteen are facing the danger of acute malnutrition.[492] The World Food Programme believes almost half the population faces food insecurity.[493]

The aftermath of the coup saw many internally displaced persons, some 350,000 by April 2021, according to one estimate.[494] Managing the humanitarian needs of displaced populations has become far more challenging. Aid groups are scrambling to modify their operations and adapt their approach to cooperation with the de facto authorities, while still delivering emergency services to vulnerable populations. Households in the country are facing food insecurity and a severe lack of healthcare services.

Medical services were affected by the military's targeting of health workers and medical professionals, who played a key role in launching the Civil Disobedience Movement (CDM). One such medical professional, Dr Troy Maung, founder of the Myanmar Doctors for Human Rights Network, recounts a 'brutalizing' attack by security forces on a group of female medics during a protest in Yangon. '[W]hen the junta began pushing health professionals underground, the situation started to get even more severe for people fleeing violence in rural areas.'[495]

By July 2021, Burma had reported over 280,000 infections and 8,200 deaths.[496] But these were gross underestimates due to the limited availability of testing and the fact that the official death toll only counts those who die at medical facilities. As a result, estimates of infections and deaths vary widely, a situation which can also be found in other countries, including neighbouring India. The third wave of COVID-19 in 2021 was particularly lethal for the country. The NUG claims that at least 43,500 people died of COVID-19 between 1 June and 30 September 2021.[497] The Yangon-based *Frontier Myanmar* magazine, which conducted its own investigation, concluded: '[T]he true death toll may be in the hundreds of thousands, as most were never counted.'[498] The Reuters news service in May 2022 put the COVID-19 numbers in Burma at 613,000 for infections and 19,434 for deaths.[499]

The coup also disrupted COVID-19 vaccination roll-out and the upgrading of public hospitals to provide COVID-19 treatment services.[500] Refusal of healthcare workers to report for work under a military government compounded the problem.[501] Those who refused to work were subjected to arrests and harassment by military units, which were deployed to medical facilities. The regime prioritized treatment and vaccines for military personnel, while denying access to its own hospitals to civilian COVID patients and limiting oxygen supplies to civilians and humanitarian agencies.[502] Vaccination became a political issue; refusing the vaccine provided by the military regime became an act of defiance. By May 2022, only about 45 per cent of the population (52.7 per cent according to the Reuters COVID-19 Tracker) had been vaccinated, according to the Vaccine Tracker of the Johns Hopkins University Coronavirus Resource Centre.[503]

The economic plight of the Burmese is well captured by the Thought Warriors. Here are some responses:

> *Youths become futureless. Economy turns downwards. The oppressors have become oppressive more than ever. Mostly, the worker class, lower class have to suffer food shortage and poverty more than usual.*
>
> *Unemployment, diseases and commodity prices have risen. Domestic violence, crime, theft, fraud, robbery, homicide and suicide are on the rise, and job opportunities are declining.*

By the first anniversary of the coup, according to the UN human rights office, military repression had killed at least 1,500 protesters, including 200 who died during torture while in military custody. These numbers do include those killed during the armed conflict, which could be 'in the thousands'. Out of 11,787 people detained by the military after the coup, 8,800 remained in prison.[504] Appendix 3, drawing on publicly available data, provides some accounts of these killings and atrocities, although this should be taken as indicative, not definitive.

Burma's economic and humanitarian situation is fluid, and it might worsen or improve in the coming years depending on the scale of the civil war, the degree of international assistance and the ease of its delivery to the needy, as well as the international economic situation, which has worsened since the outbreak of the Russia-Ukraine conflict (which would, among other things preoccupy Western nations and limit their capacity to provide economic aid). But the country has already seen much disruption and devastation, which could take decades to recover from, if at all.

## Will Burma's Military Revolt?

Those looking at Burma's future prospects are naturally interested in the prospects for an internal revolt from within the ranks of the armed forces. There are signs that the military is facing mounting challenges in keeping its hold on power. As described by the US Institute of Peace in a report issued on the first anniversary of the coup:[505]

> The Myanmar military is severely depleted and, due to popular resentment, faces mounting difficulty recruiting troops and administrative staff for the State Administrative Council (SAC), the caretaker government formed by the junta. The country's economic deterioration further constrains the resources available to the military to consolidate control. Negotiated efforts to squeeze the generals with an expanded international arms embargo and coordinated sanctions would go a step further. The military's domestic legitimacy—including among its soldiers—is at an all-time low. Continuing efforts to exclude the coup regime from international forums, such as ASEAN and the United Nations, would weaken its remaining domestic legitimacy as a governing institution and increase the incentives for defections, desertions, and noncompliance.

The veteran Burma military watcher Bertil Lintner also noted, 'Dissent within the ranks of the Tatmadaw could also lead to coups or coup attempts with extremely uncertain outcomes, even a repeat of the mutinies and chaos that prevailed in the wake of independence in 1948.'[506]

Despite its united front, the Tatmadaw has never been internally uniform. There have been not only power struggles, but also divisions over ideological issues—whether democracy is good for the country or not.[507] In the past, factionalism and rivalry within Tatmadaw have been engineered to encourage mass defections. If serious, the Tatmadaw usually dealt with such divisions with leadership changes, and internal purges. Given its extremely secretive culture, it is difficult to ascertain the reformists versus hardline elements within the military. After the 2021 coup, the Tatmadaw carried out some personnel changes, such as ousting the judge advocate general of the military.[508] But wider changes in the senior ranks did not take place.

The 'military hostage system' described in Chapter 3 also inhibits defections and the immediate breakdown of the military regime. Apart from the economic levers, this system is supported by propaganda and censorship, which have significantly increased after the 2021 coup. Social media campaigns create the image of wider support for the military in society, while portraying protestors as a minority that are nothing but agents of foreign forces. These campaigns stress the benefits of relying on military law over civilian law for soldiers.[509] This is supplemented by creating and promoting pro-junta ideology, monitoring and infiltrating potential anti-coup groups through fake social media accounts,[510] linking anti-coup sentiments to treachery/terrorist action, and banning social media platforms that critique and oppose the regime. The system also prevents soldiers and officers from observing the full extent of the coup and military action, not to mention the full extent of human rights abuses and issues presented by the junta.[511]

Overall, the system continues to foster a sense of dependency and discourage defection. It is thus not surprising that the majority of soldiers willing to defect after the 2021 coup have been single young men, who are less likely to have been integrated into a privilege system due to their low ranking, and are yet to have become deeply dependent on the resources provided by the Tatmadaw.[512] At the same time, the appointment of older, entrenched loyalists into nearly all leadership positions makes the collapse of loyalty within these bodies difficult, allowing the Tatmadaw to continue operations through prior established coercive networks and dependencies.

The military hostage system is also bolstered by ethno-religious nationalist sentiments, especially in the post-coup period. Through propaganda publications, the Tatmadaw is presented as the guardian of Buddhist religion and culture, assisting and protecting the Sangha, and presenting Islam as a religious threat. Buddhist nationalists like Ashin Wirathu of the 969 Movement and members of the Patriotic Association of Myanmar were released from prison after the junta took power in February 2021.[513] The composition of the Tatmadaw is heavily skewed in favour of Bamar Buddhists.

I once asked a Burmese youth, who is not a Thought Warrior (he lives outside Burma), whose family had military links in the past, whether the Tatmadaw encounters serious internal disunity. I gave him some prompts:

*Why has there been no large-scale defections or split in the military, despite being plagued by the low morale of soldiers? Why do soldiers still support the regime that they cannot morally defend? Is the reason that the military lives in a separate sphere or bubble with its own schools, hospitals, housing, pension system, supply chain and promotion system designed to take people hostage? It has rules like unmarried people cannot be promoted. Married can. Married with children can go even higher. These discourage defections: soldiers are 'effectively hostages'. So, it is a long shot for the army to break. Is this view accurate?*

This was his answer.

*Yes, that is accurate, but doesn't fully capture everything. There is a culture of corruption embedded in the military itself as well. For soldiers who think the military is morally bankrupt, they would unlikely go up the halls of power through promotions and ranks. This is because the military pays its soldiers through a system of money requests that pervade the entire structure. It works like a mafia structure where those on the bottom need to pay their superiors, who then pay their superiors, who then pay their superiors, and this goes on and on. You keep any surplus for yourself, and you're allowed to abuse your power as a soldier to the people, so long as you get the money. Hence those who find better ways to extort, or extract money from the public, or from their resources, will receive promotions and ranks. This has been the style for nearly sixty years and is now basically expected and trained for anyone inside the bubble of the military. They are well raised in the system, and it's all they know. The general public knows this as well. Sadly, even if any person raised in this bubble doubted the teachings of the Tatmadaw, I don't see who they can turn to, because no doubt they are looked at with disdain or fear by anyone in the general public. This would also explain why many soldiers and higher-ranking officials will not break rank. Because their entire life, not just fortune, but entire way of life can be upended, and they had a taste of that during Aung San Suu Kyi's reforms from 2016 onwards. Two things she did from a policy standpoint that really targeted the military were land reforms and property taxes. Military officials had a practice of stealing farmland, and making fake papers after Ne Win's time. However, Suu Kyi started auditing land documents during her 2016 period, and these fake papers suddenly disappeared, allowing farmers to reclaim their land. Property taxes also disproportionately affected military officials, because they are the ones who owned all the property.*

He concluded:

*I am not sure, but the military may not ultimately collapse even if they win against PDF. Their soldiers are so poorly trained, which is directly caused by corruption. The misuse of their own resources as mentioned in previous emails, such as weapons and fuel, prevents training of their own soldiers. But the real advantage the Tatmadaw has, which is enormous, is the gap in military hardware. Because frankly, I don't see why anyone would want to enter the military unless it's to climb the corridors of power or make income. It does not sound like anyone in the higher levels actually care for the country, just their own life inside the bubble of the Tatmadaw, which is basically a country in and of itself. A military like that will stay fragile, even if all this fighting is over. Sadly, I just don't know how the people can take power back from the Tatmadaw, who have the ability to buy weapons from other nations openly or secretly, and withdraw into their own bubble. So, in the end, I am becoming pessimistic about the outcome here.*

The perception of the military has turned deeply negative, especially among the youth. As a student protestor who took part in my survey noted:

*'They [the military] are unable to build, develop or maintain anything. However, there is one thing they are able to do: terrorize and slaughter.'*

Another said,

*'[That military is good at] accusing, arresting and murdering people have separated many families into pieces. Burning houses and villages have caused a lot of people to become displaced and homeless. All these things are rooted from a selfish person who thinks of himself. The whole military organization is responsible for all those merciless things. They must repay all the blood that has been shed!'*

The older generation continues to have a softer view of the military. One such person, now living in Myanmar, gave me such an impression. As a relative of his summarized it: 'He knows the army is corrupt but is needed to hold the country together. In other words, he thinks the military as they are, without having staged the coup, is best for the nation.'

Another Burmese person, also not a Thought Warrior, who is in his seventies, who once worked for the military government, believes that Burma's future depends on removing the distrust between politicians and a military that continues to see itself as the heirs to the freedom fighters and the best guardian of the country's interests. As he sees it:

> The army has a mentality that it has to be involved in everything to keep the nation together. This stems from the fact that Burma gained independence through an army. In fact, those who started the army came from patriotic students joining the cause for Burmese independence (Aung San and the thirty comrades). However, after the war and the country finally had a proper army, there were many different paths and priorities they fumbled. One was that only the region around the Burman people was under military control, and the army had to figure out how to stop rebellions and gain control over the entire country. The army, being the force of independence, naturally transitioned into politics. However, it did not seem like there was a good boundary made between military choices and political ones.
>
> Additionally, the military also didn't like politicians for two reasons. One, because politicians were seen as making money and choices based on corruption. Military at the time made basically no money . . . there was more of a philosophical disconnect between soldiers and politicians. Politicians would often be corrupt, making deals with all sorts of people to accomplish their goals. And so my dad pointed out that the military failed to appreciate that sometimes politicians can help the people through corruption. Making deals with

*businesses to provide jobs, things of that nature. Thus, the military, to become more like the US army, needed to step away from politics to give space for politicians, but that was difficult since they were seen as the protectors of the nation. They also were actively fighting other ethnic groups to keep the country together, further enforcing that narrative. And to make things worse, politicians already had a stigma among soldiers, leaving the military to believe it was their burden to take care of the country. In the end, my father thinks the politicians and the army need to figure out how to share power, and something like that takes a whole generation. The dictatorship of Ne Win put a long pause on that, because there were other people in the military trying to figure things out, who were kicked out of power, and Ne Win took full control of the country. In any case, no one today can figure it out, and it's something that takes a long time.*

## Federalist Dreams

As noted in Chapter 7, the political and military response of Burma's ethnic parties and militias to the coup differ considerably. These differences, stemming from varied self-interests, are compounded by their continuing distrust of the NLD. This weakens the prospect of a unified or highly coordinated armed struggle against the military regime.[514]

An equally important question is whether the coup has led to greater prospects for inter-ethnic reconciliation, as many inside and outside Burma hope for? To some extent, this has happened. The Committee Representing Pyidaungsu Hluttaw (CRPH) and the NUG have appointed members of ethnic groups to its cabinet positions. The CRPH not only abolished the 2008 Constitution, but also pledged to create a federal system. Relations between the NLD government and the ethnic groups were strained after the failure of the peace process to make progress. It revived the suspicion among ethnic groups that the Bamar-led NLD had little interest in devolution of power, and they resented what they saw as the NLD's overly accommodating posture towards the military, including its support for the brutal campaign against the Arakan Army. Several Thought Warriors insist that the coup will create awareness among the majority Bamar people of the neglect and discrimination that ethnic minorities in the country suffer from. As one noted, one positive outcome was the *'realization of the negligence on other ethnicities, increased open-mindedness'*. Another put it more strongly:

> *The only good thing is that people can now clearly see the true sight of the Myanmar military. For example, we have learnt about how the military really did the genocide and repression on indigenous people.*

The differing positions of the EAOs, stemming from varied self-interests and their continuing distrust of the NLD, mean there is little prospect for the creation of a federal army or a coordinated nationwide armed struggle against the junta. It is important to keep in mind that the coup has not only put an end to negotiation for a formal peace agreement, but also called into question the continuing relevance of the NCA and the bilateral ceasefire agreements between the Tatmadaw and the ethnic groups.

## Prospects

The situation in Burma is grim, with no foreseeable prospects for an end to the political stalemate and violence. This seems to be the prevailing consensus among many observers, both inside and outside. As the International Crisis Group noted in a January 2022 report, the country 'likely faces a protracted period of increased conflict, as neither the Tatmadaw nor the opposition appears likely to prevail'.[515] One Thought Warrior stressed the *'possibility for full-scale civil war'*.

Yet, some Thought Warrior remain relatively hopeful. Their opinions seem mixed, with some hoping for some sort of normalization within two to three years after the coup, while others foreseeing an indefinite conflict:

Overall, when asked to comment on when and how the coup might end, the Thought Warriors responded in a variety of ways, with varying degrees of pessimism. A number of them thought it might end fairly soon, perhaps in two to three years. The power of the people would prevail, and cooperation among various resistance groups and outside support would repel those generals:

*Maybe next three years, we people will win.*

*The strong relations and strategic cooperation between UGs, PDFs, EAOs and NUG can bring this coup to an end very soon. CDM was part of the answer, but now armed revolution is the way towards our victory.*

Others are not so sure. It will take longer for the coup makers to give in to the will of the people:

*It's hard to tell yet. It seems to be a matter of which side will give up first. I think it's going to take longer than two years at least.*

The resistance movement's military weaknesses loom large. The military regime would endure for a while.

*To be honest, I think the coup will take another one or two years. I often tend to think that if the military is weakened by the PDF attacks, Min Aung Hlaing will not be able to stand it and the people would win. However, it might take time as there are no sufficient weapons for PDF. Moreover, people begin to lack enthusiasm as time goes on. Older generations are the worst. I think the younger generation will be left alone in the revolution. And yes, the international community has nothing to rely on.*

At the same time, there is expectation and hope that armed resistance to the regime will grow:

> *I don't know how this will end, but if things get worse, more people might arm themselves to revolt against the junta forces.*
>
> *The coup must fail at all costs; we cannot live under it. They are not winning at this point, which means they do not gain any legitimacy both domestically and internationally. Resistance of people is not a joke; the power comes from people.*

Duwa Lashi La, the Acting President of the NUG, claimed in May 2022 that 'within a year, we achieved significant success on the military and administrative fronts'. The People's Defence Forces, he claimed, already controlled '15 per cent of Myanmar' and the 'collective resistance forces', which includes the Bamar and other ethnic resistance groups, control 'almost 50 per cent' of the country.[516]

These numbers are impossible to verify, but they do not mean a victory by the resistance forces is on the horizon. A few Thought Warriors see a prolonged stalemate between the opposition and the regime, which might plunge Burma into a perpetual state of civil war.

> *Not for a couple of years, I think it might not end at all and there would be no clear victory for both sides.*

This is the worst-case outcome for Burma. And it is not far-fetched. But a fight till the bitter end until a victory over the military is achieved can also be good for the country in the long-term.

> *We have only one way. It's 'do or die', with no choice. There's no way to step back, either for us or the juntas. The one who can fight till the last minute would win and bring the end. Maybe we would lose. I don't know. The military council will face failure for sure. And I think we will be able to accomplish the federal union eventually.*

*It might take a lot of time, and the country will be wrecked too. In the end, the ruined country will be rebuilt by the hands of youths. [The goal should be] to build Federal Democracy and work for transitional justice after all of this is over. If we do not revolt with unity, the country will always be under military government, where there is no light of development and future. To gain its glory back among the world's developing countries, the military dictatorship must fail.*

Outside observers have been generally pessimistic about the future of Burma. The aforementioned USIP report lists five possible outcomes:[517]

- continuation over the short to medium term of chaotic and increasingly bloody civil war that could become internecine;
- partial or complete secession from the union by some of the ethnic minority groups as their armies gain ground against the military;
- consolidation of harsh military control over some parts of the country;
- failure of the opposition movement to unite effectively around an agreed future for the country; or
- emergence of an empowered opposition government conceived as an inclusive federal democracy with security forces reconfigured along federal lines, some early signs of which are already emerging in conflict areas where opposition forces and EAOs are increasingly taking over local administration, health services, and security control.

These scenarios parallel the possible outcomes that a Thought Warrior had outlined to me:

1. *It will end within a year or two by releasing DASSK and going back to the negotiating table, the military still taking part in politics. I don't call it an end, but many people do.*

2. *Military continued the coup for decades, like after 1990. They might hold a general election again but might abolish the NLD or try to completely control the winning party or not hand over the authority to the winning party. They can do anything with their hands. That could be decades long.*

3. *Military loses, the NLD come back and continue ruling. That could be like a dictator losing and a dictator coming back. Not very different. Revolution must continue. This could happen if the revolution ends in a year or two, but I think under this occasion, military coup can happen anytime again, like the 1958–60 Caretaker Government led by Ne Win returning power to U Nu in 1960–62 and doing a coup again in 1962.*

4. *Third Party Organizations such as Students' Union, Workers' Unions and others leading the revolution (NUG stepping aside) and fighting for all the claims and sayings of this revolution till the end. There is a very small percentage that this could happen and may take more than a decade. But, what's the matter? Revolutions always take a long time.*

Of these, the second point deserves particular attention: the military regime organizing an election under the 2008 Constitution in the coming years. While the NLD and many other parties under the NUG would surely boycott the election, the military regime could flaunt the election as fulfilling its promise of 'a free and fair multiparty general election', as announced in the official notification of the military takeover on 1 February 2021. A new government led by the military-backed party (USDP or another name) would run the country, thereby continuing with de facto military control of Burma. It may then co-opt some opposition elements; as another Thought Warrior puts it:

*I don't believe that the coup will end with a complete triumph of one side. Considering the intelligence I have, the fight between the NUG and the military will end in a reconciliation method.*

*(The old method that NLD, previous civil government, pursued.)*
*Or the country will remain as a failed state between political clashes*
*for a really long duration.*

But such an outcome implies there would be some way of engaging the military by the resistance forces and outside actors. Some analysts believe such an approach is necessary and could be fruitful. They have called for reaching out to the regime. But this remains a sensitive issue and there is no agreement on whether engaging the military is morally justifiable or would be productive if undertaken.

The USIP report, written from an explicitly US perspective, suggested several responses, such as sanctions and pressure to undercut the military regimes' resources, cooperation with ASEAN to apply pressure on the Burmese regime, organizing international humanitarian assistance to Burma, closer engagement with the opposition (not limited to NUG), including civilian non-state actors, especially those that are democratically elected, and developing plans for the transition to a civilian government in the future. These recommendations make no mention of engaging the military.

On the other hand, Nay Yan Oo, who worked for the Asia Foundation in Burma, argues that part of the blame for the crisis in Burma must be laid at the 'Western nations', who 'failed to engage with the Tatmadaw. When Myanmar enjoyed greater freedom and prosperity, soldiers did not have many opportunities to interact with the world outside of their own institution, and military propaganda was reinforced to them through training and other means of indoctrination'. He suggests, 'Engaging with the Tatmadaw is thus required, but it does not mean lifting existing arms embargos or transferring military technology to Myanmar.'[518]

ASEAN might play an important role in the diplomatic efforts to return Burma to democracy. But ASEAN's past record shows that it has been often reluctant to and divided over when and how to go about responding to military coups in its member states. While ASEAN has achieved a consensus on not including the regime in its official meetings, it has also made little progress in getting the regime to engage in conversations to return Burma to civilian rule. That might change, and ASEAN could play a slow but positive role in bringing about a peaceful end to the military takeover. But this is no Cambodia conflict of the 1980s, where ASEAN's diplomacy was, in the end, fruitful? However, that conflict was triggered by an invasion (Vietnamese invasion of Cambodia), not an internal coup. ASEAN did apply some pressure against Cambodian co-Prime Minister Hun Sen when he ousted his co-Prime Minister Norodom Ranariddh in 1997, by postponing Cambodia's accession to full membership. But in the case of Burma, the only equivalent option would be suspension or expulsion, which has not been seriously discussed, although it has been raised by analysts and policymakers. And if such a move is carried out, its effect on the military regime is not likely to be decisive.

Another possible mechanism could be a form of transitional justice plan that can be offered as an inducement to the military to give up control. Transitional justice requires cooperation with the regime's remnants, unless total victory over it is achieved by the opposition. A transitional justice plan would include assurances of non-persecution to those officers with a clean record (identifying these would be a daunting task), or those who defect to the opposition. Although difficult to implement, such a mechanism should be seriously considered.

The coup and the resistance to it do carry some hopeful signs for Burma's longer-term future. None of the factors that might have been behind the failure of democracy in Burma are unique to the country. Hence, they are not irreversible. The coup has brought about a sense of common purpose among the majority Bamars and the ethnic groups, which is unprecedented in the country's history. Until now, they had no common enemy.

Thanks to the nature and effects of British colonial rule, the Bamars and the ethnic groups remained culturally and politically apart, and never developed a sense of national unity and purpose. Now, their common resistance to the military might create the basis for a power-sharing mechanism that would serve Burma well if the current regime is deposed and democratic forces prevail.

At this point of time, the Burmese remain fiercely opposed to the coup and in general agreement that the military takeover must end. And amidst much despair for the short-term outlook for the country, there are flickers of hope for its positive, long-term transformation. Resistance is not futile, insisted a Thought Warrior:

> *Coup or not, oppressions should have never existed in the first place. I hope we could revolt against them from the root so that our next generation won't go through hell like us.*

Another said it in more heartfelt words:

> *Even if we win this revolution, people have to suffer the coup-consequences and rebuilding the country back will also take a lot of time. And those military dogs will destroy and steal the country's resources as much as they can before victory can be gained. Man, even thinking about it makes me feel exhausted. We will never have a normal life like the citizens from the developing and developed country. Why do we have to suffer like this? I also want to have a good life too . . . I just hope that our next generation will never have to experience this kind of hell like we had to. But anyway, of course, I want my country to be able to stand up and catch up with all the other countries very soon. But to be able to become like that, we, the citizens, have to work hard and unite.* (Student and civil disobedience movement activist).

While factors such as a stalemate on the ground between junta and opposition forces; strong international sanctions against the regime; genuine support from China, the US, India, and ASEAN for political normalization and democracy, can help, the key to Burma's return to relative stability and democracy is national unity and reconciliation against military rule. Without this, Burma faces a dark future, the fate of a tragic nation.

But there is hope. Democracy has failed twice in Burma, but this does not mean it will disappear. On the contrary, it might grow, as the result of the 2021 coup. The rising political consciousness of the younger generation, as confirmed by the Thought Warriors, and the fact that the majority ethnic group in Burma is not only protesting but has also taken up armed struggle, and is prepared to accommodate the aspirations of the ethnic groups, is a huge force for the country's transformation.

# Appendix 1

## Burma's Armed Forces: Origin and Evolution

Compiled by Ryan Roden and
Arabinda Acharya

The modern Burmese Army known as the Tatmadaw draws, its roots from the days of Aung San (Burmese nationalist leader and father of Aung San Suu Kyi) and the Burma Independence Army (BIA) formed in December 1941. Aung San and his 'Thirty Comrades', received military training from the Japanese Imperial Army to fight against the British colonial authority.[1] Aung San and the Thirty Comrades would then work under Commander-in-Chief Suzuki Keiji.[2] In July 1942, the Japanese occupiers disbanded BIA, which later emerged as the Burma Defence Army (BDA) in August 1942, under the command of Aung San.

In March 1945, however, Aung San switched sides and openly declared war against the Japanese, and in June 1945 formally joined the Allied forces with BDA as the Patriotic Burmese Forces (PBF). On 7 September 1945,[3] Aung San attended a two-day conference

---

[1] Myint-U Thant., *The River of Lost Footsteps: A Personal History of Burma*, London, UK: Faber and Faber, 2008.

[2] Myint-U Thant, *The River of Lost Footsteps*.

[3] Martin Smith, *Burma: Insurgency and the Politics of Ethnicity*. Dhaka, BD: University Press, 1999.

at Kandy in Sri Lanka, together with Lord Mountbatten, the Supreme Commander of the Allied Forces, and other top-ranking military and civilian officers. The negotiations at Kandy resulted in the 'Kandy Agreement' that, among others, recognized PBF as part of the Burmese Army, allowing several thousand of the PBF personnel to enlist and serve as professional armed forces.[4]

This was one of the foundational points to the origin of the contemporary Tatmadaw. However, even as such validation would endow nationalist fervour on Aung San and his Anti-Fascist People's Freedom League (AFPFL), the underline discontent with the British Army lingered due to the policy of maintaining a divided army based on ethnicity-based battalions.[5]

The Aung San-Atlee Agreement on 27 January 1947 led to the political independence of Burma. After independence, one of the major challenges was to reorganize the armed forces; shaping it from an entity divided by geography and ethnicity involving the British Burma Army and Patriotic Burma Forces. The British colonial administration had deliberately organized the armed forces in Burma along ethnic lines—class battalions based on ethnicity—to keep what they called the 'revolutionary forces', at bay.[6] Forces were drawn in a manner that kept the PBF personnel separate from Karen, Gurkha, and Chin groups, which were placed alongside former members of the British Burma Army. Commanding officers for various positions, including of the navy and the air force, as well as the high-ranking officials in the War Office, were drawn from the former officers of the British Burma

---

[4] Susanne Prager-Nyein, 'The birth of Burma's modern army', in David P. Chandler, et al., *End Of Empire: 100 days in 1945 that Changed Asia and the World*. The Nordic Institute of Asian Studies, 2016.

[5] Josef Silverstein, ed., *The Political Legacy of Aung San*. Cornell University Press, 1993.

[6] Susanne Prager-Nyein, 'The birth of Burma's modern army', in David P. Chandler, et al., *End Of Empire: 100 days in 1945 that Changed Asia and the World*. The Nordic Institute of Asian Studies 2016.

Army and Army of Burma Reserve Organization (ABRO).[7] The divisions and dissensions were so severe that in 1949 the Karen National Defence Organization incorporated the personnel of the Karen ethnicity of the Tatmadaw to help 'Kawthoolei', the movement for an independent Karen state.[8]

The consolidation and reorganization of the Tatmadaw fell on the shoulders of Ne Win. On 31 January 1949, Ne Win was appointed chief of staff of the Tatmadaw, taking control of the army from General Smith Dun. In 1956, the War Office was redesignated as the Ministry of Defence, and Ne Win became the chief of the general staff of the Burmese Army. Ne win took command of the army, navy, and air force, unifying the three positions into a single entity for the first time in Burmese history.[9]

In 1957, following large-scale political disorder, Prime Minister U Nu invited Ne Win to head the caretaker government and, in October 1958, handed him the powers of the office of the prime minister, apparently under the threat of a military coup.[10] The caretaker government of Ne Win was the first instance where the Tatmadaw yielded total political authority in post-colonial Burma. During this period, the Defence Services Act was enacted, followed by Detailed Rules for its implementation. Under the 1959 Defence Services Act, military courts and procuratorates were established.[11] The military itself was expanded with additional

---

[7] Andrew Selth, *Burma's Armed Forces: Power Without Glory*. Norwalk, CT: EastBridge, 2002.

[8] Karen Environmental Social Action Network, 'The Karen Struggle for Self-Determination in Kawthoolei', *Burma Link*, 21 August 2018, The Karen Struggle for Self-Determination in Kawthoolei (burmalink.org).

[9] Tin Maung Maung Than, 'Burma's National Security and Defence Posture', *Contemporary Southeast Asia* 11, no. 1 (June 1989).

[10] Cecil Hobbs, 'U Nu: Saturday's Son. By U Nu. Translated by U Law Yone; Edited by U Kyaw Win. New Haven; Yale University Press, 1975. Xv, 358 Pp. Index'. *The Journal of Asian Studies* 35, no. 2 (1976): 355–56. doi:10.2307/2054025.

[11] The Defence Services Act 1959, dsa1959148.pdf (asianlii.org).

brigades and divisions and with the purchase of equipment from other countries like the United States and Israel.[12]

In February 1960, following the win of U Nu and his Pyidaungsu Party (Union Party) in the parliamentary elections, the military handed over power to U Nu as prime minister, which was one of the first instances in Burma of a voluntary transition of power from military to civilian elements. The peaceful transition of authority drew widespread support for the Tatmadaw and further legitimized Ne Win's administrative authority. After the elections, several ranking military officers were dismissed allegedly due to political partisanship, further solidifying an environment of shared political engagement and thought.[13] During this period, the old system of geography and ethnicity-based brigades was abolished, and instead, five military regions—the Northwest, East, Central, Southwest, and Southeast were created. The navy received special attention with expansion in terms of areas of operations and bases.[14]

This military-civilian bonhomie, however, did not last long. On 2 March 1962, Tatmadaw staged a coup and upstaged the civilian government, and took U Nu and other senior leaders into custody. Ne Win formed the Union Revolutionary Council to replace the civilian government ostensibly for 'keeping the country's safety, owing to the greatly deteriorating conditions of the Union',[15] and to address corruption, crime, and social instability issues.[16] Ne Win's Union Revolutionary Council was to facilitate

---

[12] Ibid.

[13] Maung, Aung Myoe, *Building the Tatmadaw: Myanmar Armed Forces Since 1948*. Singapore: ISEAS, 2009.

[14] Zhong ZhiXiang and Li ChenYang, *Burmese Armed Forces Research* Military Yiwen Publishing House, 2004.

[15] General Ne Win, cited in Maung Maung, *General Ne Win and Burma* Burma: Religious Affairs Department Press, 1969.

[16] Aung-Thwin, Michael, and Maitrii Aung-Thwin. *A History of Myanmar since Ancient Times: Traditions and Transformations*. London, UK: Reaktion Books, 2013.

a 'self-sustaining democratic socialist state', in Burma. All the members were from the military. The Burma Socialist Programme Party (BSPP) was recognized as the sole political party, and most of its members were also drawn from the military.[17] The Military Intelligence unit of the Tatmadaw acted as the secret police service of the state infrastructure. It was commonplace for all government actors and servants to undergo military training. Thus, the Tatmadaw exercised absolute power in Burma until the August 1988 protests.[18]

For the most part, Ne Win's totalitarian governance created the background conditions for the 8888 Uprising or the People Power Uprising of August 1988,[19] which was a series of nationwide protests against the full-scale impoverishment of the country under military rule.[20] Initiated by students, the protests soon involved almost all sections of the civilian population.[21] It was during this crisis that Aung San Suu Kyi emerged as a prominent political figure. Ne Win resigned in July 1988 and was replaced by Saw Maung heading the State Law and Order Restoration Council (SLORC). Saw Maung repressed the 8888 uprising with an iron hand.

The SLORC comprised nineteen military officers that ruled the country and controlled the Tatmadaw. In 1990, it concentrated its efforts on military modernization opportunities, beginning with

---

[17] Martin Smith, *Burma: Insurgency and the Politics of Ethnicity*. London and New Jersey: Zed Books, 1991.

[18] Zhong ZhiXiang and Li ChenYang, *Burmese Armed Forces Research*.

[19] Chao-Tzang Yawnghwe, 'Burma: Depoliticization of the Political', in Muthiah Alagappa, *Political Legitimacy in Southeast Asia: The Quest for Moral Authority*. Stanford University Press, 1995.

[20] *Burma in 1988: There Came a Whirlwind*. Asian Survey, 29(2); Kate Woodsome, 'Burmese Way to Socialism Drives Country into Poverty', *Voice of America*, 4 October 2007.

[21] David Steinberg, *Burma: State of Myanmar*. Georgetown University Press, 2002.

a five-year plan that would build the army, with General Saw Maung acting as the supreme authority. In 1997, the SLORC renamed itself as the State Peace and Development Council (SPDC). The Chief of Intelligence Khin Nyunt was appointed as Secretary-1, who in 2003 became the prime minister of Burma. It was Khin Nyunt who unveiled the 'Roadmap to Democracy' that would envision permanent military participation in governance, though, in October 2004, he was removed from office by SPDC Chairman Than Shwe. Khin Nyunt was arrested and put under protective custody.[22]

The 2008 Constitution replaced the one enacted in 1974. It allowed opposition parties to participate in governance while ensuring that 25 per cent of the membership of the Burmese Parliament would be reserved for serving military officers. The military would appoint one of the two vice-presidents, and several ministries would need to be headed by military officers, including the Ministry of Defence, Home Affairs, and Border Affairs, in essence cutting down the role of civilians in key areas of administration.[23]

The constitution also ensured that Aung San Suu Kyi would not be allowed to hold the position of the President, and it authorized the commander-in-chief to exercise sovereign powers in several instances.

> '[The constitution allowed] the military to dissolve the civilian government and parliament and rule directly if the President declares a state of emergency. The military has the right to administer its own affairs, and members of the former military government received blanket immunity for all official acts.' [24]

---

[22] 'Burma's prime minister arrested', *BBC News*, 19 October 2004.

[23] Hunter Marston, 'Analysis: Why Is Myanmar's Military so Powerful?' *Al Jazeera*, 5 October 2021. https://www.aljazeera.com/features/2021/2/2/analysis-why-is-myanmar-military-so-powerful

[24] 'Freedom in the World 2017—Myanmar', *Freedom House*, Document #1408609, January 2017, https://freedomhouse.org/report/freedom-world/2017/myanmar

Under the new constitution, the Tatmadaw was given the authority to veto any constitutional reforms enacted by civilian legislators. This allowed the Tatmadaw to ensure independence, particularly in financial matters as its claim and authority over the nationalized mining, oil, and gas industries brought a continuous flow of income, through bodies such as the Myanmar Economic Holdings Limited (MEHL) and the Myanmar Economic Corporation (MEC), both Tatmadaw facilitated conglomerates.[25]

In 2010, conscription legislation made three-year military service mandatory for all able-bodied citizens, both male and female.[26] The same year, the Union Solidarity and Development Association became the Union Solidarity and Development Party (USDP) headed by President Thein Sein. Most of the party officials were from the military. In 2011, a Special Funds Law authorized the military to circumvent parliamentary oversight and any audit to access and use unlimited 'special funds' beyond budgetary provisions 'for the perpetuation of national sovereignty'.[27] It is also the same year that Min Aung Hlaing, 'a battle-hardened warrior of brutal Burmese Army',[28] assumed the position as the commander-in-chief of Tatmadaw succeeding Than Shwe.

Though, on the surface, Burma was transitioning to democracy, Hlaing persisted in maintaining Tatmadaw's supremacy in the country.[29] This explains his subsequent actions, especially those leading to the coup in February 2021.

---

[25] Gerard McCarthy, *Military Capitalism in Myanmar: Examining the Origins, Continuities and Evolution of 'Khaki Capital'*, Singapore, SG: ISEAS Yusof Ishak Institute, 2019.

[26] Joseph Allchin, 'Burma Introduces Military Draft', *Democratic Voice of Burma*, 10 January 2011, http://www.dvb.no/news/burma-introduces-military-draft/13640

[27] Wai Moe, 'Than Shwe Grants Himself Power to Access "Special Funds"', *The Irrawaddy*, 4 March 2011.

[28] 'Myanmar coup: Min Aung Hlaing, the general who seized power', *BBC News*, 1 February 2021.

[29] Ibid.

Following the coup on 1 February 2021, Acting President Myint Swe surrendered all powers and authority to Min Aung Hlaing and endorsed the authority of the State Administration Council (SAC), apparently under pressure from Hlaing.[30] Now Hlaing serves as the chairman of the SAC, with Soe Win serving both as deputy commander-in-chief and vice-chairman of SAC. All other council members are military officials, dissenters from the National League for Democracy, and factions of some of the ethnic-based parties.[31]

The SAC negotiated a ceasefire with the Arakan Army, letting the latter establish its own governing institutions, judicial systems, and township networks with a majority of Tatmadaw forces removed from the western state.[32] The military government has acted on cybersecurity issues with a mechanism to prosecute cybercrimes, providing a general expansion of access to the junta to online platforms to control digital information with a view to curb the spread of anti-Tatmadaw sentiments.[33]

## Financing Tatmadaw

The Tatmadaw receives about 24 per cent of the national budget, which is one of the highest among the countries in the world.

---

[30] 'Junta Watch: Old Faces Reappear, Coup Leader Declares Himself Buddhism's Savior and More'. *The Irrawaddy*, 18 March 2022. https://www.irrawaddy.com/news/burma/junta-watch-old-faces-reappear-coup-leader-declares-himself-buddhisms-savior-and-more.html

[31] Sai Wunna, 'Karenni Armed Group Urges Govt, Tatmadaw on Single Stand in Peace Talks'. *Myanmar Times*, 2 December 2020. https://www.mmtimes.com/news/karenni-armed-group-urges-govt-tatmadaw-single-stand-peace-talks.html

[32] Anthony Davis, 'Why Myanmar's Military Will Win in the End.' *Asia Times*, 25 February 2021. https://asiatimes.com/2021/02/why-myanmars-military-will-win-in-the-end/

[33] Dhevy Sivaprakasam, and Raman Jit Singh Chima, 'Analysis: The Myanmar Junta's Cybersecurity Law Would Be a Disaster for Human Rights'. *Access Now*, 27 January 2022. https://www.accessnow.org/analysis-myanmar-cybersecurity-law/

Additionally, Tatmadaw funding comes from its holdings within the two major nationalized conglomerates of the MEHL and MEC, which was approximately $18 billion US dollars in 2020.[34] The funds used by the commander-in-chief under the Special Funds Law are over and above those allocated to the military in the defence budget, as mentioned earlier.[35]

## Challenges for the Tatmadaw

Post 2021 coup, the greatest challenge to the Tatmadaw comes from defections, which have been on the rise. According to some estimates, as of February 2022, approximately 16,000 police and soldier defections have been reported.[36] The People's Defence Force (PDF) relies on local recruiting mechanisms that cannot be easily traced, networked, or controlled by single-target responses by the Tatmadaw.[37] The Tatmadaw also has an uphill task fighting ethnic armed groups, many of which act autonomously, such as the Brotherhood Alliance.[38] The militias of the various ethnic groups engage the Tatmadaw on multiple fronts, while the PDF supports both ethnic armies and urban rebels. All these present a challenge that the Tatmadaw does not appear prepared

---

[34] 'Myanmar: Military Ltd: The Company Financing Human Rights Abuses in Myanmar', *Business and Human Rights, Amnesty International*, 1 June 2021. https://www.amnesty.org/en/documents/asa16/2969/2020/en/

[35] Wai Moe, 'Than Shwe Grants Himself Power to Access Special Funds'.

[36] Khin Muang, 'Thousands of Myanmar Soldiers and Police Have Joined Anti-Junta Forces since Coup', *Radio Free Asia*, 3 September 2021. https://www.rfa.org/english/news/myanmar/defect-09022021203230.html

[37] John Geddie, 'In Myanmar Jungle, Civilians Prepare to Battle Military Rulers', *Reuters*. 22 December 2021. https://www.reuters.com/world/asia-pacific/myanmar-jungle-civilians-prepare-battle-military-rulers-2021-12-16/

[38] Bertil Lintner, 'What Has Happened to Myanmar's Tatmadaw?' *The Irrawaddy*, 13 September 2021. https://www.irrawaddy.com/opinion/guest-column/what-has-happened-to-myanmars-tatmadaw.html

to combat effectively.[39] Unlike in the past, when the Tatmadaw mainly fought the militias of ethnic minorities, it is now fighting the Bamars, most of the country's population. This is a dramatic shift in the ground reality for the military in Burma.

Since its inception, the Burmese military or the Tatmadaw has dabbled in political affairs in one way or the other. Over the years this culture has become deeply ingrained in its organization. Anytime it feels constrained by civilian oversight, it lashes out, overturns the civilian government on some pretext, and takes control of the governance in the country, as evident in 1962, 1988 and 2021.

Characteristically, Tatmadaw does not have much concern about external defence as there is no threat to Burma's sovereignty and territorial integrity from external actors yet. Arguably, it faces severe internal threats from diverse ethnic groups demanding self-determination in terms of separation, independence, or self-rule, which requires a strong security apparatus in Burma. Tatmadaw, which is the second-largest active armed force in Southeast Asia,[40] draws its legitimacy from maintaining law and order against numerous agitations, armed uprisings and subversive activities of the groups engaged in the above-mentioned activities. Unfortunately, Tatmadaw has also repeatedly gone beyond its traditional role and ventured into politics much too often, the latest episode being the coup in February 2021. There is no indication that it will not do so in the future.

---

[39] Bertil Lintner, 'Myanmar Military Struggles to Adapt to New Kind of Conflict', *The Irrawaddy*, 18 October 2021. https://www.irrawaddy.com/opinion/guest-column/myanmar-military-struggles-to-adapt-to-new-kind-of-conflict.html

[40] *The Military Balance 2021*, The International Institute for Strategic Studies. London Routledge, 2021.

# Appendix 2

## Burma's Armed Forces: Structure and Weapons

### Compiled by Ryan Roden and
### Arabinda Acharya

According to a 2021 estimate, the Tatmadaw currently has 406,000 serving personnel in total, with 375,000 in the army, 16,000 in the Navy, and 15,000 in Air Force, along with another 18,998 reserve personnel distributed among the Border Guards, hired Militia groups, and membership within the University Training Corps.[41] Other sources, however, put the number of active and voluntary military units closer to 100,000 in total, with the caveat that the officially provided numbers do not take into account forced conscripts and administrative personnel.[42]

A breakdown of the size and weapon systems of different units of the Tatmadaw is given below.

---

[41] *The Military Balance 2021*, The International Institute for Strategic Studies London Routledge, 2021.

[42] Paskorn Jumlongrach, 'Junta Brutality Triggers Desertions', *Bangkok Post*, 1 February 2022, https://www.bangkokpost.com/opinion/opinion/2256599/junta-brutality-triggers-desertions

## Army

The army has between 479–599 Tanks, including fifty MBT-2000, between 160–280 Thermal Fitted Type-59D/M MBT, 130 Type-69 MBT all from China;[43] ten T-55 Medium Tanks from both India and Russia (that were purchased for training practices), and 105 Type-63 Amphibious Tanks from China that were retrofitted in the 2018 Sin Phyu Shin joint military exercise.[44] In 2017, Myanmar introduced the MMT-40, which is a lightweight class tank outfitted with a 105 milimetre gun, produced with aid from Ukraine.[45] There is an unknown quantity of these vehicles in service.

The Tatmadaw operates a minimum of 300 'Tank Destroyers' including 150 EE-9 Cascavel purchased from Israel, 150 WMA-03 purchased from China, and fifty Panhard AML also purchased from Israel.[46]

There are approximately 800 Infantry Fighting Vehicles in service, including about 1,000 BTR-3U procured from Ukraine, 100 Type-92 heavy machine guns from China, and 100 Myanmar-produced MAV (scout cars). There are approximately 500 Armoured Personnel Carriers (APC) in use, with 250 Type-86, 150 YW-531H, and fifty Type-90 AFV all from China. Thirty-three Amphibious BRDM-2MS were purchased from Russia in 2020, and ten M-3 VTT are suspected to have come from Israel in 2011. An unknown quantity of GAIA Thunder MRAPs was given by Israel in 2019 and was utilized by the Tatmadaw in the February 2021 coup.[47]

---

[43] Sarosh Bana, 'Myanmar's Military Coup: How the Tatmadaw Have Clung on to Power for More than 50 Years', Defence Procurement International, 1 April 2021. https://www.defenceprocurementinternational.com/features/air/myanmars-military-coup-enters-its-second-month-with-the-tatmadaw-killing-hundreds-of-protesters

[44] 'Myanmar's military goes shopping', Mizzima Foundation, 30 May 2019, Myanmar's military goes shopping | Mizzima Myanmar News and Insight.

[45] 'MA-MMT-40 105mm Light Tank', Globalsecurity.org.

[46] '2017 Military Strength Ranking', Globalfirepower.org, 16 March 2018.

[47] 'BTR-3E / BTR-3U Guardian-Myanmar', Globalsecurity.org.

# Navy

Burma's Naval Forces consist of four primary fleets, located in Thanlyin, Heinze, Kyaukphyu, and Haigyi. The navy has acquired one submarine in active service; an EX-INS Sindhuvir (Kilo Class), refitted with Indian systems at the Hindustan Shipyard. The vehicle possesses the capacity for eighteen 53-65KE Torpedos, as well as TEST-71MKE TV Wire-Guided Homing Torpedoes.[48]

Active vessels include the Amphibious Transport Dock (Makassar Class) UMS Moattamma, which serves as the Naval Flagship.[49] This vessel possesses 2 × 14.5 MM Gatling and 2 × QJH-02G 14.5 Heavy Machine Guns. Myanmar possesses four indigenous frigates: two Kaya Sittha Class Frigates, a 2010 Aung Zeya Class Frigate, and Project FF-135, estimated to launch in 2022, which is at least 135 metres long, and displaces approximately 4,000–4,500 tonnes.[50] The navy also possesses two Type-053H1 (Jianghu-II) Class Frigates purchased from China in 2012 and produced in the Hudong Shipyard and three Anawartha class (Myanmar Indigenous) Corvettes.[51]

The navy also has several River Patrol Crafts that are most often employed against internal actors: this includes six PBR Class vessels which were constructed between 1978–1982 and purchased from the United States, two Myanmar-Constructed twenty-one M River Patrol Crafts from 2019, ten 1970 Yan Naing Class vessels, and twenty-five Michao Class purchases from Yugoslavia in the 1960s.[52]

---

[48] Huma Siddiqui, 'India's naval diplomacy: Myanmar gets Kilo Class submarine INS Sindhuvir from India', *Financial Express*, 15 October 2020.

[49] Rahmat, Ridzwan, 'South Korean shipyard launches landing platform dock for Myanmar Navy'. IHS Jane's, 4 September 2019.

[50] 'Myanmar Shipyard Building 4th Frigate', RSS. Army Recognition Group SPRL, March 2021. https://www.navyrecognition.com/index.php/news/defence-news/2021/march/9906-myanmar-shipyard-building-4th-frigate.html.

[51] Mrityunjoy Mazumdar, Alameda. 'Myanmar Navy Commissions First Stealth Corvette.' Thai Military and Asian Region, 29 December 2016. https://thaimilitaryandasianregion.wordpress.com/2016/12/30/myanmar-navy-commissions-first-stealth-corvette/

[52] Aung Myoe, *Building the Tatmadaw: Myanmar Armed Forces since 1948*. New Delhi: KW Publishers, 2011.

## Air Force

The Burmese Air Force, in total, consists of eighty active Combat Aircraft, thirty-nine Transport Vessels, seventy-five Helicopters, and several Trainer Aircraft and UAVs.[53]

The Air Force has fifteen combat aircrafts on order in 2022 (Multirole Sukhoi Su-30 from Russia and nine Multirole JF-17 Thunder from Pakistan to accompany seven already in the inventory). This is in addition to having been in possession of thirty-one MiG-29 SE/SM/UB Combat Aircrafts acquired from Russia, twenty Nanchang Q-5 Attack Aircrafts from China, twenty-one Chengdu J-7 Fighters, and one Shenyang J-6 fighters.[54]

The Air force also possesses ten ATR-42 VIP transport vessels from France, eleven transport aircraft from China (five Shaanxi Y-8 and six Harbin Y-11), one Dutch Fokker F-27, five utility/transport Pilatus PC-6 from Switzerland (which are STOL Capable), seven utility/transport Beechcraft 1900 from the United States, and five Britten-Norman BN-2 from the UK for maritime patrol. Twenty-two Mil Mi-1 Liaison helicopters were acquired from Poland, twenty-one Mil series Attack helicopters from Russia (twelve Mi-17 and nine Mi-24), twenty-five Utility Helicopters from Europe (Thirteen Alouette III's from France, and twelve PZl W-3 Sokół from Poland) and seven Utility helicopters from the United States (four Bell-206, two Bell Uh-1, and one Bell 212).[55]

The Air Force's armaments include 540 Air-to-Air Missiles acquired from China and 445 AAM beyond-visual-range missiles acquired from both China and Russia.[56]

---

[53] 'World Air Forces 2022', *FlightGlobal*, https://www.flightglobal.com/reports/world-air-forces-directory-2022/146695.article, Retrieved 5 January 2022.

[54] 'World Air Forces 2022', *FlightGlobal*, https://www.flightglobal.com/reports/world-air-forces-directory-2022/146695.article, Retrieved 5 January 2022.

[55] 'World Air Forces 2022', *FlightGlobal*, https://www.flightglobal.com/reports/world-air-forces-directory-2022/146695.article, Retrieved 5 January 2022.

[56] 'World Air Forces 2022', *FlightGlobal*, https://www.flightglobal.com/reports/world-air-forces-directory-2022/146695.article, Retrieved 5 January 2022.

## The Border Guard

The Border Guard numbers approximately 7,498. Its battalion commanders are often appointed from localized ethnic armed organizations and groupings, yet overall command remains in the hands of the central command of the Tatmadaw.[57] Defection among Border Guard Forces, presumably because of these ethnic appointments and dependencies on localized leadership, has been rampant since the coup, mostly facilitated by the PDF. Therefore, the exact number of operating BGFs is unknown.[58]

## Sources of Weapons

As of 2021, fourteen companies from China, Russia, Ukraine, Israel, North Korea, India, and the Philippines have been active contributors and suppliers of arms and ammunition to the Tatmadaw. Other sources include South Korea for a post-2008 modernization endeavour of major weapons capacity.[59]

---

[57] 'Border Guard Force Scheme 'Myanmar Peace Monitor'', Myanmar Peace Monitor. Burma News International, 18 March 2020. https://www.mmpeacemonitor.org/border-guard-force-scheme/

[58] 'Burma Army Fights DKBA and Its Allies: 600 Villagers Displaced in Myawaddy Township', Karen News, 2 June 2021. https://karennews.org/2021/06/burma-army-fights-dkba-and-its-allies-600-villagers-displaced-in-myawaddy-township

[59] Sarosh Bana, 'Myanmar's Military Coup: How the Tatmadaw Have Clung on to Power for More than 50 Years', Defence Procurement International, 1 April 2021. https://www.defenceprocurementinternational.com/features/air/myanmars-military-coup-enters-its-second-month-with-the-tatmadaw-killing-hundreds-of-protesters

# Appendix 3

## Reported Atrocities in Burma: February 2021-March 2022

### Compiled by Karina Martinez

(Note: AAPP stands for Assistance Association for Political Prisoners, a non-profit group of former Burmese political prisoners based in Thailand.)

## February

2/7

- Peaceful demonstrations against the coup took place in Rangoon, Bago, Mandalay, Sagaing, Ayeryarwady, Tanintharyi and Magway Regions, Naypyidaw, Mon, Shan, Karen and Kachin States, which consisted of activists, students, and civilians; rioting broke out after police fired in the air at protesters in Myawaddy Town in Karen State, and one woman was shot in Myawaddy.[60] Fourteen civilians were arrested but were released later that evening.[61]

---

[60] Reuters, 'Shots heard as police break up protest in southeastern town of Myawaddy—video', *Reuters*, 7 February 2021. https://www.reuters.com/world/asia-pacific/shots-heard-police-break-up-protest-southeastern-town-myawaddy-video-2021-02-07/

[61] 'Daily Briefing in Relation to the Military Coup', *Assistance Association for Political Prisoners (AAPP)*, 7 February 2021. https://aappb.org/?p=13026

**2/9**

- Tens of thousands of people across Burma rallied against the coup. In Naypyidaw, police fired water cannons without warning, used rubber bullets, and fired live ammunition, which left four people injured and killed one student (gunshot wound to the head).[62,63] Protests in Bago and Mandalay were also met with water cannons and rubber bullets.[64,65]

**2/20**

- In Mandalay, security forces opened fire on demonstrators trying to stop the arrest of workers taking part in the growing anti-coup movement. Three civilians, including a sixteen-year-old, were killed and twenty were wounded in demonstrations in Mandalay.[66,67,68]

---

[62] 'Daily Briefing in Relation to the Military Coup', *Assistance Association for Political Prisoners (AAPP)*, 8 February 2021. https://aappb.org/?p=13052

[63] 'Recent Fatality List for November 20 2021', *Assistance Association for Political Prisoners (AAPP)*, 20 November 2021. https://aappb.org/wp-content/uploads/2021/11/Recent-Fatality-List-for-November-20-2021-English.pdf

[64] 'Myanmar forces fire rubber bullets, warning shots at protesters', *Aljazeera*, 9 February 2021. https://www.aljazeera.com/news/2021/2/9/myanmar-protesters-defiant-amid-ban-on-large-gatherings

[65] Reuters, 'Myanmar police fire to disperse protest, four hurt, one critical', *Reuters*, 8 February 2021. https://www.reuters.com/world/asia-pacific/myanmar-police-fire-disperse-protest-four-hurt-one-critical-2021-02-09/

[66] 'Recent Fatality List for November 20 2021', *Assistance Association for Political Prisoners (AAPP)*, 20 November 2021. https://aappb.org/wp-content/uploads/2021/11/Recent-Fatality-List-for-November-20-2021-English.pdf

[67] 'Myanmar police kill 2 in bloodiest day of anti-coup protests', *Aljazeera*, 20 February 2021. https://www.aljazeera.com/news/2021/2/20/two-myanmar-protesters-killed-by-police-fire-reports

[68] 'Police Shoot Myanmar Demonstrators, Two People Killed in Mandalay', *Archyde*, 20 February 2021. https://www.archyde.com/police-shoot-myanmar-demonstrators-two-people-killed-in-mandalay/

2/28

- Deaths: Fifteen (AAPP),[69] eighteen killed and thirty wounded (UN human rights official), nineteen confirmed dead in nine cities, with another ten deaths unconfirmed (Democratic Voice of Burma).[70,71] Military forces used tear gas, flash-bang grenades, stun grenades, and live ammunition to fire into crowds in Yangon, Dawei, Mandalay, Myeik, Bago, and Pokokku. In Yangon, medical students and teachers marched in protest and were met with tear gas and rubber bullets from the police.[72] One protester recalled that the police started shooting without warning.[73] In Dawei, four people were killed.[74,75]

---

[69] 'Recent Fatality List for November 20 2021', *Assistance Association for Political Prisoners (AAPP)*, 20 November 2021. https://aappb.org/wp-content/uploads/2021/11/Recent-Fatality-List-for-November-20-2021-English.pdf

[70] The Associated Press, 'Crackdown on Myanmar protests sees at least 18 killed: UN Human Rights office', *Alarabiya News*, 28 February 2021. https://english.alarabiya.net/News/world/2021/02/28/Protests-Crackdown-on-Myanmar-protests-sees-at-least-18-killed-UN-Human-Rights-office    https://english.alarabiya.net/News/world/2021/02/28/Protests-Crackdown-on-Myanmar-protests-sees-at-least-18-killed-UN-Human-Rights-office

[71] 'UN: At least 18 killed by Myanmar forces in several cities', *Associated Press News*, 28 February 2021. https://apnews.com/article/arrests-yangon-myanmar-asia-pacific-f6538173ae8df3a7707966a3cb4cb503

[72] The Associated Press, 'Crackdown on Myanmar protests sees at least 18 killed: UN Human Rights office', *Alarabiya News*, 28 February 2021. https://english.alarabiya.net/News/world/2021/02/28/Protests-Crackdown-on-Myanmar-protests-sees-at-least-18-killed-UN-Human-Rights-office

[73] 'Myanmar coup: Deadliest day of protests as police open fire', *Citi Newsroom*, 28 February 2021. https://citinewsroom.com/2021/02/myanmar-coup-deadliest-day-of-protests-as-police-open-fire/

[74] 'Myanmar coup: Deadliest day of protests as police open fire', *Citi Newsroom*, 28 February 2021. https://citinewsroom.com/2021/02/myanmar-coup-deadliest-day-of-protests-as-police-open-fire/

[75] 'Recent Fatality List for November 20 2021', *Assistance Association for Political Prisoners (AAPP)*, 20 November 2021. https://aappb.org/wp-content/uploads/2021/11/Recent-Fatality-List-for-November-20-2021-English.pdf

# March

Total number of deaths according to AAPP data: 281

3/3

- Deaths: Thirty-eight total,[76] eighteen in Yangon, eight in Monywa, three in Mandalay, two in Salin, one in Mawlamyine, one in Myingyan, and one in Kalay.[77] In Yangon, Myanmar security forces fired slingshots at protesters, chased them down, and even brutally beat an ambulance crew. Videos from security cameras show police brutally beating members of an ambulance crew, apparently after they were arrested.[78,79]

  The military used live ammunition against protesters in at least seven towns and cities. Photographs and videos from the crackdowns show soldiers holding

[76] Helen Regan, Sandi Sidhu, and Paula Hancocks, 'Increasing evidence that Myanmar's military forces are shooting to kill as country mourns young victims', *CNN*, 5 March 2021. https://www.cnn.com/2021/03/05/asia/myanmar-military-shoot-to-kill-intl-hnk/index.html

[77] 'UN: 38 died on deadliest day yet for Myanmar coup opposition', *Associated Press News*, 3 March 2021. https://apnews.com/article/myanmar-security-forces-kill-multiple-protesters-e378d9bc703f7363c71ca639d47df738

[78] 'UN: 38 died on deadliest day yet for Myanmar coup opposition', *Associated Press News*, 3 March 2021. https://apnews.com/article/myanmar-security-forces-kill-multiple-protesters-e378d9bc703f7363c71ca639d47df738

[79] Associated Press, 'Myanmar security forces kill at least 33 protesters', *New York Post*, 3 March 2021. https://nypost.com/2021/03/03/myanmar-security-forces-kill-at-least-33-protesters/

automatic weapons, long-range sniper rifles, and other firearms.[80,81,82,83]

**3/8**

- In Myitkyina, security forces used tear gas and opened fire during street clashes with stone-throwing protesters, who sought to paralyse the economy with strike action. Two people were killed.[84,85]

**3/11**

- Deaths: Six in Myaing, one in Yangon, one in Mandalay, one in Bago, and one in Taungoo.[86] At least five to six people

---

[80] Richard Roth, Angela Dewan, and Helen Regan, 'Myanmar a "war zone" as security forces open fire on peaceful protesters, killing 38', *CNN*, 4 March 2021. https://www.cnn.com/2021/03/03/asia/myanmar-protest-deaths-intl/index.html

[81] Reuters, 'Police in Myanmar shoot protesters, killing at least nine', *The Japan Times*, 3 March 2021. https://www.japantimes.co.jp/news/2021/03/03/asia-pacific/myanmar-protest-deaths/

[82] 'Recent Fatality List for November 20 2021', *Assistance Association for Political Prisoners (AAPP)*, 20 November 2021. https://aappb.org/wp-content/uploads/2021/11/Recent-Fatality-List-for-November-20-2021-English.pdf

[83] Reuters, 'Police in Myanmar shoot protesters, killing at least nine', *The Japan Times*, 3 March 2021. https://www.japantimes.co.jp/news/2021/03/03/asia-pacific/myanmar-protest-deaths/

[84] 'Two killed as Myanmar workers go on strike', *Asia Times*, 8 March 2021. https://asiatimes.com/2021/03/two-killed-as-myanmar-workers-go-on-strike/

[85] 'Recent Fatality List for November 20 2021', *Assistance Association for Political Prisoners (AAPP)*, 20 November 2021. https://aappb.org/wp-content/uploads/2021/11/Recent-Fatality-List-for-November-20-2021-English.pdf

[86] Myanmar junta kills more protesters, adds Suu Kyi accusation (wsls.com).

were killed, and eight others were injured in a riot in front of Myaing Police Station in Magway.[87],[88]

**3/14**

- Deaths: 115, approximately sixty-five from the Hlaing Tharyar strike.[89] In Hlaing Tharyar, protests were planned by factory workers, a large portion of the industrial area's residents. HRW documented that police and soldiers with assault rifles deliberately surrounded the protesters, killing at least sixty-five protesters and bystanders. Witnesses said the security forces emerged from different directions to trap them.[90],[91]

**3/15**

- Deaths: Thirty-two. Marches took place in Mandalay, Myingyan, and Aunglan, where police opened fire and killed one person in Mandalay, three in Myingyan, and two in Aunglan.[92]

---

[87] 'Recent Fatality List for November 20 2021', *Assistance Association for Political Prisoners (AAPP)*, 20 November 2021. https://aappb.org/wp-content/uploads/2021/11/Recent-Fatality-List-for-November-20-2021-English.pdf

[88] The Mratt's blog, 'Six people killed by the police in Myaing, Pakokku district (Myanmar)', *Myanmar Coup—Translated News*, 11 March 2021. https://myanmarcouptranslatednews.wordpress.com/2021/03/11/six-people-killed-by-the-police-in-myaing-pakokku-district-myanmar/

[89] 'Recent Fatality List for November 20 2021', *Assistance Association for Political Prisoners (AAPP)*, 20 November 2021. https://aappb.org/wp-content/uploads/2021/11/Recent-Fatality-List-for-November-20-2021-English.pdf

[90] Manny Maung, 'A Year On, No Justice for Myanmar Massacre', *Human Rights Watch*, 14 March 2022. https://www.hrw.org/news/2022/03/14/year-no-justice-myanmar-massacre

[91] 'NGO claims junta forces deliberately targeted Yangon protestors in March', *Mizzima*, 4 December 2021.

[92] Reuters, 'Security forces fire on Myanmar protests, martial law tightens military grip', *New York Post*, 15 March 2021. https://nypost.com/2021/03/15/security-forces-fire-on-myanmar-protests-martial-law-tightens-military-grip/

Another report claims that six people, three of whom were teenage boys, were killed in the Myingyan crackdown and at least seventeen were injured.[93]

3/24–25

- Deaths: Eleven.[94,95] Anti-coup silent strike was held across Burma during the day on 3/24 and was followed by night protests in several towns, some of which were violently cracked down. In Kyaukpadaung Township, Mandalay Region, a youth was killed. In Mandalay City, a sixteen-year-old child was killed. Ambulance vehicles attempting to aid the injured were also shot at unprovoked.[96]

3/26

- Deaths: Eight. Protests in Mohnyin and Myitkyina, Kachin state, Hpa-an Township in Karen State, Mawlamyine Township in Mon State, Taunggyi Township in Shan State, Khin-U Township in Sagaing Region, Mandalay City, and Thingangyun and Tamwe Township in Yangon Region were violently cracked down. The junta used live ammunition to create a combat zone in Taungyi Township, raided houses and killed civilians in Thuwanna, used live

---

[93] 'Three teenagers among six killed by regime's forces in Myingyan on Monday', *Myanmar Now*, 16 March 2021. https://www.myanmar-now.org/en/news/three-teenagers-among-six-killed-by-regimes-forces-in-myingyan-on-monday

[94] 'Daily Briefing in Relation to the Military Coup 53 Days ago', *Assistance Association for Political Prisoners*, 25 March 2021. https://aappb.org/?p=13871

[95] Associated Press, 'Myanmar protest deaths reach 320 as US, UK, impose sanctions', *Washington Times*, https://www.washingtontimes.com/news/2021/mar/26/myanmar-protest-deaths-top-300-as-us-uk-impose-san/

[96] 'Daily Briefing in Relation to the Military Coup 53 Days ago', *Assistance Association for Political Prisoners*, 25 March 2021. https://aappb.org/?p=13871

ammunition to suppress dissenters in Phyu Township, and a violently suppressed gathering strike in Hpa-an Township.[97,98]

3/27

- Deaths: At least ninety were killed according to the AAPP,[99] but other sources report between 114 *(Reuters)* and 160 people killed, seventy-eight from Mandalay.[100,101] Most people were shot in the head; military jets also launched air strikes on a village in territory controlled by an armed group (Karen National Union) and at least two people were killed. The resistance group had overrun an army post earlier, killing ten people.[102, 103]

---

[97] 'Daily Briefing in Relation to the Military Coup 53 Days ago', *Assistance Association for Political Prisoners*, 25 March 2021. https://aappb.org/?p=13871

[98] Associated Press, 'Myanmar protest deaths reach 320 as US, UK, impose sanctions', *Washington Times*, https://www.washingtontimes.com/news/2021/mar/26/myanmar-protest-deaths-top-300-as-us-uk-impose-san/

[99] 'Daily Briefing in Relation to the Military Coup', *Assistance Association for Political Prisoners*, 28 March 2021. https://aappb.org/?p=13901

[100] Reuters, 'Myanmar security forces kill over 100 protesters in horrifying day of bloodshed', *CNBC*, 27 March 2021. https://www.cnbc.com/2021/03/27/more-than-60-protesters-killed-in-myanmar-on-day-of-shame-for-armed-forces.html

[101] Wa Lone, Poppy McPherson, Aditi Bhandari, and Shoon Naing, 'Military crackdowns sent hundreds to their deaths', *Reuters*, 27 August 2021. https://graphics.reuters.com/MYANMAR-POLITICS/zjpqkkoaqpx/

[102] "Day of shame': Dozens of anti-coup protesters killed in Myanmar', *Aljazeera*, 27 March 2021. https://www.aljazeera.com/news/2021/3/27/myanmar-coup-leaders-put-on-show-of-force

[103] Reuters, 'Myanmar security forces kill over 100 protesters in horrifying day of bloodshed', *CNBC*, 27 March 2021. https://www.cnbc.com/2021/03/27/more-than-60-protesters-killed-in-myanmar-on-day-of-shame-for-armed-forces.html

- Individual accounts from Fortify Rights' report:[104]
  - ○ Myanmar Army soldiers opened fire on protesters in Bhamo (Bamaw) Township in Kachin State. The police had rubber bullets, the military had long firearms and snipers.
  - ○ A young man witnessed another peaceful protester shot next to him, and saw the police and soldiers preventing the ambulances from coming down the road.

3/28

- Activist Ah Khu was shot at a protest in Sagaing Division.[105]

## April

Total number of deaths according to AAPP data: 223

4/7

- Troops opened fire on pro-democracy protesters, killing at least fifteen people and wounding dozens.[106] In Kale,

---

[104] Fortify Rights and The Orville H. Schell, Jr. Center for International Human Rights at Yale Law School, Myanmar Human Rights Project, ' "Nowhere is Safe" The Myanmar Junta's Crimes Against Humanity Following the Coup d'état', March 2022. https://www.fortifyrights.org/downloads/Nowhererper cent20isper cent20Safeper cent20-per cent20Fortifyper cent20Rightsper cent20Report.pdf

[105] Wa Lone, Poppy McPherson, Aditi Bhandari, and Shoon Naing, 'Military crackdowns sent hundreds to their deaths', *Reuters*, 27 August 2021. https://graphics.reuters.com/MYANMAR-POLITICS/zjpqkkoaqpx/

[106] Reuters Staff, 'Myanmar security forces kill 15 protesters, junta leader says opposition aims to 'destroy' country', *Reuters*, 7 April 2021. https://www.reuters.com/article/us-myanmar-politics/myanmar-security-forces-kill-15-protesters-junta-leader-says-opposition-aims-to-destroy-country-idUSKBN2BU0F3

security forces fired live rounds, grenades, and machine guns on protesters, thirteen were killed.[107]

4/9

- Deaths: At least eighty protesters.[108] In Bago, over 250 regime soldiers raided four residential wards (Shinsawpu, Nantawya, Hmawkan, and Ponnasu) where anti-coup demonstrations had taken place. While trying to remove roadblocks erected by the protesters, troops opened fire with automatic weapons on civilians and protesters defending themselves with slingshots, fireworks, and homemade airguns. After the raids, the regime blocked the area for days, so the wounded could not receive medical treatment and the bodies of the deceased could not be removed.[109]

## May

Total number of deaths according to AAPP data: Eighty-one
- Resistance forces (Southern Pauk Guerilla Force) reportedly assassinated two perceived regime sympathizers in Pauk Township: a USDP organizer (killed 5/25), and a local government clerk (killed 5/30).[110]

---

[107] Devjyot Ghoshal and Chanchinmawia, 'Local uprisings emerge to challenge Myanmar's army', *Reuters*, 19 April 2021. https://www.reuters.com/world/asia-pacific/local-uprisings-emerge-challenge-myanmars-army-2021-04-19/

[108] 'Myanmar security forces kill over 80 anti-coup protesters—group', *Reuters*, 10 April 2021. https://www.reuters.com/world/asia-pacific/myanmar-security-forces-kill-over-80-anti-coup-protesters-group-2021-04-10/

[109] 'Myanmar Junta's Worst Massacres of 2021', *Military Coup Myanmar*, 6 January 2022. https://militarycoupmyanmar.com/2022/01/06/myanmar-juntas-worst-massacres-of-2021/

[110] 'Disputing junta narrative, Magway villagers blame security forces for massive fire', *Frontier Myanmar*, 23 August 2021. https://www.frontiermyanmar.net/en/disputing-junta-narrative-magway-villagers-blame-security-forces-for-massive-fire/

# June

Total number of deaths according to AAPP data: Forty-four
- First clash between the military and local militias in a major city. In Mandalay, troops reportedly raided a boarding school being used as a base by the militia, which led to an exchange of gunfire. Four protesters were killed in the raid, and eight were arrested.[111],[112]
- In Taze, three former local administrators were killed after being accused of acting as military informants.[113]

6/15

- The resistance group Southern Pauk Guerrilla Force (SPGF) attacked regime forces near Kinma Village, killing at least ten soldiers and police. The police and soldiers burnt most of Kinma Village down in response to the attack and assassinations by the SPGF in May.[114]

# July

Total number of deaths according to AAPP data: Fifty-six

---

[111] 'Myanmar army clashes with anti-junta militia in major city', *BBC*, 22 June 2021. https://www.bbc.com/news/world-asia-57567789

[112] Reuters Staff, 'Myanmar army clashes with anti-junta militia in Mandalay city', *Nasdaq*, 22 June 2021. https://www.nasdaq.com/articles/myanmar-army-clashes-with-anti-junta-militia-in-mandalay-city-2021-06-22

[113] 'Gunmen in Sagaing kill entire family, including 12-year-old boy, accused of helping junta', *Myanmar Now*, 21 September 2021. https://www.myanmar-now.org/en/news/gunmen-in-sagaing-kill-entire-family-including-12-year-old-boy-accused-of-helping-junta

[114] 'Disputing junta narrative, Magway villagers blame security forces for massive fire', *Frontier Myanmar*, 23 August 2021. https://www.frontiermyanmar.net/en/disputing-junta-narrative-magway-villagers-blame-security-forces-for-massive-fire/

## August

Total number of deaths according to AAPP data: Ninety-nine

8/6

- In Yangon, two people were killed, and two were injured during a series of attacks targeting informants and officials working for the military regime. The regime blamed the PDFs, but many people claim the junta forces are behind the attacks in an effort to blacken the name of the PDFs.[115]

8/13

- One article reported that at least 1,130 Myanmar soldiers were killed and 443 wounded in more than 700 clashes between junta forces and local militias across the country between 1 June and 31 July. At least five soldiers were killed in a clash the day before (8/12) in Kalay.[116]

## September

Total number of deaths according to AAPP data: 106

9/9

- Resistance fighters (Civilian Defence and Security Organization of Myaung) in Sagaing Region's Myaung

---

[115] The Irrawaddy, 'Myanmar Junta Informants and Officials Killed in Yangon Attacks', *The Irrawaddy*, 6 August 2021. https://www.irrawaddy.com/news/burma/myanmar-junta-informants-and-officials-killed-in-yangon-attacks.html

[116] 'More than 1,100 Myanmar Troops Killed in Clashes With Local Militias Over Two Months', *Radio Free Asia*, 13 August 2021. https://www.rfa.org/english/news/myanmar/killed-08132021181109.html

Township said they killed twelve junta soldiers and captured three police officers on 9/8, while ten more troops were killed the following day as they travelled to Myaung as reinforcements.[117]

9/14

- Resistance forces allegedly snatched, blindfolded and tortured a man accused of participating in the killing of a resistance leader in Pauk Township.[118]

9/21

- An unidentified group of armed men shot and killed a family of five following accusations that some of its members had helped junta soldiers during a raid on the village. The leader of the Taze People's Defence Force denied his group's involvement.[119]

9/22

- Resistance forces reportedly killed a family in Sagaing Region's Taze Township, including an alleged Pyusawhti

---

[117] 'PDF fighters "kill 22" soldiers and capture three police officers during clashes in central Myanmar', *Myanmar Now*, 9 September 2021. https://www.myanmar-now.org/en/news/pdf-fighters-kill-22-soldiers-and-capture-three-police-officers-during-clashes-in-central

[118] 'Resisting the Resistance: Myanmar's Pro-military Pyusawhti Militias', *International Crisis Group*, 6 April 2022. https://www.crisisgroup.org/asia/south-east-asia/myanmar/b171-resisting-resistance-myanmars-pro-military-pyusawhti-militias

[119] 'Gunmen in Sagaing kill entire family, including 12-year-old boy, accused of helping junta', *Myanmar Now*, 21 September 2021. https://www.myanmar-now.org/en/news/gunmen-in-sagaing-kill-entire-family-including-12-year-old-boy-accused-of-helping-junta

leader. In revenge, the man's surviving daughter and husband, both police officers, reportedly led a raid on the village the next day, burning down fifteen houses belong to NLD members.[120]

## October

Total number of deaths according to AAPP data: seventy-seven

10/6

- Anti-junta forces (Yaw Defence Force) attacked a fifty-vehicle military convoy, killing more than forty soldiers and injuring thirty others.[121]

10/15
- A resistance group (Zero Guerrilla Force) ambushed a military outpost in Mandalay Region's Natogyi Township, killing eleven soldiers and wounding three.[122]

## November

Total number of deaths according to AAPP data: seventy-seven

---

[120] 'Resisting the Resistance: Myanmar's Pro-military Pyusawhti Militias', *International Crisis Group*, 6 April 2022. https://www.crisisgroup.org/asia/south-east-asia/myanmar/b171-resisting-resistance-myanmars-pro-military-pyusawhti-militias

[121] 'Forty Junta Soldiers Are Killed in Attack on Military Convoy, Militia Group Says', *Radio Free Asia*, 6 October 2021. https://www.rfa.org/english/news/myanmar/fighting-10062021160655.html

[122] '11 soldiers killed in raid on military outpost in Natogyi', *Myanmar Now*, 20 October 2021. https://www.myanmar-now.org/en/news/11-soldiers-killed-in-raid-on-military-outpost-in-natogyi

## 11/5

- Resistance forces (People's Defence Forces) managed to kill dozens of soldiers from the Myanmar military regime in Kalay.[123]

# December

Total number of deaths according to AAPP data: eighty-five (Christmas massacre not included in data pulled from daily briefings)

## 12/7

- Deaths: Eleven. In Sagaing Region, regime forces opened fire on farmers, raided nearby Don Taw Village, and seized ten residents after a military convoy was ambushed with mines. An opposition leader said the civilians were burnt alive. A video of the aftermath showed the charred bodies of eleven people lying in a circle amid what appeared to be the remains of a hut.[124,125,126]

---

[123] 'Attacked by People's Defense Forces (PDF), At Least fifty Myanmar Military Regime Soldiers Killed in Kalay', *VOI*, 5 November 2021. https://voi.id/en/news/101201/attacked-by-peoples-defense-forces-pdf-at-least-50-myanmar-military-regime-soldiers-killed-in-kalay

[124] David Pierson and Kyaw Hsan Hlaing, '"My friends are being burned": Atrocities mount under Myanmar's junta', *Los Angeles Times*, 14 December 2021. https://www.latimes.com/world-nation/story/2021-12-14/myanmar-villagers-burned-alive

[125] Tassanee Vejpongsa, 'Massacre of Civilians in Myanmar Fuels Outrage', *The Diplomat*, 27 December 2021. https://thediplomat.com/2021/12/massacre-of-civilians-in-myanmar-fuels-outrage/

[126] 'Myanmar Junta's Worst Massacres of 2021', *Military Coup Myanmar*, 6 January 2022. https://militarycoupmyanmar.com/2022/01/06/myanmar-juntas-worst-massacres-of-2021/

- The villagers were rounded up and beaten by soldiers hunting down resistance fighters. The killings were reportedly in retaliation for a nearby bomb attack on a military convoy by guerrilla fighters, who have used land mines and improvised explosive devices to kill a growing number of soldiers.[127]

## 12/17

- Deaths: Nine. In Magwe, Nine civilians were killed by junta airstrikes that involved five aircraft on Hnan Khar Village in Gangaw Township. Two helicopter gunships attacked the village using machine guns, while around 100 junta soldiers were airlifted into the village by two other choppers. The junta launched the attack in an attempt to kill or capture leaders of local PDFs who were meeting in the village. Two PDF members were killed in the raid. Five civilians in a vehicle passing through the village also died after being shot by regime troops. Two Hnan Khar villagers who were farming and tending cattle outside the village were executed with shots to their heads while detained and tied up.[128]
- In Lay Kay Kaw, at least eighteen junta soldiers had died and eight had been captured during a fight with two resistance groups (Karen National Liberation Army and People's Defence Force).[129]

---

[127] David Pierson and Kyaw Hsan Hlaing, '"My friends are being burned": Atrocities mount under Myanmar's junta', *Los Angeles Times*, 14 December 2021. https://www.latimes.com/world-nation/story/2021-12-14/myanmar-villagers-burned-alive

[128] 'Myanmar Junta's Worst Massacres of 2021', *Military Coup Myanmar*, 6 January 2022. https://militarycoupmyanmar.com/2022/01/06/myanmar-juntas-worst-massacres-of-2021/

[129] The Irrawaddy, 'Myanmar Junta Forces See Heavy Casualties in Lay Kay Kaw Clashes', *The Irrawaddy*, 17 December 2021. https://www.irrawaddy.com/news/burma/myanmar-junta-forces-see-heavy-casualties-in-lay-kay-kaw-clashes.html

12/24

- The junta's official statements on the Christmas massacre blamed PDFs for the incident, asserting that resistance forces threw bombs and exchanged fire but the aftermath of the incident doesn't match up with that narrative, as most of the victims had their hands tied behind their backs. [130]

## January 2022

Total number of deaths according to AAPP data: 116

## February 2022

Total number of deaths according to AAPP data: Eighty-three

2/3

- A resistance group (Zero Guerrilla Force) in Sagaing Region's Ayadaw Township killed a poet and prominent pro-democracy activist in front of his children. The group claimed that the individual was helping the regime despite the lack of evidence.[131]

---

[130] Esther J, 'As details of Christmas Eve massacre emerge, calls for justice grow', *Myanmar Now*, 24 January 2022. https://www.myanmar-now.org/en/news/as-details-of-christmas-eve-massacre-emerge-calls-for-justice-grow

[131] Wathone Nyein Aye, 'Anti-junta guerrillas draw outrage for killing respected democracy activist', *Myanmar Now*, 15 February 2022. https://www.myanmar-now.org/en/news/anti-junta-guerrillas-draw-outrage-for-killing-respected-democracy-activist

2/5

- In Sagaing, junta forces torched houses in Inn Ma The village after a local pro-junta militia was attacked by anti-coup fighters who then fled.[132]

2/11

- Sagaing: regime soldiers near Sanabyin Village were raided by a resistance group on early Wednesday (2/9) morning, which killed three junta troops and injured two others. Junta forces torched most of the houses in four villages and detained then killed three PDF fighters in retaliation.[133]

2/17

- Two resistance groups reportedly killed over forty regime troops in attacks on two bases of Pyu Saw Htee, a pro-junta militia group, in Sagaing Region. Resistance groups also attacked a Pyu Saw Htee outpost in Pale, killing at least four fighters.[134]

[132] Agence France-Presse, 'Myanmar junta troops burning hundreds of homes, villagers say', *South China Morning Post*, 5 February 2022. https://www.scmp.com/news/asia/southeast-asia/article/3165947/myanmar-junta-troops-burning-hundreds-homes-villagers-say

[133] 'Thousands Flee as Myanmar Regime Raids Villages in Sagaing Region', *The Irrawaddy*, 11 February 2022. https://www.irrawaddy.com/news/burma/thousands-flee-as-myanmar-regime-raids-villages-in-sagaing-region.html

[134] 'Regime Soldiers and Pro-Junta Militia Reportedly Killed in Upper Myanmar Raids', *The Irrawaddy*, 17 February 2022. https://www.irrawaddy.com/news/burma/regime-soldiers-and-pro-junta-militia-reportedly-killed-in-upper-myanmar-raids.html#:~:text=Regimeper cent20Soldiersper cent20andper cent20Proper cent2DJuntaper cent20Militiaper cent20Reportedlyper cent20Killedper cent20inper cent20Upperper cent20Myanmarper cent20Raids,-

- Around twenty junta soldiers and twenty resistance fighters were killed in Mobye town.[135]

## March 2022

Total number of deaths according to AAPP data: 139

3/14

- In Hlaing Tharyar, protests planned by factory workers were deliberately surrounded and shot by police and soldiers. At least sixty-five people were killed.[136]

3/21

- Five junta privates were killed, and a captain was injured in a clash with a resistance group in Gangaw (Gangaw People's Defence Force).[137]

3/24

- Military deserters told Fortify Rights and the Schell Centre that the military had deployed snipers to kill protesters as a

---

Resistanceper        cent20groupsper        cent20attacked&text=Resistanceper cent20groupsper   cent20reportedper   cent20killingper   cent20over,inper cent20Sagaingper cent20Region'sper cent20Paleper cent20Township.

[135] 'Both Sides Sustain Casualties as Fighting Rages Between PDFs and Myanmar Junta', *The Irrawaddy*, 18 February 2022. https://www.irrawaddy.com/news/burma/both-sides-sustain-casualties-as-fighting-rages-between-pdfs-and-myanmar-junta.html

[136] Manny Maung, 'A Year On, No Justice for Myanmar Massacre', *Human Rights Watch*, 14 March 2022. https://www.hrw.org/news/2022/03/14/year-no-justice-myanmar-massacre

[137] 'Myanmar Junta Tortures Civilians to Death in Magwe', *The Irrawaddy*, 29 March 2022. https://www.irrawaddy.com/news/burma/myanmar-junta-tortures-civilians-to-death-in-magwe.html

matter of state policy to deliberately instil fear among those opposed to its rule.[138]

## April 2022

Total number of deaths according to AAPP data: Seventy-five.

- Resistance forces have assassinated more than 1,000 allegedly pro-regime individuals since mid-2021, including almost 200 known or rumoured to be involved with pro-regime militias.[139]

[138] 'Myanmar military deliberately killed civilians after coup: Report', *Aljazeera*, 24 March 2022. https://www.aljazeera.com/news/2022/3/24/military-committing-crimes-against-humanity-in-myanmar-report

[139] 'Resisting the Resistance: Myanmar's Pro-military Pyusawhti Militias', *International Crisis Group*, 6 April 2022. https://www.crisisgroup.org/asia/south-east-asia/myanmar/b171-resisting-resistance-myanmars-pro-military-pyusawhti-militias

# Acknowledgements

I owe much debt to a number of people without whom this book would have been impossible.

This begins with the encouragement and support of Nora Nazerene Abu Bakar of Penguin Random House Southeast Asia. Valuable research assistance was provided by Shagun Gupta, Ryan Roden, Alison Adams and Karina Martinez, and Manaswini Ramkumar, all graduate students at American University in Washington DC. Further research assistance came from Arabinda Acharya, Shristi Acharya, Yuhang Wei and Sripathi Narayanan. I am particularly indebted to Dr Arabinda Acharya, formerly Associate Professor at the National Defense University in the US, for his advice, for helping me to organize my research, and providing considerable research and editorial assistance. I am also grateful for the editorial work on the manuscript by Amberdawn Manaois at Penguin Random House SEA. Conversations and correspondence with noted writer and Burma expert Thant Myint-U, former Canadian Ambassador to Burma Mark McDowell, former US Ambassador to Burma Scot Marciel and Professor David Steinberg, at different stages of writing the book, were invaluable in shaping my thinking and understanding of Burma. Manaswini Ramkumar offered considerable help with research and proof reading in the final stages of the book.

Over the years, I have had conversations with scores of citizens, students, experts, journalists, entrepreneurs and political leaders of Burma, including during my two teaching stints at two of the leading universities in Burma. I cannot name them, given the sensitivities and risks involved. But suffice it to say that they represent a cross-section of the society and polity of Burma, including those now divided into the military and opposition camps. One name that stands out in my mind is Maung Thura (stage name Zarganar, or 'tweezers'), Burma's leading comedian and long-time political prisoner. It was at his invitation that in the summer of 2012, I gave a series of lectures to a group of recently released political prisoners. It was this interaction that gave me profound and first-hand insights into hearts and minds of political activism in Burma and got me interested in writing a book about Burma's unfinished quest for freedom. At the end of my research, another group, whom I never personally met, but who provided a raw sense of the tragedy unfolding in Burma, are the youths that I call Thought Warriors, as explained on the dedication page of the book.

Amitav Acharya
Washington, DC

# Bibliography

## Books

Acharya, Amitav. *Constructing a Security Community in Southeast Asia: ASEAN and the Problem of Regional Order*. London: Routledge, 2014.

Acharya, Amitav. *ASEAN and Regional Order: Revisiting Security Community in Southeast Asia*. London: Routledge, 2021.

Aung San. *Burma's Challenge, 1946*. South Okklapa: Tathetta Sarpay, 1974.

Suu Kyi, Aung San. *Freedom from Fear*. London: Penguin Books, 1995.

Aung-Thwin, Michael and Maitrii Aung-Thwin. *A History of Myanmar Since Ancient Times: Traditions and Transformations*. London: Reaktion Books, 2012.

Ayoob, Mohammed. 'Regional Security and the Third World.' In *Regional Security in the Third World: Case Studies from Southeast Asia and the Middle East*, edited by Mohammed Ayoob. London: Croom Helm Publishers, 1986.

Brown, David and David Martin Jones. 'Democratization and the Myth of the Liberalizing Middle Classes.' In *Towards Illiberal Democracy in Pacific Asia*, edited by Daniel A. Bell, David Brown, Kanishka Jayasuriya and David Martin Jones, 78–106. London: Palgrave Macmillan, 1995.

Buzan, Barry. *People, States & Fear: The National Security Problem in International Relations*. London: Wheatsheaf Books, 1983.

Buzan, Barry. 'People, States and Fear: The National Security Problem in the Third World.' In *National Security in the Third World: The Management of Internal and External Threats*, edited by Edward E. Azar and Chung-in Moon. Aldershot: Edward Elgar, 1988.

Callahan, Mary P. 'On Time Warps and Warped Time: Lessons from Burma's Democratic Era.' In *Burma: Prospects for a Democratic Future*, edited by Robert I. Rotberg, pp. 49–68. Washington DC: Brookings Institution Press, 1998.

Chachavalpongpun, Pavin and Moe Thuzar. *Myanmar: Life After Nargis*. Singapore: Institute of Southeast Asian Studies, 2009.

Crouch, Melissa. 'Ethnic Rights and Constitutional Change: The Recognition of Ethnic Nationalities in Myanmar/Burma.' In *Central-Local Relations in Asian Constitutional Systems*, pp. 105–24. Oxford: Hart Publishing, 2015.

Furnivall, J.S. *An Introduction to the Political Economy of Burma*. Rangoon: Peoples' Literature Committee & House, 1957.

Hall, D.G.E. *Burma*. London: Hutchinson's University Library, 1950.

Harvey, G.E. *Outline of Burmese History*. Calcutta: Longmans, Green & Co., 1929.

Myat Thein. *Economic Development of Myanmar*. Singapore: ISEAS Publishing, 2004.

Nyi Nyi Kyaw. 'Myanmar's Pluralist Constitution: Nation-Building versus State-Building.' In *Pluralist Constitutions in Southeast Asia*, edited by Jaclyn L. Neo and Bui Ngoc Son. New York: Hart Publishing, 2019.

Rajah, Ananda. 'Ethnicity and Civil War in Burma: Where is the Rationality?' In *Burma: Prospects for a Democratic Future*, edited by Robert I. Rotberg, 135–50. Washington DC: Brookings Institution Press, 1998.

Saw David Taw. 'Choosing to Engage: Strategic Considerations for the Karen National Union.' In *Choosing to Engage: Armed Groups and Peace Processes*, edited by Robert Ricigliano, pp. 40–43. London: Conciliation Resources, 2005.

Silverstein, Josef. *The Political Legacy of Aung San*. Ithaca: Department of Asian Studies, Cornell University, 1972.

Silverstein, Josef. 'The Evolution and Salience of Burma's National Political Culture.' In *Burma: Prospects for a Democratic Future*, edited by Robert I. Rotberg, pp. 11–32. Washington DC: Brookings Institution Press, 1998.

Stamp, Elsa C. *A First Geography of Burma*. Hyderabad: Orient Longman Publisher, 1957.

Steinberg, David I. 'Burma-Myanmar: The US-Burmese Relationship and its Vicissitudes.' In *Short of the Goal: US Policy and Poor Performing States*, edited by Nancy Birdsall, Milan Vaishnav and Robert L. Ayres, pp. 209–44. Washington DC: Center for Global Development, 2006.

Steinberg, David I. *Burma/Myanmar: What Everyone Needs to Know*. New York City: Oxford University Press, 2010.

Taylor, Robert H. *Foreign and Domestic Consequences of the KMT Intervention in Burma*. Ithaca: Department of Asian Studies, Cornell University, 1973.

Thant Myint-U. *The Hidden History of Burma: Race, Capitalism and the Crisis of Democracy in the 21st Century*. New York: W.W. Norton & Company, 2019.

U Nu. *Saturday's Son: Memoirs of the Former Prime Minister of Burma*, translated by U Law Yone and edited by U Kyaw Win. New Haven: Yale University Press, 1975.

## Journal Articles

Acharya, Amitav. 'Democracy in Burma: Does Anybody Really Care?' *Yale Global*, 1 September 2005. https://archive-yaleglobal.yale.edu/content/democracy-burma-does-anybody-really-care.

Acharya, Amitav. 'ASEAN and Burma/Myanmar: Past and Prologue.' *Rising Powers Initiative Blog*, 22 April 2012.

https://www.risingpowersinitiative.org/2012/04/22/asean-and-burmamyanmar-past-and-prologue/.

Albert, Eleanor and Lindsay Maizland. 'The Rohingya Crisis.' *CFR Backgrounder*, 23 January 2020. https://www.cfr.org/backgrounder/rohingya-crisis.

Aung-Thwin, Maureen and Thant Myint-U. 'The Burmese Ways to Socialism.' *Third World Quarterly* 13, no. 1 (1992): 67–75. DOI 10.1080/01436599208420262.

Ayoob, Mohammed. 'Security in the Third World: The Worm About to Turn?' *International Affairs* 60, no. 1 (Winter 1983–84): 41–51.

Bhanu Singh, Udai. 'Post-Coup Myanmar and India's Response.' *Manohar Parrikar Institute for Defence Studies and Analyses Comment*, 21 May 2021. https://idsa.in/idsacomments/post-coup-myanmar-indias-response-ubsingh-210521.

Bland, Ben. 'ASEAN Muddles Through on Myanmar.' *The Interpreter*, 22 October 2021. https://www.lowyinstitute.org/the-interpreter/asean-muddles-through-myanmar.

Bunte, Marco and Jorn Dosch. 'Myanmar: Political Reforms and the Recalibration of External Relations.' *Journal of Current Southeast Asian Affairs* 34, no. 2 (2015): 3–19. DOI 10.1177/186810341503400201.

Burke, Adam. 'New Political Space, Old Tensions: History, Identity and Violence in Rakhine State, Myanmar.' *Contemporary Southeast Asia* 38, no. 2 (2016): 258–83. DOI:10.1355/cs38-2d.

Carr, Thomas. 'Supporting the Transition: Understanding Aid to Myanmar Since 2011.' *The Asia Foundation Report*, February 2018. file:///C:/Users/manur/Downloads/Understanding_Aid_to_Myanmar_Since_2011_-_Asia_Foundation_2018.pdf.

'Desk Brief: The Shared Constitutional Heritage of India & Myanmar.' *Centre for Law and Policy Research*, 3 July 2020. https://www.constitutionofindia.net/blogs/desk_brief__the_shared_constitutional_heritage_of_india___myanmar.

Cribb, Robert. 'Burma's Entry into ASEAN: Background and Implications.' *Asian Perspective* 22, no. 3 (1998): 49–62.

Crouch, Melissa. "Ethnic Rights and Constitutional Change: The Constitutional Recognition of Ethnic Nationalities in Myanmar/Burma." *SSRN*, 30 March 2015. https://papers.ssrn.com/sol3/papers.cfm?abstract_id=2592474.

Crouch, Melissa. 'Pre-emptive Constitution-Making: Authoritarian Constitutionalism and the Military in Myanmar.' *Law & Society Review* 54, no. 2 (June 2020): 487–515. DOI 10.1111/lasr.12471.

Currie, Kelley. 'Can a Dam Deal Buy Beijing's Support for Myanmar's Junta?' *Foreign Policy*, 23 February 2021. https://foreignpolicy.com/2021/02/23/myanmar-china-dam-deal-junta-democracy.

Diller, Janelle. 'Constitutional Reform in a Repressive State: The Case of Burma.' *Asian Survey* 33, no. 4 (April 1993): 393–407. https://doi.org/10.2307/2645105.

Ford, Billy and Zarchi Oo. 'Myanmar Coup: Military Regime Seeks to Weaponize Religion.' *USIP Analysis and Commentary*, 16 December 2021. https://www.usip.org/publications/2021/12/myanmar-coup-military-regime-seeks-weaponize-religion.

Frankel, Laura. 'Power & Money: Economics and Conflict in Burma.' *Cultural Survival Quarterly* 24, no. 3 (September 2000). https://www.culturalsurvival.org/publications/cultural-survival-quarterly/power-money-economics-and-conflict-burma.

Gravers, Mikael. 'A Tentative Unity Among Myanmar's Anti-Coup Forces.' *East Asia Forum*, 8 June 2021. https://www.eastasiaforum.org/2021/06/08/a-tentative-unity-among-myanmars-anti-coup-forces/.

Herath, Dhammika. 'Constructing Buddhists in Sri Lanka and Myanmar: Imaginary of a Historically Victimised Community.' *Asian Studies Review* 44, no. 2 (2020): 315–34. DOI 10.1080/10357823.2020.1717441.

Htet Myet Min Tun, Moe Thuzar and Michael Montesano. 'Buttressing the Anti-NLD Project: Data on the Civilian Members of Myanmar's State Administration Council Junta.' *ISEAS Perspective* 119 (September 2021). https://www.iseas.edu.sg/articles-commentaries/iseas-perspective/2021-119-buttressing-the-anti-nld-project-data-on-the-civilian-members-of-myanmars-state-administration-council-junta-by-htet-myet-min-tun-moe-thuzar-and-michael-montesano/.

Htet Myet Min Tun, Moe Thuzar and Michael Montesano. 'An Attempt to Lead Myanmar Back to the Future? Data on the State Administration Council Regime's Union Ministers.' *ISEAS Perspective* 137 (October 2021). https://www.iseas.edu.sg/articles-commentaries/iseas-perspective/2021-137-an-attempt-to-lead-myanmar-back-to-the-future-data-on-the-state-administration-council-regimes-union-ministers-by-htet-myet-min-tun-moe-thuzar-and-michael-montesano/.

Kennedy, Lindsey and Nathan Paul Southern. 'Myanmar's Opposition is Forming Fragile Alliances with Armed Ethnic Groups.' *Foreign Policy*, 4 September 2021. https://foreignpolicy-com.proxyau.wrlc.org/2021/09/04/myanmar-coup-opposition-armed-ethnic-groups/.

Kipgen, Nehginpao. 'Political Change in Burma: Transition from Democracy to Military Dictatorship (1948–1962).' *Economic and Political Weekly* 46, no. 20 (May 2011): 48–55.

Kipgen, Nehginpao. 'Ethnic Nationalities and the Peace Process in Myanmar.' *Social Research* 82, no. 2 (2015): 399–425.

Korany, Bahgat. 'Strategic Studies and the Third World: A Critical Evaluation.' *International Social Science Journal* 38, no. 4 (1986): 547–62.

Landis, Taylor. 'Beyond the Coup in Myanmar: A Northern View.' *Human Rights@Harvard Law Blog*, 7 May 2021. https://hrp.law.harvard.edu/myanmar/beyond-the-coup-in-myanmar-a-northern-view/.

Lee Huang, Roger. 'Myanmar's Way to Democracy and the Limits of the 2015 Elections.' *Asian Journal of Political Science* 25, no. 1 (2017): 25–44. DOI: 10.1080/02185377.2016.1245154.

Malik, Mohan. 'Regional Reverberations from Regime Shake-up in Rangoon.' *Daniel K. Inouye Asia-Pacific Center for Security Studies Perspectives* 6 (2005). https://apcss.org/nexus_articles/regional-reverberations-from-regime-shake-up-in-rangoon/.

Martin, Michael. 'The Importance of Ethnic Minorities to Myanmar's Future.' *Stimson's Civil-Military Relations in Myanmar Series*, 3 June 2021. https://www.stimson.org/2021/the-importance-of-ethnic-minorities-to-myanmars-future/.

Maung Aung Myoe. 'The Road to Naypyitaw: Making Sense of the Myanmar Government's Decision to Move its Capital.' *Asian Research Institute Working Paper Series* 79 (November 2006). https://ari.nus.edu.sg/publications/wps-79-the-road-to-naypyitaw-making-sense-of-the-myanmar-governments-decision-to-move-its-capital/.

McCarthy, Stephen. 'Burma and ASEAN: Estranged Bedfellows.' *Asian Survey* 48, no. 6 (2008): 911–35. https://doi.org/10.1525/as.2008.48.6.911.

Meehan, Patrick. 'How the Military Benefits from Myanmar's Growing Opium Economy.' *East Asia Forum*, 14 June 2016. https://www.eastasiaforum.org/2016/06/14/how-the-military-benefits-from-myanmars-growing-opium-economy/.

Moe, David. 'Is Buddhism a Democratic Religion? Religious Nationalism and Military Violence in Myanmar.' *Berkley Forum*, 6 April 2021. https://berkleycenter.georgetown.edu/responses/is-buddhism-a-democratic-religion-religious-nationalism-and-military-violence-in-myanmar.

Moe Thuzar and Htet Myet Min Thun. 'Myanmar's National Unity Government: A Radical Arrangement to Counteract the Coup.' *ISEAS Perspective* 8 (January 2022). https://

www.iseas.edu.sg/wp-content/uploads/2021/12/ISEAS_
Perspective_2022_8.pdf.

Moeller, Anders Kirstein. 'Peering Under the Hood:
Coup Narratives and Tatmadaw Factionalism.' *Tea Circle
Oxford*, 10 January 2022. https://teacircleoxford.com/politics/
peering-under-the-hood-coup-narratives-and-tatmadaw-
factionalism/.

Mya Maung. 'The Burma Road to the Past.' *Asian Survey* 39, no.
2 (March-April 1999): 265–86.

Myanmar Study Group. 'Final Report: Anatomy of the Military
Coup and Recommendations for U.S. Response.' *USIP Report*,
1 February 2022. https://www.usip.org/publications/2022/02/
myanmar-study-group-final-report.

Nay Yan Oo. 'Order from Chaos: Don't Give Up on Myanmar.'
*Brookings Blog*, 16 December 2021. https://www.brookings.
edu/blog/order-from-chaos/2021/12/16/dont-give-up-
on-myanmar/.

Nyi Nyi Kyaw. 'Putting their Guns on Sale: Constitution-Making
in Burma/Myanmar under Military Command.' *The Chinese
Journal of Comparative Law* 7, no. 2 (September 2019): 309–
32. https://doi.org/10.1093/cjcl/cxz010.

Ong, Andrew. 'Ethnic Armed Organisations in Post-Coup
Myanmar: New Conversations Needed.' *ISEAS Perspective* 79
(June 2021). https://www.iseas.edu.sg/articles-commentaries/
iseas-perspective/2021-79-ethnic-armed-organisations-
in-post-coup-myanmar-new-conversations-needed-by-
andrew-ong/.

'This Day in History: Burmese Independence.' *OUP Blog*,
4 January 2011. https://blog.oup.com/2011/01/burma-
myanmar/.

Publish What You Pay. 'Financing the Military in Myanmar:
Analysis of Gas Revenues.' *Policy Brief* (June 2021). https://
www.pwyp.org/wp-content/uploads/2021/06/Financing-
the-Military-in-Myanmar.pdf.

Rau, B.N. 'The Constitution of the Union of Burma.' *India Quarterly* 4, no. 2 (April-June 1948): 109–20.

Rodrik, Dani. 'Is Liberal Democracy Feasible in Developing Countries?' *Studies in Comparative International Development* 51, no. 1 (March 2016): 50–9. DOI 10.1007/s12116-016-9218-6.

Selth, Andrew. 'Race and Resistance in Burma, 1942–1945.' *Modern Asian Studies* 20, no. 3 (1986): 483–507.

Selth, Andrew. 'Myanmar's Military Mindset: An Exploratory Survey.' *Griffith Asia Institute Research Paper* 2021. https://www.griffith.edu.au/__data/assets/pdf_file/0023/1418333/Military-mindset-web.pdf.

Siemers, Gunter. 'MYANMAR 1992: Heading for "Guided Democracy"?' *Southeast Asian Affairs* (1993): 245–66.

Silverstein, Josef. 'Burma: Ne Win's Revolution Considered.' *Asian Survey* 6, no. 2 (February 1966): 95–102.

Silverstein, Josef. 'The Burma Socialist Program Party and its Rivals: A One-Plus Party System.' *Journal of Southeast Asian History* 8, no. 1 (1967): 8–18. DOI 10.1017/S0217781100003434.

Silverstein, Josef. 'The Idea of Freedom in Burma and the Political Thought of Daw Aung San Suu Kyi.' *Pacific Affairs* 69, no. 2 (Summer 1996): 211–28.

Simpson, Adam. 'Myanmar's Exile Government Signs up to ICC Prosecutions.' *East Asia Forum*, 17 September 2021. https://www.eastasiaforum.org/2021/09/17/myanmars-exile-government-signs-up-to-icc-prosecutions/.

Sint Sint Myat. 'Explaining Myanmar's Policy of Non-Alignment: An Analytic Eclecticism Approach.' *Journal of Current Southeast Asian Affairs* 40, no. 3 (2021): 379–99. DOI 10.1177/1868103421992068.

Spandler, Kilian. 'Lessons from ASEAN's Rakhine Response.' *East Asia Forum*, 5 February 2020. https://www.eastasiaforum.org/2020/02/05/lessons-from-aseans-rakhine-response/.

Steinbach, Udo. 'Sources of Third World Conflict.' *The Adelphi Papers* 21, no. 166 (1981): 21–8. DOI: 10.1080/05679328108448604.

Steinberg, David. 'Globalization, Dissent, and Orthodoxy: Burma/Myanmar and the Saffron Revolution.' *Georgetown Journal of International Affairs* 9, no. 2 (Summer/Fall 2008): 51–8.

Steinberg, David. 'Myanmar's Military Coup Redux.' *East Asia Forum*, 28 December 2021. https://www.eastasiaforum.org/2021/12/28/myanmars-military-coup-redux/.

Sundararaman, Shankari. 'From SLORC to SPDC: Political Continuity Versus Economic Change in Myanmar.' *IDSA*. http://www.idsa-india.org/an-jan10.html.

Taylor, Robert H. 'Burma's National Unity Problem and the 1974 Constitution.' *Contemporary Southeast Asia* 1, no. 3 (December 1979): 232–48.

'Independent Burma: Years of Lost Opportunity.' *The Round Table: The Commonwealth Journal of International Affairs* 56, no. 221 (1965): 14–22. DOI: 10.1080/00358536508452578.

Tin Maung Maung Than. 'Burma/Myanmar in 2001: A Year of Waiting.' *Asian Survey* 42, no. 1 (2002): 115–23. https://doi.org/10.1525/as.2002.42.1.115.

Tin Maung Maung Than. 'Myanmar's 2012 By-Elections: The Return of NLD.' *Southeast Asian Affairs* (2013): 204–19.

Tower, Jason. 'In Myanmar, the State the Generals Seized is Coming Apart.' *USIP Analysis and Commentary*, 19 August 2021. https://www.usip.org/publications/2021/08/myanmar-state-generals-seized-coming-apart.

Turnell, Sean. 'Myanmar's Fifty-Year Authoritarian Trap.' *Journal of International Affairs* 65, no. 1 (Fall/Winter 2011): 79–92.

van Noort, Sam. 'Industrialization and Democracy.' *SSRN*, 15 September 2020. http://dx.doi.org/10.2139/ssrn.3693044.

Von der Mehden, Fred R. 'The Burmese Way to Socialism.' *Asian Survey* 3, no. 3 (March 1963): 129–35.

Wade, Francis. 'How Myanmar's Military Wields Power from the Shadows.' Interview by Eleanor Albert. CFR, 2 October 2017. https://www.cfr.org/interview/how-myanmars-military-wields-power-shadows.

Williams, David C. and Lian H. Sakhong. 'Designing Federalism in Burma.' *Books & Book Chapters by Maurer Faculty* 122 (2005). https://www.repository.law.indiana.edu/facbooks/122/.

Williams, David C. 'Constitutionalism Before Constitutions: Burma's Struggle to Build a New Order.' *Articles by Maurer Faculty* 492 (2009). https://www.repository.law.indiana.edu/cgi/viewcontent.cgi?article=1492&context=facpub.

Win, Sandar. 'Myanmar's Historically "Incomplete" Market Reforms and their Consequences in Post-Military Coup Era.' *LSE Blog*, 9 December 2021. https://blogs.lse.ac.uk/seac/2021/12/09/myanmars-historically-incomplete-market-reforms-and-their-consequences-in-post-military-coup-era/.

## Official Documents

Association of Southeast Asian Nations. *The ASEAN Charter*. Jakarta: Public Affairs Office, The ASEAN Secretariat. January 2008. https://asean.org/wp-content/uploads/images/archive/publications/ASEAN-Charter.pdf.

Australia Minister for Foreign Affairs. *Statement on Myanmar*. Marise Payne. 1 February 2021. https://www.foreignminister.gov.au/minister/marise-payne/media-release/statement-myanmar.

Australia Minister for Foreign Affairs. *Statement on Myanmar*. Marise Payne. 7 March 2021. https://www.foreignminister.gov.au/minister/marise-payne/media-release/statement-myanmar-0.

Australia Minister for Foreign Affairs. *Joint Statement on Increasing Violence in Myanmar*. Marise Payne. 26 November 2021.

https://www.foreignminister.gov.au/minister/marise-payne/media-release/joint-statement-increasing-violence-myanmar.

CIA The World Factbook. *Burma*. 13 July 2022. https://www.cia.gov/the-world-factbook/countries/burma/#people-and-society.

The Constitution of the Union of Burma. 24 September 1947. https://www.ilo.org/dyn/natlex/docs/ELECTRONIC/79573/85699/F1436085708/MMR79573.pdf.

The Constitution of the Republic of the Union of Myanmar 2008. https://www.wipo.int/edocs/lexdocs/laws/en/mm/mm009en.pdf.

Consulate-General of the People's Republic of China in Mumbai. *Foreign Ministry Spokesperson Wang Wenbin's Regular Press Conference on June 7, 2021*. 7 June 2021. https://www.fmprc.gov.cn/ce/cgmb/eng/fyrth/t1881926.htm.

Council of the European Union. *Myanmar: Declaration by the High Representative on Behalf of the European Union*. 2 February 2021. https://www.consilium.europa.eu/en/press/press-releases/2021/02/02/myanmar-declaration-by-the-high-representative-on-behalf-of-the-european-union/.

Council of the European Union. *Myanmar/Burma: Council Adopts Conclusions*. 22 February 2021. https://www.consilium.europa.eu/en/press/press-releases/2021/02/22/myanmar-burma-council-adopts-conclusions/.

Council of the European Union. *Myanmar/Burma: EU Sanctions 11 People over the Recent Military Coup and Ensuing Repression*. 22 March 2021. https://www.consilium.europa.eu/en/press/press-releases/2021/03/22/myanmar-burma-eu-sanctions-11-people-over-the-recent-military-coup-and-ensuing-repression//.

Council of the European Union. *Myanmar/Burma: EU Imposes Sanctions on 10 Individuals and Two Military-Controlled Companies over the February Military Coup and Subsequent Repression*. 19 April 2021. https://www.consilium.europa.

eu/en/press/press-releases/2021/04/19/myanmar-burma-eu-imposes-sanctions-on-10-individuals-and-two-military-controlled-companies-over-the-february-military-coup-and-subsequent-repression/.

Council of the European Union. *Myanmar/Burma: Council Extends Sanctions for Another Year.* 29 April 2021. https://www.consilium.europa.eu/en/press/press-releases/2021/04/29/myanmar-burma-council-extends-sanctions-for-another-year/.

Council of the European Union. *Myanmar/Burma: Declaration by the High Representative on Behalf of the European Union to Support the Work of the ASEAN Special Envoy.* 13 October 2021. https://www.consilium.europa.eu/en/press/press-releases/2021/10/13/myanmar-burma-declaration-by-the-high-representative-on-behalf-of-the-european-union-to-support-the-work-of-the-asean-special-envoy/.

CRS Report for Congress. *China–Southeast Asia Relations: Trends, Issues, and Implications for the United States*, by Bruce Vaughn and Wayne E. Morrison. Washington DC: 4 April 2006.

CRS. *Burma's 2020 Parliamentary Elections.* 16 November 2020. https://crsreports.congress.gov/product/pdf/IF/IF11687/1.

Embassy of the People's Republic of China in the Republic of the Union of Myanmar. *Chinese Ambassador to Myanmar H.E. Mr. Chen Hai Gives Interview to Myanmar Media on the Current Situation in Myanmar.* 16 February 2021. https://www.mfa.gov.cn/ce/cemm/eng/sgxw/t1854268.htm.

Embassy of the People's Republic of China in the United States of America. *Foreign Ministry Spokesperson Wang Wenbin's Regular Press Conference on February 1, 2021.* 1 February 2021. http://us.china-embassy.gov.cn/eng/fyrth/202102/t20210202_4475653.htm.

Embassy of the People's Republic of China in the United States of America. *Foreign Ministry Spokesperson Chao Lijian's Regular Press Conference on May 20, 2021.* 20 May 2021. http://us.china-embassy.gov.cn/eng/fyrth/202105/t20210520_9016369.htm.

Embassy of the People's Republic of China in the United States of America. *Wang Yi: China Supports ASEAN's Appointment of Special Envoy on Myanmar Affairs.* 5 August 2021. http://us.china-embassy.gov.cn/eng/zgyw/202108/t20210805_9015393.htm.

European Union. *Council Decision (CFSP) 2021/482 of 22 March 2021 amending Decision 2013/184/CFSP Concerning Restrictive Measures against Myanmar/Burma.* LI 99/37. 22 March 2021. https://eur-lex.europa.eu/legal-content/EN/TXT/?uri=CELEX%3A32021D0482.

European Union. *Council Decision (CFSP) 2021/1000 of 21 June 2021 amending Decision 2013/184/CFSP Concerning Restrictive Measures in view of the Situation in Myanmar/Burma.* LI 219/57. 21 June 2021. https://eur-lex.europa.eu/legal-content/EN/TXT/?uri=uriserv%3AOJ.LI.2021.219.01.0057.01.ENG&toc=OJ%3AL%3A2021%3A219I%3ATOC.

European Union External Action. *Myanmar: Statement by the Spokesperson on the General Elections.* 9 November 2020. https://www.eeas.europa.eu/eeas/myanmar-statement-spokesperson-general-elections_en.

Report of the Frontier Areas Committee of Inquiry, 1947. https://www.burmalibrary.org/docs14/Frontier_Areas_Committee_of_Enquiry-1947-full.pdf.

Government of India Ministry of External Affairs. *Question No. 2651 Military Rule in Myanmar.* 18 March 2021. https://mea.gov.in/rajya-sabha.htm?dtl/33672/QUESTION_NO2651_MILITARY_RULE_IN_MYANMAR.

Government of India Ministry of External Affairs. *Transcript of Special Press Briefing by Foreign Secretary before Prime Minister's Visit to Bangladesh.* 25 March 2021. https://mea.gov.in/media-briefings.htm?dtl/33760/Transcript_of_Special_Press_briefing_by_Foreign_Secretary_before_Prime_Ministers_visit_to_Bangladesh_March_24_2021.

Government of India Ministry of External Affairs. *Official Spokesperson's Response to Media Queries on the ASEAN Initiative on Myanmar Agreed to at the ASEAN Summit held on April 24.* 25 April 2021. https://mea.gov.in/response-to-queries.htm?dtl/33822/Official_Spokespersons_response_to_media_queries_on_the_ASEAN_initiative_on_Myanmar_agreed_to_at_the_ASEAN_Summit_held_on_April_24.

International Labour Organization Regional Office for Asia and the Pacific. *Employment in Myanmar Since the Military Takeover: A Rapid Impact Assessment.* 19 July 2021. https://www.ilo.org/yangon/publications/WCMS_814681/lang--en/index.htm.

Japan Joint Staff Press Release. *Joint Statement of Chiefs of Defense.* 28 March 2021. https://www.mod.go.jp/js/Press/press2021/press_pdf/p20210328_02.pdf.

Japan Ministry of Foreign Affairs. *The Internal Situation in Myanmar: Statement by Foreign Minister Motegi Toshimitsu.* 1 February 2021. https://www.mofa.go.jp/press/release/press3e_000161.html.

Japan Ministry of Foreign Affairs. *Emergency Grant Aid for Humanitarian Assistance to the Populations Affected by the Coup in the South East Area of Myanmar.* 13 July 2021. https://www.mofa.go.jp/press/release/press3e_000210.html.

Karen National Union. *The Karens and their Struggle for Freedom.* July 1992. https://www.yumpu.com/en/document/read/61727584/the-karens-and-their-struggle-for-freedom.

Myanmar Ministry of Hotels and Tourism. *The 8 Major National Ethnic Races in Myanmar.* https://web.archive.org/web/20071220174829/http:/www.myanmar.gov.mm/ministry/hotel/fact/race.htm

Myanmar Ministry of Information. 'National Convention Reconvenes in Nyaunghnapin Camp in Hmawby Township.' *The New Light of Myanmar* 12, no. 32 (May 2004). https://

www.burmalibrary.org/sites/burmalibrary.org/files/obl/docs/NLM2004-05-18.pdf.

Myanmar Ministry of Information. 'Union of Myanmar State Peace and Development Council (Announcement No. 5/2008).' *The New Light of Myanmar* 16, no. 19 (May 2008). https://www.burmalibrary.org/sites/burmalibrary.org/files/obl/docs4/NLM2008-05-07.pdf.

Myanmar Office of the Commander-in-Chief of Defence Services. *Statement on Ceasefire and Eternal Peace.* 12 November 2020. https://cincds.gov.mm/node/9793?d=2.

National Unity Government of the Republic of the Union of Myanmar. *Heads of Government.* https://www.nugmyanmar.org/en/.

People's Republic of China Ministry of Foreign Affairs. *Foreign Ministry Spokesperson Chao Lijian's Regular Press Conference on March 15, 2021.* 15 March 2021. https://www.fmprc.gov.cn/mfa_eng/xwfw_665399/s2510_665401/2511_665403/202103/t20210315_9721227.html.

Permanent Mission of the People's Republic of China to the UN. *Ambassador Zhang Jun Elaborated on China's Position on the Situation in Myanmar.* 5 March 2021. http://un.china-mission.gov.cn/eng/hyyfy/202103/t20210306_10026726.htm.

Permanent Mission of the People's Republic of China to the UN. *Ambassador Zhang Jun Elaborated China's Position on the Situation in Myanmar in the Security Council.* 31 March 2021. https://www.mfa.gov.cn/ce/ceun//eng/hyyfy/t1866062.htm.

Singapore Ministry of Foreign Affairs. *Minister for Foreign Affairs Dr. Vivian Balakrishnan's Oral Reply to Parliamentary and Supplementary Questions on the Situation in Myanmar.* 16 February 2021. https://www.mfa.gov.sg/Newsroom/Press-Statements-Transcripts-and-Photos/2021/02/20210216-Oral-Reply-to-PQ-on-Situation-in-Myanmar.

UNDP Human Development Report 2020. *The Next Frontier: Human Development and the Anthropocene—Myanmar.* https://hdr.undp.org/sites/default/files/Country-Profiles/ MMR.pdf.

UN Economic and Social Council Commission on Human Rights. *Question of the Violation of Human Rights and Fundamental Freedoms in Any Part of the World, with Particular Reference to Colonial and Other Dependent Countries and Territories—Report on the Situation of Human Rights in Myanmar.* Yozo Yokota, E/ CN.4/1996/65. 5 February 1996. http://hrlibrary.umn.edu/ commission/country52/65-mmr.htm.

UN General Assembly. *The Situation in Myanmar: Resolution / Adopted by the General Assembly.* A/RES/75/287. 18 June 2021. https://digitallibrary.un.org/record/3930690?ln=en#record-files-collapse-header.

UN General Assembly. *General Assembly Reappoints Secretary-General to Second Five-Year Term, Adopting Resolution Condemning Lethal Violence by Myanmar's Armed Forces.* GA/12339. 18 June 2021. https://press.un.org/en/2021/ ga12339.doc.htm#:~:text=The%20General%20Assembly%20 today%20unanimously,and%20allow%20the%20 sustained%20democratic.

UN Human Rights Council. *Report of the Independent International Fact-Finding Mission on Myanmar.* A/HRC/39/64. 12 September 2018. https://www.ohchr.org/sites/default/files/ Documents/HRBodies/HRCouncil/FFM-Myanmar/A_ HRC_39_64.pdf.

UN Human Rights Council. *The Economic Interests of the Myanmar Military: Independent International Fact-Finding Mission on Myanmar.* A/HRC/42/CRP.3.5 August 2019. https://www.ohchr. org/sites/default/files/Documents/HRBodies/HRCouncil/ FFM-Myanmar/EconomicInterestsMyanmarMilitary/A_ HRC_42_CRP_3.pdf.

UN Human Rights Council. *Human Rights Council Holds Dialogue with Special Rapporteur on Myanmar and Starts Dialogue with*

*Commission of Inquiry on Syria.* 22 September 2020. https://www.ohchr.org/en/statements/2020/09/human-rights-council-holds-dialogue-special-rapporteur-myanmar-and-starts?LangID=E&NewsID=26280.

UNICEF. *Rohingya Crisis.* UN0331066. https://www.unicef.org/emergencies/rohingya-crisis.

UN News. *Coup, COVID Fuelling 'Perfect Storm' in Myanmar, UN Expert Warns.* 14 July 2021. https://news.un.org/en/story/2021/07/1095822.

UN News. *Stop Weapons Supply to Myanmar, Rights Expert Urges.* 22 February 2022. https://news.un.org/en/story/2022/02/1112422.

UN Office for the Coordination of Humanitarian Affairs. *Humanitarian Needs Overview: Myanmar.* December 2021. file:///C:/Users/manur/Downloads/mmr_humanitarian_needs_overview_2022.pdf.

UN Office of the High Commissioner for Human Rights. *Myanmar: Pillay Concerned about Human Rights Situation in Rakhine State.* 27 July 2012. https://www.ohchr.org/en/press-releases/2012/07/myanmar-pillay-concerned-about-human-rights-situation-rakhine-state#:~:text=Myanmar%3A%20Pillay%20on%20Rakhine%20state&text=GENEVA%20(27%20July%202012)%20%E2%80%93,urging%20a%20prompt%2C%20independent%20investigation.

UN Office of the High Commissioner for Human Rights. *Myanmar: Bachelet Deplores Conviction and Sentencing of Aung San Suu Kyi.* 6 December 2021. https://reliefweb.int/report/myanmar/myanmar-bachelet-deplores-conviction-and-sentencing-aung-san-suu-kyi.

UN Office on Drugs and Crime. *Global Illicit Drug Trends 2001: Myanmar.* Howdidmba Major. 26 June 2001. https://www.unodc.org/pdf/report_2001-06-26_1/analysis_myanmar.pdf.

UN Office on Drugs and Crime. *Alternative Development: Myanmar.* https://www.unodc.org/unodc/en/alternative-development/myanmar.html.

UN Peacemaker. *The Nationwide Ceasefire Agreement between the Government of the Republic of the Union of Myanmar and the Ethnic Armed Organizations.* https://peacemaker.un.org/sites/peacemaker.un.org/files/MM_151510_NCAAgreement.pdf.

United Nations Population Fund. *Myanmar Country Profile.* https://myanmar.unfpa.org/en/country-profile-0#:~:text=70%20per%20cent%20of%20the%20population%20lives%20in%20rural%20areas

UN Secretary General. *Violence, Intimidation, Harassment by Myanmar Security Personnel Unacceptable, Secretary General Says, Also Expressing Concern over Restrictions on Internet.* SG/SM/20581. 14 February 2021. https://press.un.org/en/2021/sgsm20581.doc.htm.

UN Secretary General. *Secretary-General Strongly Condemns Continuing Violence by Myanmar Military as 'Utterly Unacceptable', Urging Unified International Response.* SG/SM/20639. 19 March 2021. https://press.un.org/en/2021/sgsm20639.doc.htm.

UN Secretary General. *Humanitarian Support, Coherent Global Action Still Needed 100 Days after Deadly Military Takeover in Myanmar, Secretary General Says.* SG/SM/20722. 11 May 2021. https://press.un.org/en/2021/sgsm20722.doc.htm.

UN Security Council. *Statement by the President of the Security Council.* S/PRST/2021/5. 10 March 2021. https://www.securitycouncilreport.org/atf/cf/%7B65BFCF9B-6D27-4E9C-8CD3-CF6E4FF96FF9%7D/s_prst_2021_5.pdf.

UN Security Council. *Security Council Press Statement on the Situation in Myanmar.* SC/14785. 2 February 2022. https://press.un.org/en/2022/sc14785.doc.htm.

US Department of Commerce. *Burma—Country Commercial Guide.* International Trade Administration. 27 September 2021. https://www.trade.gov/country-commercial-guides/burma-agriculture.

US Department of State. *Memorandum from the Director, Far East Region (Heinz) to the Assistant Secretary of Defense for International Security Affairs (Nitze)*. 6 March 1962. I–2674/62. https://history.state.gov/historicaldocuments/frus1961-63v23/d49#fnref3.

US Department of State. *Joint Statement by Female Foreign Ministers Condemn Violation of Aung San Suu Kyi's Human Rights*. 11 September 2000. https://1997-2001.state.gov/statements/2000/000911a.html.

US Department of State. *Burmese Military Arrests of Civilian Government Leaders*. Press Statement by Anthony J. Blinken. 31 January 2021. https://www.state.gov/burmese-military-arrests-of-civilian-government-leaders/.

US Department of State Office of the Spokesperson. *Briefing with Senior State Department Officials on the State Department's Assessment of Recent Events in Burma*. 2 February 2021. https://www.state.gov/briefing-with-senior-state-department-officials-on-the-state-departments-assessment-of-recent-events-in-burma/.

US Department of State. *Department Press Briefing—February 2, 2021*. Ned Price. 2 February 2021. https://www.state.gov/briefings/department-press-briefing-february-2-2021/.

US Department of State. *Department Press Briefing—February 3, 2021*. Ned Price. 3 February 2021. https://www.state.gov/briefings/department-press-briefing-february-3-2021/.

US Department of State. *Designating Officials and Entities in Connection with the Military Coup in Burma*. Press Statement by Anthony J. Blinken. 11 February 2021. https://www.state.gov/designating-officials-and-entities-in-connection-with-the-military-coup-in-burma/.

US Department of State. *Promoting Accountability for those Responsible for Violence Against Protestors in Burma*. Press Statement by Anthony J. Blinken. 22 February 2021.

https://www.state.gov/promoting-accountability-for-those-responsible-for-violence-against-protestors-in-burma/.

US Department of State. *Designating Officials and Military Units in Response to Escalating Violence in Burma.* Press Statement by Anthony J. Blinken. 22 March 2021. https://www.state.gov/designating-officials-and-military-units-in-response-to-escalating-violence-in-burma/.

US Department of the Treasury. *United States Targets Leaders of Burma's Military Coup Under New Executive Order.* 11 February 2021. https://home.treasury.gov/news/press-releases/jy0024.

US Department of the Treasury. *United States Targets Family Members Profiting from Connection to Burmese Coup Leader.* 10 March 2021. https://home.treasury.gov/news/press-releases/jy0051.

US Department of the Treasury. *Treasury Sanctions Military Holding Companies in Burma.* 25 March 2021. https://home.treasury.gov/news/press-releases/jy0078.

US Embassy in Burma. *Joint Statement on Attacks on Civilians in Karen State.* 24 December 2021. https://mm.usembassy.gov/joint-statement-on-attacks-on-civilians-in-karen-state/.

US Executive Office of the President. *Blocking Property with Respect to the Situation in Burma.* Executive Order 14014. 10 February 2021. https://www.federalregister.gov/documents/2021/02/12/2021-03139/blocking-property-with-respect-to-the-situation-in-burma.

US Senate Subcommittee on Asia and Pacific Affairs Hearings on Burma. *Hearings on Burma: Testimony of David I. Steinberg, Professor, School of Foreign Service, Georgetown University.* 30 September 2009. https://reliefweb.int/report/myanmar/hearings-burma-testimony-david-i-steinberg-professor-school-foreign-service.

The White House Office of the Press Secretary. *Remarks by President Obama at the University of Yangon.* 19 November 2012. https://obamawhitehouse.archives.gov/the-press-office/2012/11/19/remarks-president-obama-university-yangon

The White House. *Statement by President Joseph R. Biden, Jr. on the Situation in Burma.* 1 February 2021. https://www.whitehouse.gov/briefing-room/statements-releases/2021/02/01/statement-by-president-joseph-r-biden-jr-on-the-situation-in-burma/.

The White House. *Remarks by President Biden on the Administration's Response to the Coup in Burma.* 10 February 2021. https://www.whitehouse.gov/briefing-room/speeches-remarks/2021/02/10/remarks-by-president-biden-on-the-administrations-response-to-the-coup-in-burma/.

The White House. *Statement by National Security Advisor Jake Sullivan on Violence Against Peaceful Demonstrations in Burma.* 28 February 2021. https://www.whitehouse.gov/briefing-room/statements-releases/2021/02/28/statement-by-national-security-advisor-jake-sullivan-on-violence-against-peaceful-demonstrations-in-burma/.

The World Bank. *Poverty Report—Myanmar Living Conditions Survey 2017.* 26 June 2019. https://www.worldbank.org/en/country/myanmar/publication/poverty-report-myanmar-living-conditions-survey-2017#:~:text=The%20Poverty%20Report%20shows%20that,been%20faster%20in%20urban%20areas.

The World Bank. *Myanmar COVID-19 Emergency Response Project Information Document.* PIDA29102. 9 April 2020. https://documents1.worldbank.org/curated/en/178971586428026889/pdf/Project-Information-Document-Myanmar-COVID-19-Emergency-Response-Project-P173902.pdf.

The World Bank. *Progress Threatened; Resilience Tested.* Myanmar Economic Monitor. July 2021. https://pubdocs.worldbank.org/en/525471627057268984/Myanmar-Economic-Monitor-July-2021.pdf.

World Food Programme Myanmar. *Myanmar: Analysis of the Economic Fallout and Food Insecurity in the Wake of the Takeover—2021.* 21 April 2021. https://www.wfp.org/publications/myanmar-analysis-economic-fallout-and-food-insecurity-wake-takeover-2021.

# Notes

1 'Internet Disrupted in Myanmar amid Apparent Military Uprising'. NetBlocks, 31 January 2021. https://netblocks. org/reports/internet-disrupted-in-myanmar-amid-apparent-military-uprising-JBZrmlB6.

2 Julie Gerstein, 'Scenes from a Coup: Images from Myanmar Show How the Military Took Control in a Matter of Hours', *Business Insider*, 1 February 2021. https://www. businessinsider.com/myanmar-military-coup-photos-yangon-naypyitaw-2021-2.

3 'Myanmar Gov't Leaders Detained by Military, State-Run Radio, Television Channel Cut Off,", *Xinhua*, 1 February 2021. http:// www.xinhuanet.com/english/2021-02/01/c_139712123.htm.

4 'Republic of the Union of Myanmar Office of the Commander-in-Chief of Defence Services Notification No. 1/2021', *The Global New Light of Myanmar*, 2 February 2021. https://www. gnlm.com.mm/republic-of-the-union-of-myanmar-office-of-the-commander-in-chief-of-defence-services-notification-no-1-2021/.

5 Hannah Beech, 'Top Myanmar General Says Military Rule Will Continue into 2023', *New York Times*, 1 August 2021. https://www.nytimes.com/2021/08/01/world/asia/myanmar-state-emergency.html.

6 'Hundreds of Myanmar MPs under House Arrest', *The News International*, 3 February 2021. https://www.thenews.com.pk/ print/784319-hundreds-of-myanmar-mps-under-house-arrest.

7 'Aung San Suu Kyi, Win Myint to Face Charges as NLD Calls for
   "Unconditional" Release', *Frontier Myanmar*, 5 February 2021.
   https://www.frontiermyanmar.net/en/aung-san-suu-kyi-win-
   myint-to-face-charges-as-nld-calls-for-unconditional-release/
8 Obama did acknowledge 'huge challenges' and of the possibility
   that 'there will be those who resist the forces of change'. But he
   ended on an optimistic note: 'Over the last year and a half, a
   dramatic transition has begun, as a dictatorship of five decades
   has loosened its grip. Under President Thein Sein, the desire
   for change has been met by an agenda for reform. A civilian
   now leads the government, and a parliament is asserting itself.
   The once-outlawed National League for Democracy stood in
   an election, and Aung San Suu Kyi is a Member of Parliament.
   Hundreds of prisoners of conscience have been released, and
   forced labor has been banned. Preliminary cease-fires have
   been reached with ethnic armies, and new laws allow for
   a more open economy. The road ahead will be marked by
   huge challenges, and there will be those who resist the forces
   of change. *But I stand here with confidence that something is
   happening in this country that cannot be reversed, and the will
   of the people can lift up this nation and set a great example for
   the world.*' (emphasis added) 'Remarks by President Obama
   at the University of Yangon', 19 November 2012. https://
   obamawhitehouse.archives.gov/the-press-office/2012/11/19/
   remarks-president-obama-university-yangon..
9 Sergiy Zorya, 'A Bigger and Better Harvest: Myanmar's Rice
   Export Opportunities', *World Bank Blogs*, 11 June 2014, https://
   blogs.worldbank.org/eastasiapacific/bigger-and-better-harvest-
   myanmar-s-rice-export-opportunities
10 Dani Rodrik, 'Is Liberal Democracy Feasible in Developing
   Countries?', *Studies in Comparative International Development*, 9
   March 2016. DOI 10.1007/s12116-016-9218-6; https://drodrik.
   scholar.harvard.edu/files/dani-rodrik/files/is_liberal_democracy_
   feasible_in_developing_countries.pdf.

11 Sam Van Noort, 'Industrialization and Democracy', SSRN Research Paper, 15 September 2020. https://ssrn.com/abstract= 3693044.

12 Elsa C. Stamp, *A First Geography of Burma.* (Orient Longmans, 1957), p. 4.

13 'Factbox: Key facts about Myanmar.' *Reuters*, 6 November 2010, https://www.reuters.com/article/us-myanmar-fb/factbox-key-facts-about-myanmar-idUSTRE6A605G20101107

14 Myat Thein, *Economic Development of Myanmar* (Singapore: ISEAS Publishing, 2004).

15 'Country Profile: Myanmar', United Nations Population Fund. https://myanmar.unfpa.org/en/country-profile-0#:~: text=70per cent20perper cent20centper cent20ofper cent20theper cent20populationper cent20livesper cent20inper cent20ruralper cent20areas.

16 Michael Aung-Thwin and Maitrii Aung-Thwin. *A History of Myanmar Since Ancient Times: Traditions and Transformations* (London: Reaktion Books, 2012), p. 40.

17 The full text of Khin Nyunt's speech is available at https://www.burmalibrary.org/sites/burmalibrary.org/files/obl/docs/Roadmap-KN.htm.

18 Senior General Min Aung Hlaing, 19 February 2018. https://www.irrawaddy.com/in-person/ties-forged-brotherhood.html

19 Michael Aung-Thwin and Maitrii Aung-Thwin. *A History of Myanmar Since Ancient Times: Traditions and Transformations* (London: Reaktion Books, 2012), p. 34

20 Amitav Acharya, 'Are democracies better at reducing poverty?' *The Jakarta Post*, 17 December 2021. https://www.thejakartapost.com/opinion/2021/12/17/are-democracies-better-at-reducing-poverty-.html.

21 *China News* (Taipei), 21 November 1992. A video recording of Lee Kuan Yew's speech is available at https://www.youtube.com/watch?v=Nm3l3mHBGDo.

22 Acharya, 'Are democracies better at reducing poverty?'

23 Ramos Tells Singapore's Lee Filipinos have Rejected Dictatorship," UPI Archives, 20 Nov 1992. https://www.upi.com/Archives/1992/11/20/Ramos-tells-Singapores-Lee-Filipinos-have-rejected-dictatorship/1643722235600/.

24 Tommy Koh, 'The 10 Values That Undergird East Asian Strength and Success', *International Herald Tribune*, 11 December 1993. https://www.nytimes.com/1993/12/11/opinion/IHT-the-10-values-that-undergird-east-asian-strength-and-success.html.

25 'A Lesson from Singapore', *The Irrawaddy*, 2 December 2016. https://www.irrawaddy.com/opinion/commentary/a-lesson-from-singapore.html.

26 'Suu Kyi not angry with Lee Kuan Yew', UPI Archives, 23 June 1996. https://www.upi.com/Archives/1996/06/23/Suu-Kyi-not-angry-with-Lee-Kuan-Yew/7431835502400/.

27 'A Lesson from Singapore', 2 December 2016. https:// https://www.irrawaddy.com/opinion/commentary/a-lesson-from-singapore.html.

28 'Suu Kyi not angry with Lee Kuan Yew', UPI Archives, 23 June 1996. https://www.upi.com/Archives/1996/06/23/Suu-Kyi-not-angry-with-Lee-Kuan-Yew/7431835502400/

29 Aung San Suu Kyi, *Freedom from Fear* (London, Penguin, 1995), pp. 169–70.

30 David Moe, "Is Buddhism a Democratic Religion? Religious Nationalism and Military Violence in Myanmar," 6 April 2021. https://berkleycenter.georgetown.edu/responses/is-buddhism-a-democratic-religion-religious-nationalism-and-military-violence-in-myanmar.

31 G.E. Harvey, *Outline of Burmese History* (Bombay, Orient Longman, 1929), p. 81.

32 J.S. Furnivall, *An Introduction to the Political Economy of Burma*, 3rd edition (Peoples' Literature Committee and House, 1957), pp. 1-m.

33 Robert H. Taylor, 'Burma's National Unity Problem and the 1974 Constitution', *Contemporary Southeast Asia* 1,

no. 3 (December 1979): p. 232. https://www.jstor.org/
stable/25797574#metadata_info_tab_contents.

34 Ananda Rajah, 'Ethnicity and Civil War in Burma', in Robert
I. Rotberg, ed., *Burma: Prospects for a Democratic Future*
(Washington, DC: Brookings Institution Press, 1998), p.135.

35 'People and Society - Burma', Central Intelligence Agency.
Central Intelligence Agency, 6 April 2022. https://www.cia.
gov/the-world-factbook/countries/burma/#people-and-society.

36 https://www.embassyofmyanmar.be/ABOUT/ethnicgroups.htm.

37 Reuters Staff, 'Factbox: Key Facts About Mynmar,' *Reuters*,
13 November 2010. https://www.reuters.com/article/
us-myanmar-factbox/factbox-key-facts-about-myanmar-
idUKTRE6AC1T920101114.

38 'Factbox: Key facts about Myanmar', *Reuters*, 6 November 2010,
https://www.reuters.com/article/us-myanmar-fb/factbox-
key-facts-about-myanmar-idUSTRE6A605G20101107

39 Dinyar Godrej. 'A Short History of Burma,' *New
Internationalist*, 18 April 2008. https://newint.org/
features/2008/04/18/history.

40 Josef Silverstein, 'The Evolution and Salience of Burma's
National Political Culture', in Robert I. Rotberg, ed., *Burma:
Prospects for a Democratic Future* (Washington, DC: Brookings
Institution Press, 1998), p. 21.

41 Silverstein, 'The Evolution and Salience of Burma's National
Political Culture', p. 21.

42 Silverstein, 'The Evolution and Salience of Burma's National
Political Culture', p. 21

43 Silverstein, 'The Evolution and Salience of Burma's National
Political Culture', p. 21.

44 Sarah Yuniarni, 'Unity in Diversity: Indonesia's Six Largest
Ethnic Groups', *Jakarta Globe*, 16 July 2016, https://
jakartaglobe.id/culture/unity-diversity-indonesias-six-largest-
ethnic-groups/.

45 Nyein Nyein, 'Timeline: 70 Years of Ethnic Armed Resistance
Movements in Myanmar', *The Irrawaddy*, 1 February 2019.

https://www.irrawaddy.com/specials/timeline-70-years-
ethnic-armed-resistance-movements-myanmar.html.
46  Rajah, 'Ethnicity and Civil War in Burma', p.137.
47  Nyein Nyein, 'Timeline: 70 Years of Ethnic Armed Resistance
     Movements in Myanmar.'
48  'Rohingya       crisis',      https://www.unicef.org/emergencies/
     rohingya-crisis#:~:text=What%20is%20UNICEF%20
     doing%20to,protection%2C%20nutritious%20food%20
     and%20education.
49  'A Conversation with Aung San Suu Kyi', Organized by the
     Council on Foreign Relations, 30 November 2011, https://
     www.cfr.org/event/conversation-aung-san-suu-kyi-0.
50  Thant Myint-U, *The Hidden History of Burma* (New York:
     W.W. Norton, 2021), pp. 258–9.
51  Kyaw Ye Lynn, 'Census Data Shows Myanmar Muslims
     Population has Fallen', *Anadolu Agency*, 21 July 2016. https://
     www.aa.com.tr/en/asia-pacific/census-data-shows-myanmar-
     muslim-population-has-fallen/612764; Rachel Blomquist and
     Richard Cincotta, 'Myanmar's Democratic Deficit: Demography
     and the Rohingya Dilemma', *The Wilson Center Blog*, 12 April
     2016.     https://www.newsecuritybeat.org/2016/04/myanmars-
     democratic-deficit-demography-rohingya-dilemma/.
52  There are no definitive numbers of civilian casualties during the
     war, but one private source (C. Peter Chen, 'Burma', https://
     ww2db.com/country/burma) estimates 250,000 civilian deaths
     out of a pre-war (1939) population of 16.1 million. One window
     to the effect of the war on the rural Burmese economy is the
     massive deaths of domesticated elephants, a vital resource for
     agriculture and transport, which were also used to carry heavy
     combat equipment. About 18,000 of the estimated 20,000
     domesticated elephants perished during the war. Many civilian
     deaths resulted from forced labour at the hands of the Japanese
     for construction projects as well as malnutrition and disease.
53  D.G.E. Hall, *Burma* (London: Hutchinson University Library,
     1950), pp. 172–3.

54 Cited in Andrew Selth, 'Race and Resistance in Burma, 1942–1945', *Modem Asian Studies* 20, no. 3 (1986): 502.

55 Ibid.

56 Ibid., pp. 506-06.

57 Bruce Vaughn and Wayne M. Morrison, 'China-Southeast Asia Relations: Trends, Issues, and Implications for the United States', Washington DC: Congressional Research Service Report, The Library of Congress, 4 April 2006, p. 6.

58 'The Day Chinese Invaders Were Forced Out of Myanmar', n. d., https://www.irrawaddy.com/specials/on-this-day/day-chinese-invaders-forced-myanmar.html.

59 David I. Steinberg, *Burma/Myanmar: What Everyone Needs to Know* (New York: Oxford University Press, 2010), p. 47.

60 Robert H. Taylor 'Foreign and Domestic Consequences of the KMT Intervention in Burma', Data Paper No. 93 (Ithaca, NY: Southeast Asia Program, Cornell University, 1973), pp. 63–4. https://ecommons.cornell.edu/bitstream/handle/1813/57561/093.pdf?sequen

61 Aung San, *Burma's Challenge* (South Okklapa, Myanmar: 1974), p. 192.

62 'Defence of Burma, January 30, 1945'. Defence Services Historical Research Institute, Rangoon, Burma DSHRI Classification: GR60/P III c/1945 Jan DR 49 / P III c/ 1945 Jan. Reprinted in Josef Silverstein, ed., *The Political Legacy of Aung San* (Ithaca, New York: Department of Asian Studies, Southeast Asian Program Cornell University [Data paper 86], 1972), pp. 23–4.

63 Amitav Acharya, 'Aung San's Vision of a New Asian Order: Reconciling Nationalism, Regionalism and Internationalism in Myanmar's Foreign Policy', TRANSCEND Global Brief 1/2014 (Washington, DC: The UNESCO Chair in Transnational Challenges and Governance, American University, 2014).

64 'Independent Burma: Years of Lost Opportunity,' *The Round Table* 56, no. 221 (1965): 14. DOI: 10.1080/00358536508452578.

65 Stephen McCarthy, 'Burma and ASEAN: Estranged Bedfellows,' *Asian Survey* 48, no. 6 (2008): 914.

66 Sint Sint Myat, 'Explaining Myanmar's Policy of Non-Alignment: An Analytic Eclecticism Approach', *Journal of Current Southeast Affairs* 40, no. 3 (2021): 379.

67 McCarthy, 'Burma and ASEAN', p. 915.

68 Robert Cribb, 'Burma's Entry into ASEAN: Background and Implications,' *Asian Perspective* 22, no. 3 (1998): 50; Michael Richardson, 'A Green Light for Burma to Join ASEAN's Ranks', *The New York Times*, 25 January 1997.

69 David Brown and David Martin Jones, 'Democratization and the Myth of the Liberalizing Middle Classes', in Daniel Bell et al., eds., *Towards illiberal democracy in Pacific Asia* (New York: St. Martin's Press, 1995), pp. 78–106.

70 U Nu, *Saturday's Son: Memoirs of the Former Prime Minister of Burma*, translated by U Law Yone and edited by U Kyaw Win (New Haven, CT: Yale University Press, 1975), p. 221–2.

71 Barry Buzan, *People, States and Fear: The National Security Problem in International Relations* (Brighton: Wheatsheaf Books, 1983), Chapter 2; Mohammed Ayoob, 'Security in the Third World: The Worm About to Turn?', *International Affairs*, 60, no. 1 (Winter 1983/84).

72 Mohammed Ayoob, 'Regional Security and the Third World', in Mohammed Ayoob, in *Regional Security in the Third World* (London: Croom Helm, 1986), pp. 9–10.

73 Udo Steinbach, 'Sources of Third World Conflict', in *Third World Conflict and International Security*, Adelphi Paper no. 166 (London: International Institute for Strategic Studies, 1981), p. 21.

74 Barry Buzan, 'People, States and Fear: The National Security Problem in the Third World', in Edward Azar and Chung-in Moon, eds., *National Security in the Third World: The*

*Management of Internal and External Threats* (Aldershot: Edward Elgar, 1988), p. 26.

75 Ayoob, 'Regional Security and the Third World', op. cit., p. 10.

76 Bahgat Korany, 'Strategic Studies and the Third World: A Critical Evaluation', *International Social Science Journal* 38, no. 4 (1986): p. 553.

77 Andrew Selth, 'Myanmar's Military Mindset: An Exploratory Survey', Brisbane, Griffith Asia Institute Research Paper, 2021, pp. 20–21 https://www.griffith.edu.au/__data/assets/pdf_file/0023/1418333/Military-mindset-web.pdf.

78 Alexander McLaughlin, 'A Look Inside the Myanmar Military', *Foreign Affairs Review*, St Andrews University, 30 April 2021, at https://www. foreignaffairsreview.com/home/a-look-inside-themyanmar-military.

79 Amitav Acharya, 'ASEAN and Burma/Myanmar: Past and Prologue,' Policy Brief, Rising Powers Initiative, George Washington University, 22 April 2012.

80 Melissa Crouch, 'Pre-emptive Constitution-Making: Authoritarian Constitutionalism and the Military in Myanmar', *Law & Society Review* 54, no. 2 (2020): 487.

81 'This Day in History: Burmese Independence', *Oxford University Press Blog*, 4 January 2011. https://blog.oup.com/2011/01/burma-myanmar/.

82 'Burma Independence Bill, HC Deb 05 November 1947 vol 443 cc1836-961', 5 November 1947. https://api.parliament.uk/historic-hansard/commons/1947/nov/05/burma-independence-bill.

83 Ibid.

84 Aung San, 'An Address to the Anglo-Burmans', 8 December 1946, pp. 96–7.

85 'Problems of Burma's Freedom', Presidential Address to the First Congress of Anti-Fascist People's Freedom League (AFPFL), 20 January 1946, p. 47.

86 David Williams, 'Constitutionalism Before Constitutions: Burma's Struggle to Build a New Order', *Articles by Maurer Faculty* (2009) p. 1660. https://www.repository.law.indiana.edu/facpub/492/.

87 Josef Silverstein, ed., *The Political Legacy of Aung San*, Revised Edition, Southeast Asia Program, Cornell University, 1973, p. 158.

88 David C. Williams and Lian H. Sakhong, 'Federalism in the Burmese Context: Lessons Learned from the 1947 Union Constitution' Bloomington, Maurer School of Law, Indiana University, 2005, p. 40. https://www.repository.law.indiana.edu/facbooks/122/.

89 Nehginpao Kipgen, 'Political Change in Burma: Transition from Democracy to Military Dictatorship (1948–62)', *Economic and Political Weekly* 46, no. 20 (May 2011), p. 48–55. http://www.jstor.org/stable/23018213.

90 https://www.burmalibrary.org/docs14/Frontier_Areas_Committee_of_Enquiry-text.pdf.

91 Editorial Team, 'Desk Brief: The Shared Constitutional Heritage of India & Myanmar', *Constitution of India*, 3 July 2020. https://www.constitutionofindia.net/blogs/desk_brief__the_shared_constitutional_heritage_of_india___myanmar.

92 Janelle Diller, 'Constitutional Reform in a Repressive State: The Case of Burma', *Asian Survey* 33, no. 4 (April 1993): 393–407. https://doi.org/10.2307/2645105.

93 'The Constitution of the Union of Burma', 24 September 1947, Effective 4 January 1948, https://www.ilo.org/dyn/natlex/docs/ELECTRONIC/79573/85699/F1436085708/MMR79573.pdf.

94 Melissa Crouch, 'Ethnic Rights and Constitutional Change: The Constitutional Recognition of Ethnic Nationalities in Myanmar/Burma', SSRN Papers, 11 April 2015, p. 4. https://papers.ssrn.com/sol3/papers.cfm?abstract_id=2592474.

95  B.N. Rau, 'The Constitution of the Union of Burma', *India Quarterly* 4, no.2 (April-June 1948): 109.

96  Robert H. Taylor, 'Burma's National Unity Problem and the 1974 Constitution', *Contemporary Southeast Asia* 1, no. 3 (December 1979): 232. https://www.jstor.org/stable/25797574?seq=1.

97  Mary P. Callahan, 'On Time Warps and Warped Time: Lessons from Burma's "Democratic Era",' in Robert Rotberg, ed., *Burma: Prospects for a Democratic Future* (Washington, DC: Brookings Institution Press and World Peace Foundation, 1998), p. 52.

98  Ibid., p. 53.

99  'Southeast Asian Politics: Speech, Burmese Democracy', https://chnm.gmu.edu/wwh/p/119.html

100  Alessandro Demarchi, 'From the Burmese Way to Socialism to Myanmar's current crisis', *Milton Friedman Society*, 3 May 2021.         https://www.friedmansociety.com/post/from-the-burmese-way-to-socialism-to-myanmar-s-current-crisis.

101  Maureen Aung-Thwin, Thant Myint-U and Thant Mynt-U, 'The Burmese Ways to Socialism', *Third World Quarterly* 13, no. 1 (1992): 69.

102  Nehginpao Kipgen, 'Political Change in Burma: Transition from Democracy to Military Dictatorship (1948–62)', *Economic and Political Weekly* 46, no. 20 (May 2011): 52.

103  Rear Admiral L.C. Heinz, 'Memorandum from the Director, Far East Region (Heinz) to the Assistant Secretary of Defense for International Security Affairs (Nitze)', 6 March 1962 https://history.state.gov/historicaldocuments/frus1961-63v23/d49.

104  Josef Silverstein, 'Burma: Ne Win's Revolution Considered', *Asian Survey* 6, no. 2 (February 1966): 95–102.

105  'Memorandum From the Director, Far East Region (Heinz) to the Assistant Secretary of Defense For International Security Affairs (Nitze)', Foreign Relations of the United States, 1961–63, Volume XXIII, Document 49,

6 March 1962. https://history.state.gov/historicaldocuments/
frus1961-63v23/d49.

106 Fred von der Mehden, 'The Burmese Way to Socialism',
*Asian Survey* 3, no. 3 (March 1963): 131. https://www.jstor.
org/stable/3023620#metadata_info_tab_contents.

107 Maureen Aung-Thwin, Thant Myint-U and Thant Mynt-U,
'The Burmese Ways to Socialism', *Third World Quarterly* 13,
no. 1 (1992): 72. https://www.jstor.org/stable/3992410.

108 Fred von der Mehden, 'The Burmese Way to Socialism',
*Asian Survey* 3, no. 3 (March 1963): 129. https://www.jstor.
org/stable/3023620#metadata_info_tab_contents.

109 Cited in Fred von der Mehden, 'The Burmese Way to
Socialism', *Asian Survey* 3, no. 3 (March 1963): 129. https://
www.jstor.org/stable/3023620#metadata_info_tab_contents.

110 Josef Silverstein, 'The Burma Socialist Program Party and its
Rivals: A One-Plus Party System', *Journal of Southeast Asian
History* no. 1 (1967): 16–17. https://www.cambridge.org/
core/journals/journal-of-southeast-asian-history/article/
abs/burma-socialist-program-party-and-its-rivals-a-
oneplus-party-system/2F5878F741D28D9BA96ACECF2
E6B8919.

111 Maureen Aung-Thwin, Thant Myint-U and Thant
Mynt-U, 'The Burmese Ways to Socialism', *Third World
Quarterly* 13, no. 1 (1992): 68. https://www.jstor.org/
stable/3992410..

112 Robert Taylor, 'Burma's National Unity Problem and the 1974
Constitution', *Contemporary Southeast Asia* 1, no. 3 (December
1979): 235. https://www.jstor.org/stable/25797574?seq=1.

113 Ibid., p. 234–35.

114 David Steinberg, 'Burma-Myanmar: The U.S.-Burmese
Relationship and Its Vicissitudes', in *Nancy Birdsall*, Milan
Vaishnav, Robert L. Ayres, eds., *Short of the Goal: U.S. Policy
and Poorly Performing States* (Washington, DC: Center for
Global Development, 2006), p. 210–11.

115  BBC, 'Myanmar Profile—Timeline', *BBC*, 3 September 2018. https://www.bbc.com/news/world-asia-pacific-12992883.

116  Sein Win, 'Burmese Leader Ne Win Resigns in Surprise Move', *The Washington Post*, 24 July 1988. https://www.washingtonpost.com/archive/politics/1988/07/24/burmese-leader-ne-win-resigns-in-surprise-move/1b5896ff-3997-4472-8ffd-d49753838d39/..

117  David Steinberg, 'Burma-Myanmar: The U.S.-Burmese Relationship and Its Vicissitudes', in Milan Vaishnav, Robert L. Ayres, eds., *Short of the Goal: U.S. Policy and Poorly Performing States* (Washington, DC: Center for Global Development, 2006), p. 210–11.

118  Mya Maung, 'The Burma Road to the Past', *Asian Survey* 39, no. 2 (1999): 265–86. https://doi.org/10.2307/2645455..

119  Ibid.

120  'Southeast Asian Politics: Speech, Burmese Democracy', https://chnm.gmu.edu/wwh/p/119.html.

121  Cited in Josef Silverstein, 'The Idea of Freedom in Burma and the Political Thought of Daw Aung San Suu Kyi', *Pacific Affairs* 69, no. 2 (Summer 1996): 211–28. https://doi.org/10.2307/2760725.

122  https://www.refworld.org/docid/3df097254.html.

123  David Steinberg, 'Burma-Myanmar: The U.S.-Burmese Relationship and Its Vicissitudes', in Nancy Birdsall, Milan Vaishnav, Robert L. Ayres, eds., *Short of the Goal: U.S. Policy and Poorly Performing States* (Washington, DC: Center for Global Development, 2006), p. 210–11.

124  https://www.hrw.org/news/2002/10/16/burma-worlds-highest-number-child-soldiers#:~:text=Burma's%20army%20has%20doubled%20in,under%20the%20age%20of%2018.

125  'Burma: Chronology of Aung San Suu Kyi's Detention,' *Human Rights Watch*, 13 November 2010. https://www.hrw.

org/news/2010/11/13/burma-chronology-aung-san-suu-kyis-detention#.

126  BBC, 'Myanmar Profile—Timeline,' *BBC*, 3 September 2018, https://www.bbc.com/news/world-asia-pacific-12992883.

127  Mya Maung, 'The Burma Road to the Past,' *Asian Survey* 39, no. 2 (1999): 265–86. https://doi.org/10.2307/2645455.

128  'Aung San Suu Kyi—Facts,' *NobelPrize.org*, Nobel Prize Outreach AB 2022. https://www.nobelprize.org/prizes/peace/1991/kyi/facts/.

129  Gunter Siemers, 'MYANMAR 1992: Heading For 'Guided Democracy'?' *Southeast Asian Affairs*, 1993, p. 246. https://www.jstor.org/stable/27912078#metadata_info_tab_contents.

130  Nyi Nyi Kyaw, 'Putting Their Guns on the Scale: Constitution-Making in Burma/Myanmar under Military Command', *The Chinese Journal of Comparative Law* 7, no. 2 (September 2019): 318–19. https://academic.oup.com/cjcl/article/7/2/309/5551418.

131  Shankari Sundararaman, 'From SLORC to SPDC: Political Continuity Versus Economic Change in Myanmar', *Strategic Analysis*, 21, no. 10, January 1998.

132  Dinyar Godrej. 'A Short History of Burma.' *New Internationalist*, 18 April 2008. https://newint.org/features/2008/04/18/history.

133  Aung Naing Oo, 'Burma's National Convention: New Resolve, Same Hurdles', *The Irrawaddy* 18 September 2003. https://www2.irrawaddy.com/opinion_story.php?art_id=383.

134  Mya Maung, 'The Burma Road to the Past', *Asian Survey* 39, no. 2 (1999): 272. https://doi.org/10.2307/2645455.

135  Reuters Staff, 'TIMELINE - Myanmar's Suu Kyi clocks up 12 years in detention', *Reuters*, 24 October 2007. https://www.reuters.com/article/uk-myanmar-suu-kyi/timeline-myanmars-suu-kyi-clocks-up-12-years-in-detention-idUKBKK19328320071024.

136 U.S. Department of State, 'Joint Statement by Female Foreign Ministers Condemn Violation of Aung San Suu Kyi's Human Rights', 11 September 2000. https://1997-2001.state.gov/global/oes/health/000911_albright_hiv-aids.html.

137 'UN Envoy Continues Mission to Burma', Voice of America. 1 November 2009. https://www.voanews.com/a/a-13-2007-11-05-voa20/331260.html.

138 Tin Maung Maung Than, 'Burma/Myanmar in 2001: A Year of Waiting', *Asian Survey* 42, no. 1 (2002): 115–23. https://online.ucpress.edu/as/article-abstract/42/1/115/92647/Burma-Myanmar-in-2001-A-Year-of-Waiting?redirectedFrom=fulltext.

139 The full text of Khin Nyunt's 30 August 2003 speech is available at https://www.burmalibrary.org/sites/burmalibrary.org/files/obl/docs/Roadmap-KN.htm.

140 Ibid.

141 Ibid.

142 Nyi Nyi Kyaw, 'Putting Their Guns on the Scale: Constitution-Making in Burma/Myanmar under Military Command', *The Chinese Journal of Comparative Law* 7, no. 2 (September 2019): 322. https://academic.oup.com/cjcl/article/7/2/309/5551418.

143 Aung Naing Oo, 'Burma's National Convention: New Resolve, Same Hurdles', *The Irrawaddy*, 18 September 2003. https://www2.irrawaddy.com/opinion_story.php?art_id=383.

144 Reuters Staff, 'TIMELINE - Myanmar's Suu Kyi clocks up 12 years in detention', *Reuters*, 24 October 2007. https://www.reuters.com/article/uk-myanmar-suu-kyi/timeline-myanmars-suu-kyi-clocks-up-12-years-in-detention-idUKBKK19328320071024.

145 Saw David Taw, 'Choosing to Engage Strategic Considerations for the Karen National Union', in Robert Ricigliano, ed., Choosing to engage: Armed groups and

peace processes (London: Conciliation Resources, 2005), pp. 42-43.

146 The Karen National Union (KNU), 'The Karens and their Struggle for Freedom', *Karen History and Culture Preservation Society*, July 1992, p. 39. https://www.burmalibrary.org/en/ the-karens-and-their-struggle-for-freedom.

147 Myint Shwe, 'In His Own Words: The Rise and Fall of Khin Nyunt', *Bangkok Post*, 8 April 2012. https://www. bangkokpost.com/thailand/special-reports/287955/in-his- own-words-the-rise-and-fall-of-khin-nyunt

148 'The Day Myanmar's Military Intelligence Chief was Sacked', *The Irrawaddy*, 19 October 2020. https://www. irrawaddy.com/specials/on-this-day/day-myanmars- military-intelligence-chief-sacked.html.

149 'National Convention reconvenes in Nyaunghnapin Camp in Hmawby Township', *The New Light of Myanmar*, Vol. XII, No. 32, 18 May 2004. https://www.burmalibrary.org/docs/ NLM2004-05-18.pdf.

150 Nyi Nyi Kyaw, 'Putting Their Guns on the Scale: Constitution- Making in Burma/Myanmar under Military Command', *The Chinese Journal of Comparative Law* 7, no. 2 (September 2019): 322. https://academic.oup.com/cjcl/article/7/2/309/5551418.

151 Amitav Acharya, 'Democracy in Burma: Does Anybody Really Care?', *YaleGlobal*, 1 September 2005. https://archive- yaleglobal.yale.edu/content/democracy-burma-does- anybody-really-care

152 Inter-Parliamentary Union, 'Resolution Adopted by Consensus by the IPU Governing Council at Its 179th Session' (18 October 2006), cited in Nyi Nyi Kyaw, 'Putting Their Guns on the Scale: Constitution-Making in Burma/ Myanmar under Military Command', *The Chinese Journal of Comparative Law* 7, no. 2 (September 2019): 322. https:// academic.oup.com/cjcl/article/7/2/309/5551418.

153 Ibid.

154 Maung Aung Myoe, 'The Road to Naypyitaw: Making Sense of the Myanmar Government's Decision to Move its Capital', *Asia Research Institute*, November 2006. https://ari.nus.edu.sg/publications/wps-79-the-road-to-naypyitaw-making-sense-of-the-myanmar-governments-decision-to-move-its-capital/.

155 Amitav Acharya, 'Democracy in Burma: Does Anybody Really Care?', *YaleGlobal*, 1 September 2005. https://archive-yaleglobal.yale.edu/content/democracy-burma-does-anybody-really-care.

156 David Steinberg, 'Globalization, Dissent, and Orthodoxy: Burma/Myanmar and the Saffron Revolution', *Georgetown Journal of International Affairs* 9, no. 2 (Summer/Fall 2008): 51–58. http://www.jstor.org/stable/43133778.

157 Dhammika Herath, 'Constructing Buddhists in Sri Lanka and Myanmar: Imaginary of a Historically Victimised Community', *Asian Studies Review* 44, no. 2 (February 2020): 315–334. https://doi.org/10.1080/10357823.2020.1717441.

158 Angela Zhang, 'Burma's Difficult Path to Democracy', *Stanford Politics*, 1 February 2016. https://stanfordpolitics.org/2016/02/01/burma-difficult-path-democracy/.

159 https://www.hrw.org/report/2008/04/30/vote-nowhere/may-2008-constitutional-referendum-burma.

160 Ibid; https://www2.irrawaddy.com/article.php?art_id=12026.

161 https://www.hrw.org/report/2008/04/30/vote-nowhere/may-2008-constitutional-referendum-burma.

162 Nyi Nyi Kyaw, 'Myanmar's Pluralist Constitution: Nation-Building versus State-Building', in Jaclyn L. Neo and Bui Ngoc Son, *Pluralist Constitutions in Southeast Asia* (Oxford: Hart, 2019), p. 143; Melissa Crouch, 'Ethnic Rights and Constitutional Change: The Recognition of Ethnic Nationalities in Myanmar/Burma', in Andrew Harding and Mark Sidel, eds., *Central-Local Relations in Asian Constitutional Systems* (Hart 2015), p. 105; Nyi Nyi Kyaw, 'Putting Their

Guns on the Scale: Constitution-Making in Burma/Myanmar under Military Command', *The Chinese Journal of Comparative Law* 7, no. 2 (September 2019): 329–30.

163  Kyaw, 'Myanmar's Pluralist Constitution'.

164  Kyaw, 'Myanmar's Pluralist Constitution'.

165  'Hearings on Burma: Testimony of David I. Steinberg, Professor, School of Foreign Service, Georgetown University', *United States Senate*, 30 September 2009. https://reliefweb. int/report/myanmar/hearings-burma-testimony-david-i-steinberg-professor-school-foreign-service.

166  Based on electoral statistics released by the Union Election Commission on 8 and 11–18 November 2010 in Nyi Nyi Kyaw, 'Putting Their Guns on the Scale: Constitution-Making in Burma/Myanmar under Military Command', *The Chinese Journal of Comparative Law* 7, no. 2 (September 2019): 329–30. https://academic.oup.com/cjcl/article/7/2/309/5551418.

167  Tin Maung Maung Than, 'Myanmar's 2012 By-Elections: The Return of NLD', *Southeast Asian Affairs*, 2013, p. 204–19. http://www.jstor.org/stable/23471145.

168  Marco Bunte and Jorn Dosch, 'Myanmar: Political Reforms and the Recalibration of External Relations', *Journal of Current Southeast Asian Affairs* 34, no. 2 (2015): 3–19; International Crisis Group, 'Reform in Myanmar: One Year On, Asia Briefing no 136', 11 April 2012. https://www.crisisgroup.org/asia/south-east-asia/myanmar/reform-myanmar-one-year.

169  Nyi Nyi Kyaw, 'Putting Their Guns on the Scale: Constitution-Making in Burma/Myanmar under Military Command', *The Chinese Journal of Comparative Law* 7, no. 2 (September 2019): 329–30. https://academic.oup.com/cjcl/article/7/2/309/5551418.

170  'Burma's Opposition Party Wins By-Election in Landslide', *Voice of America*, 1 April 2012. https://www.voanews. com/a/burmas-opposition-party-wins-by-election-in-landslide-145727485/181259.html

171 'Suu Kyi Won Because of Father', *Radio Free Asia*, 4 April 2012. https://www.rfa.org/english/news/myanmar/usdp-04042012184529.html.

172 Dean Nelson, 'Burma Elections: President Thein Sein Happy with Result', *The Telegraph*, 3 April 2012. https://www.telegraph.co.uk/news/worldnews/asia/burmamyanmar/9183220/Burma-elections-President-Thein-Sein-happy-with-result.html.

173 'Myanmar: Pillay concerned about human rights situation in Rakhine state', *United Nations Office of the High Commissioner for Human Rights*, 27 July 2012. https://www.ohchr.org/en/press-releases/2012/07/myanmar-pillay-concerned-about-human-rights-situation-rakhine-state.

174 Cited in Adam Burke, 'New Political Space, Old Tensions: History, Identity and Violence in Rakhine State, Myanmar', *Contemporary Southeast Asia* 38, no. 2 (2016): 274.

175 Nehginpao Kipgen, 'Ethnic Nationalities and the Peace Process in Myanmar', *Social Research* 82, no. 2 (2015): 401. http://www.jstor.org/stable/44282110.

176 Naw Zipporah Sein, 'A Brief NCA History, the NCA's Flaws and Failings by Naw Zipporah Sein', *Burma Link*, 14 January 2016. https://www.burmalink.org/a-brief-nca-history-the-ncas-flaws-and-failings/.

177 Ibid.

178 Ibid.

179 Ibid.

180 Adam Simpson, Nyein Chan Naing, 'Myanmar's Military Reverts To Its Old Strong-Arm Behaviour — And The Country Takes A Major Step Backwards', *The Conversation*, 1 February 2021. https://theconversation.com/myanmars-military-reverts-to-its-old-strong-arm-behaviour-and-the-country-takes-a-major-step-backwards-154368.

181 David Steinberg, 'Transition, competition and trust in Myanmar', *Nikkei Asia*, 14 May 2016. https://asia.nikkei.

com/Politics/David-I.-Steinberg-Transition-competition-and-trust-in-Myanmar.

182 Roger Lee Huang, 'Myanmar's Way to Democracy and the Limits of the 2015 Elections', *Asian Journal of Political Science*, 25, no. 1 (2017): 25–44. https://www.tandfonline.com/doi/abs/10.1080/02185377.2016.1245154.

183 Thu Thu Aung, 'Muslim Community Condemns Rakhine Violence', *The Irrawaddy*, 28 August 2017. https://www.irrawaddy.com/news/burma/muslim-community-condemns-rakhine-violence.html.

184 Sergio Peçanha and Jeremy White, 'Satellite Images Show More Than 200 Rohingya Villages Burned in Myanmar', 18 September 2017. https://www.nytimes.com/interactive/2017/09/18/world/asia/rohingya-villages.html?mtrref=www.google.com&gwh=69CE746AB85FB7B210 65B9037585E87&gwt=regi&assetType=REGIWALL.

185 'MSF surveys estimate that at least 6,700 Rohingya were killed during the attacks in Myanmar', *Medecins Sans Frontieres*, 12 December 2017. https://www.msf.org/myanmarbangladesh-msf-surveys-estimate-least-6700-rohingya-were-killed-during-attacks-myanmar.

186 Human Rights Council, 'Report of the independent international fact-finding mission on Myanmar', *United Nations Office of the High Commissioner for Human Rights*, 10–28 September 2018. https://www.ohchr.org/en/hr-bodies/hrc/myanmar-ffm/index.

187 BBC, 'Myanmar Rohingya: What You Need to Know About the Crisis', *BBC*, 23 January 2020. https://www.bbc.com/news/world-asia-41566561.

188 Eleanor Albert and Lindsay Maizland, 'The Rohingya Crisis', *Council on Foreign Relations*, 23 January 2020. https://www.cfr.org/backgrounder/rohingya-crisis.

189 Rebecca Wright, Katie Hunt, and Joshua Berlinger, 'Aung San Suu Kyi breaks silence on Rohingya, sparks storm of

criticism', *CNN*, 19 September 2017. https://edition.cnn.
com/2017/09/18/asia/aung-san-suu-kyi-speech-rohingya/
index.html

190 Sarah Wildman, 'Aung San Suu Kyi's disappointing
speech about Myanmar's humanitarian catastrophe',
*Vox*, 19 September 2017. https://www.vox.com/
world/2017/9/19/16332582/rohingya-aung-san-suu-kyi-
speech-humanitarian-crisis-refugees.

191 Ibid.

192 Rebecca Wright, Katie Hunt, and Joshua Berlinger, 'Aung
San Suu Kyi breaks silence on Rohingya, sparks storm of
criticism', *CNN*, 19 September 2017. https://edition.cnn.
com/2017/09/18/asia/aung-san-suu-kyi-speech-rohingya/
index.html.

193 'Aung San Suu Kyi Defends Myanmar Against Rohingya
Genocide Accusations', *The New York Times*, 11 December
2019. https://www.nytimes.com/2019/12/11/world/asia/
aung-san-suu-kyi-rohingya-myanmar-genocide-hague.html.

194 Ibid.

195 Human Rights Council, 'The economic interests of the
Myanmar military. Independent International Fact-Finding
Mission on Myanmar', *United Nations Office of the High
Commissioner for Human Rights*, 5 August 2019. https://
www.ohchr.org/Documents/HRBodies/HRCouncil/
FFM-Myanmar/EconomicInterestsMyanmarMilitary/A_
HRC_42_CRP_3.pdf.

196 'Myanmar: The Military Regime's View of the World',
*International Crisis Group*, 7 December 2021. https://www.
crisisgroup.org/asia/south-east-asia/myanmar/myanmar-
military-regimes-view-world.

197 Sean Turnell, 'Myanmar's Fifty-year Authoritarian Trap',
*Journal of International Affairs* 65, no. 1 (2011): 79–90.
https://www.jstor.org/stable/24388183#metadata_info_
tab_contents.

198  https://www.pwyp.org/pwyp-resources/financing-the-military-in-myanmar-analysis-of-gas-revenues/.

199  Howdidmba Major, 'How did Myanmar Become a Major Supplier of Illicit Opium', *Global Illicit Drug Trends.* https://www.unodc.org/pdf/report_2001-06-26_1/analysis_myanmar.pdf.

200  https://www.unodc.org/unodc/en/alternative-development/myanmar.html.

201  Vijitra Duangdee, 'Meth "Super Labs" Said to Thrive in Myanmar Coup Chaos, Spilling Drugs Across Mekong', *Voice of America*, 9 September 2021. https://www.voanews.com/a/meth-super-labs-said-to-thrive-in-myanmar-coup-chaos-spilling-drugs-across-mekong/6219494.html

202  Patrick Meehan, 'How the military benefits from Myanmar's growing opium economy', *East Asia Forum,* 14 June 2016. https://www.eastasiaforum.org/2016/06/14/how-the-military-benefits-from-myanmars-growing-opium-economy/.

203  Htwe Htwe Thein, 'Taking care of business: the coup in Myanmar is partly about protecting the economic interests of the military elite', *The Conversation*, 14 February 2021. https://theconversation.com/taking-care-of-business-the-coup-in-myanmar-is-partly-about-protecting-the-economic-interests-of-the-military-elite-154727.

204  'New legislation expected to regulate Myanmar's gemstone industry', *Oxford Business Group.* https://oxfordbusinessgroup.com/analysis/ongoing-process-new-legislation-aims-better-regulate-gemstone-industry.

205  Eleanor Albert and Francis Wade, 'How Myanmar's Military Wields Power From the Shadows', *Council on Foreign Relations,* 2 October 2017. https://www.cfr.org/interview/how-myanmars-military-wields-power-shadows.

206  Joshua Cheetham, 'Myanmar Coup: The Shadowy Business Empire Funding the Tatmadaw', *BBC News*, 9 March 2021. https://www.bbc.com/news/world-asia-56133766.

207  Ibid.

208  'GDP Growth (annual per cent)—Myanmar'. https://data.
     worldbank.org/indicator/NY.GDP.MKTP.KD.ZG.

209  'Foreign Direct Investment, New Inflows (BoP, current US$-
     Myanmar).  https://data.worldbank.org/indicator/BX.KLT.
     DINV.CD.WD?locations=MM.

210  The World Bank, 'GDP Per Capita (Current US$)—
     Myanmar'.  https://data.worldbank.org/indicator/NY.GDP.
     PCAP.CD?locations=MM.

211  'Myanmar Economic Monitor December 2019: Resilience
     Amidst   Risk'.   https://www.worldbank.org/en/country/
     myanmar/publication/myanmar-economic-monitor-
     december-2019-resilience-amidst-risk.

212  Thomas Carr, *Supporting the Transition: Understanding Aid
     to Myanmar Since 2011* (The Asia Foundation, Myanmar,
     February  2018)  https://reliefweb.int/sites/reliefweb.int/
     files/resources/Understanding_Aid_to_Myanmar_Since_
     2011_-_Asia_Foundation_2018.pdf.

213  'The Human Development Report 2020, Myanmar', United
     Nations Development Agency'. https://hdr.undp.org/sites/
     default/files/Country-Profiles/MMR.pdf.

214  'Myanmar',   *Transparency   International*.   https://www.
     transparency.org/country/MMR.

215  The World Bank, 'Poverty Report- Myanmar Living
     Conditions Survey 2017', 26 June 2019 https://www.
     worldbank.org/en/country/myanmar/publication/
     poverty-report-myanmar-living-conditions-survey-
     2017#:~:text=Theper cent20Povertyper  cent20Reportper
     cent20showsper     cent20that,beenper     cent20fasterper
     cent20inper cent20urbanper cent20areas.

216  Laura Frankel, 'Power & Money: Economics and Conflict
     in Burma', *Cultural Survival Quarterly Magazine*, September
     2000.          https://www.culturalsurvival.org/publications/

cultural-survival-quarterly/power-money-economics-and-conflict-burma.

217 Sandar Win, 'Myanmar's historically 'incomplete' market reforms and their consequences in post-military coup era', *London School of Economics Southeast Asia Blog*, 9 December 2021. https://blogs.lse.ac.uk/seac/2021/12/09/myanmars-historically-incomplete-market-reforms-and-their-consequences-in-post-military-coup-era/.

218 'Myanmmar's 202 General Election Results in Numbers', *The Irrawaddy*, 11 November 2020. https://www.irrawaddy.com/elections/myanmars-2020-general-election-results-numbers.html.

219 'Burma's 2020 Parliamentary Elections', *Congressional Research Services.* 16 November 2020. https://crsreports.congress.gov/product/pdf/IF/IF11687/1.

220 Emily Fishbein and Kyaw Hsan Hlaing, 'Vote Cancellations Trigger Outrage Among Myanmar Minority Voters', *Al Jazeera*, 28 October 2020. https://www.aljazeera.com/news/2020/10/28/vote-cancellations-trigger-outrage-among-myanmar-minority-voters.

221 'Burma's 2020 Parliamentary Elections', *Congressional Research Services.* 16 November 2020. https://crsreports.congress.gov/product/pdf/IF/IF11687/1.

222 'Election Observation Mission Myanmar, General Election, November 8, 2020', *Carter Center.* 10 November 2020. https://www.cartercenter.org/resources/pdfs/news/peace_publications/election_reports/myanmar-preliminary-statement-112020.pdf.

223 'The 2020 Myanmar General Elections: Democracy Under Attack: ANFREL International Election Observation Mission Report', *The Asian Network for Free Elections (ANFREL).* https://anfrel.org/wp-content/uploads/2021/05/ANFREL_Democracy-Under-Attack-F.pdf; 'Myanmar election: No

evidence fraud in 2020 vote, observers say', *BBC*. 17 May 2021. https://www.bbc.com/news/world-asia-57144397.

224 Office of the High Commissioner, 'Human Rights Council Holds Dialogue with Special Rapporteur on Myanmar and Starts Dialogue with Commission of Inquiry on Syria', *United Nations Human Rights Office of the High Commissioner*. 22 September 2020. https://www.ohchr.org/en/statements/2020/09/human-rights-council-holds-dialogue-special-rapporteur-myanmar-and-starts?LangID=E&NewsID=26280.

225 'Myanmar: Statement by the Spokesperson on the General Elections', *European Union External Action*. 9 November 2020. https://www.eeas.europa.eu/eeas/myanmar-statement-spokesperson-general-elections_en.

226 Samuel Stolton, 'EU Slammed for Funding 'discriminatory' Myanmar Voting Application', *EURACTIV*. 14 October 2020. https://www.euractiv.com/section/digital/news/eu-slammed-for-funding-discriminatory-myanmar-voting-application/.

227 Kristina Kironska, 'Myanmar's Pandemic-era Election is Plagued with Difficulties, and the EU has made things Worse', *Myanmar Now*. 4 November 2020. https://www.myanmar-now.org/en/news/myanmars-pandemic-era-election-is-plagued-with-difficulties-and-the-eu-has-made-things-worse.

228 Samuel Stolton, 'EU Slammed for Funding 'discriminatory' Myanmar Voting Application', *EURACTIV*, 14 October 2020. https://www.euractiv.com/section/digital/news/eu-slammed-for-funding-discriminatory-myanmar-voting-application/.

229 'Carter Center Preliminary Statement on the 2020 Myanmar General Elections', *Carter Center*, 10 November 2020. https://www.cartercenter.org/news/pr/2020/myanmar-111020.html; 'Election Observation Mission Myanmar, General

Election, November 8, 2020', *Carter Center*, 10 November 2020. https://www.cartercenter.org/resources/pdfs/news/peace_publications/election_reports/myanmar-preliminary-statement-112020.pdf.

230 Ibid.
231 Ibid.
232 'Burma's 2020 Parliamentary Elections', Washington DC, Congressional Research Service, 15 November 2020. These numbers are based on Union Election Commission, 'Announcement of the Results of the 2020 Multi-Party Democratic General Election,' November 15, 2020 (in Burmese).
233 'Official Results Show Another Election Landslide for Myanmar's Ruling NLD', *The Irrawaddy*, 16 November 2020. https://www.irrawaddy.com/elections/official-results-show-another-election-landslide-myanmars-ruling-nld.html.
234 'The 2020 General Election in Myanmar: A Time for Ethnic Reflection', *Transnational Institute*, 24 December 2020. https://www.tni.org/en/publication/the-2020-general-election-in-myanmar-a-time-for-ethnic-reflection.
235 VS Seshadri, 'Myanmar Results Point to Aung San Suu Kyi's Enduring Popularity Despite Her Party's Patchy Record', *The Indian Express*, 19 November 2020. https://indianexpress.com/article/opinion/myanmar-election-aung-san-suu-kyi-7056510/.
236 'Myanmar army chief accuses government of 'unacceptable mistakes' ahead of election', *Reuters*, 3 November 2020. https://www.reuters.com/article/us-myanmar-election-idUSKBN27J2EE.
237 'Briefing with Senior State Department Officials on the State Department's Assessment of the Recent Events in Burma', *U.S. Department of State*, 2 February 2021. https://www.state.gov/briefing-with-senior-state-department-officials-on-the-state-departments-assessment-of-recent-events-in-burma/.

238 Nan Lwin Hnin Pwint, 'Myanmar's Ethnic Parties Cautiously Optimistic About Outreach From Victorious NLD', *The Irrawaddy*, 25 November 2020. https://www.irrawaddy.com/opinion/analysis/myanmars-ethnic-parties-cautiously-optimistic-outreach-victorious-nld.html.

239 Nan Lwin Hnin Pwint, 'Myanmar's Ethnic Parties Cautiously Optimistic About Outreach From Victorious NLD', *The Irrawaddy*, 25 November 2020. https://www.irrawaddy.com/opinion/analysis/myanmars-ethnic-parties-cautiously-optimistic-outreach-victorious-nld.html.

240 Nyan Hlaing Lin and Min Min, 'Military chief Min Aung Hlaing vows to accept election results after public spat with government', *Myanmar Now*, 8 November 2020. https://www.myanmar-now.org/en/news/military-chief-min-aung-hlaing-vows-to-accept-election-results-after-public-spat-with.

241 Ibid.

242 'Myanmar's opposition USDP party rejects 'unfair' election, demands new vote', *Mizzima*, 11 November 2020. https://www.mizzima.com/article/myanmars-opposition-usdp-party-rejects-unfair-election-demands-new-vote.

243 Shoon Naing and Sam Aung Moon, 'Suu Kyi's party pledges unity government after election "landslide"', *Reuters*, 13 November 2020. https://www.reuters.com/article/uk-myanmar-election-idUKKBN27T0BU.

244 Arakan Army, 'Statement No. (41/2020)', *Arakan Army*, 12 November 2020. https://www.arakanarmy.net/post/statement.

245 Office of the Commander-in-Chief of Defence Services, 'Statement on Ceasefire and Eternal Peace', *Office of the Commander-in-Chief of Defence Services*, 12 November 2020. https://cincds.gov.mm/node/9793?d=1.

246 Office of the Commander-in-Chief of Defence Services, 'Statement on Ceasefire and Eternal Peace', *Office of the*

*Commander-in-Chief of Defence Services*, 12 November 2020. https://cincds.gov.mm/node/9793?d=1.

247 'Military refuses to rule out a coup after claiming possible "vote rigging" during election', *Myanmar Now*, 26 January 2021. https://www.myanmar-now.org/en/news/military-refuses-to-rule-out-a-coup-after-claiming-possible-vote-rigging-during-election.

248 'Tension Grows Following Military's Coup Talk', *The Irrawaddy*, 28 January 2021. https://www.irrawaddy.com/opinion/analysis/tension-grows-following-militarys-coup-talk.html.

249 Nyein Nyein, 'Myanmar Military Chief Warns Constitution Should Be Revoked If Laws Not Followed', *The Irrawaddy*, 28 January 2021. https://www.irrawaddy.com/news/burma/myanmar-military-chief-warns-constitution-revoked-laws-not-followed.html.

250 Ministry of Information, 'Constitution of the Republic of the Union of Myanmar (2008)', *Ministry of Information*, September 2008, p. 6. https://www.wipo.int/edocs/lexdocs/laws/en/mm/mm009en.pdf.

251 Ministry of Information, 'Constitution of the Republic of the Union of Myanmar (2008)', *Ministry of Information*, September 2008, pp. 10–11. https://www.wipo.int/edocs/lexdocs/laws/en/mm/mm009en.pdf.

252 Ministry of Information, 'Constitution of the Republic of the Union of Myanmar (2008)', *Ministry of Information*, September 2008, p. 167.

253 Sebastian Strangio, 'Melissa Crouch on Myanmar's Coup and the Rule of Law', *The Diplomat*, 23 March 2021. https://thediplomat.com/2021/03/melissa-crouch-on-myanmars-coup-and-the-rule-of-law/.

254 Victoria Milko, 'EXPLAINER: Why did the military stage a coup in Myanmar?', *AP News*, 2 February 2021. https://apnews.com/article/military-coup-myanmar-explained-f3e8a294e63e00509ea2865b6e5c342d.

255 Kyaw Lynn, 'Reflections on military coups in Myanmar: and why political actors in Arakan chose a different path', *The Transnational Institute*, 1 March 2021. https://www.tni.org/en/article/reflections-on-military-coups-in-myanmar.

256 David I. Steinberg, 'Myanmar's military coup redux', *East Asia Forum*, 28 December 2021. https://www.eastasiaforum.org/2021/12/28/myanmars-military-coup-redux/.

257 Antoni Slodkowski, 'Newsmaker: Ambitious but cornered, Myanmar army chief took full power', *Reuters*, 1 February 2021. https://www.reuters.com/article/us-myanmar-politics-min-aung-hlaing-news/newsmaker-ambitious-but-cornered-myanmar-army-chief-took-full-power-idUSKBN2A139A.

258 'Myanmar Junta Scraps Retirement Age for Its Leaders', *The Irrawaddy*, 20 May 2021. https://www.irrawaddy.com/news/burma/myanmar-junta-scraps-retirement-age-for-its-leaders.html.

259 Nehginpao Kipgen, 'What's next for Myanmar's military chief after 65?', *The Bangkok Post*, 8 December 2020. https://www.bangkokpost.com/opinion/opinion/2031635/whats-next-for-myanmars-military-chief-after-65-.

260 Dominic Faulder, 'Who is Myanmar junta chief Min Aung Hlaing? 5 things to know', *Nikkei Asia*, 6 February 2021. https://asia.nikkei.com/Spotlight/Myanmar-Crisis/Who-is-Myanmar-junta-chief-Min-Aung-Hlaing-5-things-to-know.

261 Shibani Mahtani and Timothy McLaughlin, 'In Myanmar coup, grievance and ambition drove military chief's power grab', *The Washington Post*, 9 February 2021. https://www.washingtonpost.com/world/asia_pacific/myanmar-coup-military-suu-kyi/2021/02/09/ac385fca-675b-11eb-bab8-707f8769d785_story.html.

262 'Myanmar Junta Chief's Personal Hatred of Daw Aung San Suu Kyi Runs Deep', *The Irrawaddy*, 15 October 2021. https://www.irrawaddy.com/opinion/editorial/myanmar-

junta-chiefs-personal-hatred-of-daw-aung-san-suu-kyi-runs-deep.html.

263 Richard C. Paddock, 'In Myanmar, A Cult of Personality Meets Its Downfall', *New York Times*, 20 February 2021. https://www.nytimes.com/2021/02/04/world/asia/myanmar-coup.html.

264 Shibani Mahtani and Timothy McLaughlin, 'In Myanmar coup, grievance and ambition drove military chief's power grab', *The Washington Post*, 9 February 2021. https://www.washingtonpost.com/world/asia_pacific/myanmar-coup-military-suu-kyi/2021/02/09/ac385fca-675b-11eb-bab8-707f8769d785_story.html.

265 Dominic Faulder, 'Who is Myanmar junta chief Min Aung Hlaing? 5 things to know', *Nikkei Asia*, 6 February 2021. https://asia.nikkei.com/Spotlight/Myanmar-Crisis/Who-is-Myanmar-junta-chief-Min-Aung-Hlaing-5-things-to-know.

266 'Myanmar army ruler takes prime minister role, again pledges elections', *Reuters*, 1 August 2021. https://www.reuters.com/world/asia-pacific/myanmar-military-ruler-promises-elections-says-ready-work-with-asean-2021-08-01/.

267 Khine Lin Kyaw, 'Myanmar Junta Chief Calls for Self-Reliance Amid Political Woes', *Bloomberg*, 1 November 2021. https://www.bloomberg.com/news/articles/2021-11-01/myanmar-junta-chief-calls-for-self-reliance-amid-political-woes.

268 Htet Myet Min Tun, Moe Thuzar and Michael Montesano, 'An Attempt to Lead Myanmar Back to the Future? Data on the State Administration Council Regime's Union Ministers', *ISEAS Perspective*, no. 137 (22 October 2021), https://www.iseas.edu.sg/articles-commentaries/iseas-perspective/2021-137-an-attempt-to-lead-myanmar-back-to-the-future-data-on-the-state-administration-council-regimes-union-ministers-by-htet-myet-min-tun-moe-thuzar-and-michael-montesano/.

269 'Myanmar: Thousands call for "spring revolution",' *Deutsche Welle*, 2 May 2021. https://www.dw.com/en/myanmar-thousands-call-for-spring-revolution/a-57401915.

270 'Myanmar's Shadow Govt Declares War on Military Regime', *The Irrawaddy*, 7 September 2021. https://www.irrawaddy.com/news/burma/myanmars-shadow-govt-declares-war-on-military-regime.html.

271 'Taking Aim at the Tatmadaw: The New Armed Resistance to Myanmar's Coup', *International Crisis Group*, 28 June 2021. https://www.crisisgroup.org/asia/south-east-asia/myanmar/b168-taking-aim-tatmadaw-new-armed-resistance-myanmars-coup.

272 Htet Myet Min Tun, Moe Thuzar and Michael Montesano, 'Buttressing the Anti-NLD Project: Data on the Civilian Members of Myanmar's State Administration Council Junta', *ISEAS Perspective*, No. 119 (2021). https://www.iseas.edu.sg/articles-commentaries/iseas-perspective/2021-119-buttressing-the-anti-nld-project-data-on-the-civilian-members-of-myanmars-state-administration-council-junta-by-htet-myet-min-tun-moe-thuzar-and-michael-montesano/.

273 Htet Myet Min Tun, Moe Thuzar and Michael Montesano, 'An Attempt to Lead Myanmar Back to the Future? Data on the State Administration Council Regime's Union Ministers', *ISEAS Perspective*, no. 137 (22 October 2021). https://www.iseas.edu.sg/articles-commentaries/iseas-perspective/2021-137-an-attempt-to-lead-myanmar-back-to-the-future-data-on-the-state-administration-council-regimes-union-ministers-by-htet-myet-min-tun-moe-thuzar-and-michael-montesano/.

274 Ibid.

275 https://www.reuters.com/investigates/special-report/myanmar-politics-youth-resistance.

276 'Myanmar: What has been happening since the 2021 coup?', *BBC*, 1 February 2022. https://www.bbc.com/news/world-asia-55902070.

277 Poppy McPherson and Shoon Naing, 'The young generation risking all to topple the Myanmar junta', *Reuters*, 10 November 2021. https://www.reuters.com/investigates/special-report/myanmar-politics-youth-resistance

278 Moe Thuzar and Htet Myet Min Tun, 'Myanmar's National Unity Government: A Radical Arrangement to Counteract the Coup', *ISEAS Perspective*, =Yusof Ishak Institute, 28 January 2022.

279 National Unity Government of the Republic of Myanmar, 'Heads of Government', National Unity Government of the Republic of the Union of Myanmar. https://www.nugmyanmar.org/en/.

280 'Myanmar's Shadow Government Forms People's Defense Force', *The Irrawaddy*, 5 May 2021. https://www.irrawaddy.com/news/burma/myanmars-shadow-government-forms-peoples-defense-force.html.

281 'Attacks on Military on The Rise in Myanmar's Ethnic Regions After NUG Declaration of War', *Radio Free Asia*, 23 May 2021. https://www.rfa.org/english/news/myanmar/attacks-09212021185957.html.

282 John Liu and Rory Wallace, 'Six months after Myanmar coup, battle for diplomatic recognition', *Aljazeera*, 1 August 2021. https://www.aljazeera.com/news/2021/8/1/six-months-after-myanmar-coup-battle-for-diplomatic-recognition.

283 'Myanmar will not address world leaders at UN General Assembly', *Aljazeera*, 25 September 2021. https://www.aljazeera.com/news/2021/9/25/myanmar-will-not-address-world-leaders-at-u.

284 Adam Simpson, 'Myanmar's exile government signs up to ICC prosecutions', East Asia Forum, 7 September 2021.

https://www.eastasiaforum.org/2021/09/17/myanmars-exile-government-signs-up-to-icc-prosecutions/.

285 John Liu and Frontier, 'Six Months On, Pressure Builds on NUG to Turn Talk into Action', Frontier MYANMAR, 24 August 2021. https://www.frontiermyanmar.net/en/six-months-on-pressure-builds-on-nug-to-turn-talk-into-action/.

286 John Liu and Frontier, 'Six Months On, Pressure Builds on NUG to Turn Talk into Action', Frontier MYANMAR, 24 August 2021. https://www.frontiermyanmar.net/en/six-months-on-pressure-builds-on-nug-to-turn-talk-into-action/.

287 'Head of Myanmar's Shadow Govt Vows to Continue "Second Struggle for Independence"', *The Irrawaddy*, 5 January 2022. https://www.irrawaddy.com/news/burma/head-of-myanmars-shadow-govt-vows-to-continue-second-struggle-for-independence.html.

288 'PDF Forms Civilian Administration in Sagaing Region', *Kachin News Group*, 6 January 2022. https://kachinnews.com/2022/01/06/pdf-forms-civilian-administration-in-sagaing-region/.

289 'PDF Forms Civilian Administration in Sagaing Region', *Kachin News Group*, 6 January 2022. https://kachinnews.com/2022/01/06/pdf-forms-civilian-administration-in-sagaing-region/.

290 'Myanmar Ruling Party Follows Election Win With Unity Appeal to Ethnic Parties', *Radio Free Asia*, 11 November 2020. https://www.rfa.org/english/news/myanmar/unity-appeal-11132020181340.html.

291 Hay Man Pyae, 'Despite landslide victory, NLD appeals to ethnic parties to join its "national unity government"', *Myanmar Now*, 13 November 2020. https://www.myanmar-now.org/en/news/despite-landslide-victory-nld-appeals-to-ethnic-parties-to-join-its-national-unity-government.

292  Min Wathan, 'NLD to Focus on Principles, Not Personalities in Ethnic Meetings', *Myanmar Times*, 17 December 2020. https://www.mmtimes.com/news/nld-focus-principles-not-personalities-ethnic-meetings.html.

293  Nyein Nyein, 'NLD Reaches Out to Myanmar's Ethnic Parties Seeking Federal Union and an End to Civil War', *The Irrawaddy*, 13 November 2020. https://www.irrawaddy.com/elections/nld-reaches-myanmars-ethnic-parties-seeking-federal-union-end-civil-war.html.

294  Hay Man Pyae, 'Despite landslide victory, NLD appeals to ethnic parties to join its "national unity government"', *Myanmar Now*, 13 November 2020. https://www.myanmar-now.org/en/news/despite-landslide-victory-nld-appeals-to-ethnic-parties-to-join-its-national-unity-government.

295  Ibid.

296  'Myanmar Ruling Party Follows Election Win With Unity Appeal to Ethnic Parties', Radio Free Asia. 13 November 2020. https://www.rfa.org/english/news/myanmar/unity-appeal-11132020181340.html.

297  Ibid.

298  'Armed Ethnic Groups', Myanmar Peace Monitor, 2016. https://www.mmpeacemonitor.org/1426/armed-ethnic-groups/.

299  Altaf Parvez, 'We recognize the human rights and citizen rights of the Rohingyas', *Prothomalo*, 2 January 2022. https://en.prothomalo.com/amp/story/opinion/interview/we-recognise-the-human-rights-and-citizen-rights-of-the-rohingyas.

300  The Brotherhood Alliance declared a unilateral ceasefire in September 2019.

301  'NCA signatories suspend political negotiations with junta, says steering team', *BNI Multimedia Group*, 22 February 2021. https://www.bnionline.net/en/news/nca-signatories-suspend-political-negotiations-junta-says-steering-team.

302 'Myanmar Ceasefire Agreement is Void: KNU Concerned Group', *The Irrawaddy*, 3 September 2021. https://www.irrawaddy.com/news/burma/myanmar-ceasefire-agreement-is-void-knu-concerned-group.html.

303 David Scott Mathieson, 'The rebels who will and won't fight Myanmar's coup', *Asia Times*, 31 March 2021. https://asiatimes.com/2021/03/the-rebels-who-will-and-wont-fight-myanmars-coup/.

304 'Thousand flee homes once again as two Shan armed groups fight for control of territory', *Myanmar Now*, 25 September 2021. https://www.myanmar-now.org/en/news/thousands-flee-homes-once-again-as-two-shan-armed-groups-fight-for-control-of-territory.

305 Tom Fawthrop, 'Myanmar's Ethnic Groups Join Together to Reject Military Rule', *The Diplomat*, 27 February 2021. https://thediplomat.com/2021/02/myanmars-ethnic-groups-join-together-to-reject-military-rule/.

306 'Myanmar Junta Calls "Goodwill" Cease-fire with Ethnic Armed Groups, Omits Anti-Coup Militias', RFA, 29 September 2021. https://www.rfa.org/english/news/myanmar/cease-fire-09282021184553.html.

307 Tom Fawthrop, 'Myanmar's Ethnic Groups Join Together to Reject Military Rule', *The Diplomat*, 27 February 2021. https://thediplomat.com/2021/02/myanmars-ethnic-groups-join-together-to-reject-military-rule/.

308 Andrew Ong, 'Ethnic Armed Organisations in Post-Coup Myanmar: New Conversations Needed', *ISEAS Perspective*, no. 79 (June 2021): 1–9. https://www.iseas.edu.sg/articles-commentaries/iseas-perspective/2021-79-ethnic-armed-organisations-in-post-coup-myanmar-new-conversations-needed-by-andrew-ong/; Mikael Gravers, 'A tentative unity among Myanmar's anti-coup forces', East Asia Forum, 8 June 2021. https://www.eastasiaforum.org/2021/06/08/a-tentative-unity-among-myanmars-anti-coup-forces/.

309 Jason Tower, 'In Myanmar, the State the Generals Seized Is Coming Apart', United States Institute of Peace, 19 August 2021. https://www.usip.org/publications/2021/08/myanmar-state-generals-seized-coming-apart.

310 The Karen National Union, The Restoration Council of Shan State, the Chin National Front, All Burma Students Democratic Front, Arakan Liberation Party, Democratic Karen Benevolent Army, Karen National Liberation Army-Peace Council, the Pa-O National Liberation Organization, Lahu Democratic Union, and New Mon State Party. The last two were not original signatories in 2015, but joined later. 'NCA-signatory EAOs discuss how to prevent further bloodshed by regime', *Myanmar Now*, 12 March 2021, https://www.myanmar-now.org/en/news/nca-signatory-eaos-discuss-how-to-prevent-further-bloodshed-by-regime.

311 The Government of the Republic of the Union of Myanmar, 'The Nationwide Ceasefire Agreement Between the Government of The Republic of The Union of Myanmar and The Ethnic Armed Organizations', United Nations. https://peacemaker.un.org/sites/peacemaker.un.org/files/MM_151510_NCAAgreement.pdf.

312 Salai Samuel Hmung, 'New friends, old enemies: Politics of Ethnic Armed Organisations after the Myanmar Coup', *New Mandala*, 10 June 2021. https://www.newmandala.org/new-friends-old-enemies-politics-of-ethnic-armed-organisations-after-the-myanmar-coup/.

313 Ibid.

314 Michael F. Martin, 'The Importance of Ethnic Minorities to Myanmar's Future', *Stimson Center*, 3 June 2021. https://www.stimson.org/2021/the-importance-of-ethnic-minorities-to-myanmars-future/.

315 Linn Htin, 'Karen National Union 'killed 267' junta soldiers in December clashes', *Myanmar Now*, 7 January 2022. https://www.myanmar-now.org/en/news/karen-national-union-killed-267-junta-soldiers-in-december-clashes.

316 'Myanmar Regimes Shore up Ties with Two Powerful Northern Ethnic Armies', *The Irrawaddy*, 10 April 2021. https://www.irrawaddy.com/news/burma/myanmar-regime-shores-ties-two-powerful-northern-ethnic-armies.html.

317 Jason Tower, 'In Myanmar, the State the Generals Seized Is Coming Apart', United States Institute of Peace, 19 August 2021. https://www.usip.org/publications/2021/08/myanmar-state-generals-seized-coming-apart.

318 Mikael Gravers, 'A tentative unity among Myanmar's anti-coup forces', *Mainstream* LIX, no. 26 (12 June 2021). https://mainstreamweekly.net/article11019.html.

319 Ibid.

320 Jason Tower, 'In Myanmar, the State the Generals Seized Is Coming Apart', United States Institute of Peace, 19 August 2021. https://www.usip.org/publications/2021/08/myanmar-state-generals-seized-coming-apart.

321 'Myanmar Ceasefire Agreement is Void: KNU Concerned Group', *The Irrawaddy*, 3 September 2021. https://www.irrawaddy.com/news/burma/myanmar-ceasefire-agreement-is-void-knu-concerned-group.html.

322 'Myanmar Ceasefire Agreement is Void: KNU Concerned Group', *The Irrawaddy*, 3 September 2021. https://www.irrawaddy.com/news/burma/myanmar-ceasefire-agreement-is-void-knu-concerned-group.html.

323 Lindsey Kennedy and Nathan Paul Southern, 'Myanmar's Opposition Is Forming Fragile Alliances With Armed Ethnic Groups', *Foreign Policy*, 4 September 2021. https://foreignpolicy.com/2021/09/04/myanmar-coup-opposition-armed-ethnic-groups/.

324 Ye Myo Hein, 'Visions of a Federal Future for Myanmar are Fading Fast', *The Irrawaddy*, 1 September 2021. https://www.irrawaddy.com/opinion/guest-column/visions-of-a-federal-future-for-myanmar-are-fading-fast.html.

325 Ye Myo Hein, 'Visions of a Federal Future for Myanmar are Fading Fast', *The Irrawaddy*, 1 September 2021. https://www.irrawaddy.com/opinion/guest-column/visions-of-a-federal-future-for-myanmar-are-fading-fast.html.

326 'Rakhine Party Under Pressure for Taking Position on Military Regime's Governing Body', *The Irrawaddy*, 9 February 2021. https://www.irrawaddy.com/news/burma/rakhine-party-pressure-taking-position-military-regimes-governing-body.html?__cf_chl_jschl_tk__=pmd_fyjWeceURLT3lHSq54dXRRXvDR_J6h66ci8v0t8R61U-1635824464-0-gqNtZGzNAnujcnBszQq9.

327 Lawi Weng, 'The rule of the Wa', *The Irrawaddy*, 2 March 2017. https://www.irrawaddy.com/opinion/commentary/the-rule-of-the-wa.html.

328 'An End to Peace Efforts: Recent fighting in Doo Tha Htoo District between the KNLA and the Tatmadaw following the 2021 Myanmar military coup (March and April 2021)', *Relief Web*, 5 May 2021. https://reliefweb.int/report/myanmar/end-peace-efforts-recent-fighting-doo-tha-htoo-district-between-knla-and-tatmadaw.

329 Allegra Mendelson and Alastair Mccready, 'We are not naïve anymore: Mynamar EAOs skeptical about federal army', Globe, 23 April 2021. https://southeastasiaglobe.com/myanmar-federal-army/.

330 Taylor Landis, 'Beyond the Coup in Myanmar: A Northern View', *Human Rights @ Harvard Law*, 7 May 2021. https://hrp.law.harvard.edu/myanmar/beyond-the-coup-in-myanmar-a-northern-view/.

331 Taylor Landis, 'Beyond the Coup in Myanmar: A Northern View', *Just Security*, 6 May 2021. https://www.justsecurity.org/76016/beyond-the-coup-in-myanmar-a-northern-view/.

332 'Myanmar Junta Media Accuses EAOs of Terrorism', *The Irrawaddy*, 11 October 2021. https://www.irrawaddy.

com/news/burma/myanmar-junta-media-accuses-eaos-of-terrorism.html?__cf_chl_jschl_tk__=pmd_B2kGdxpFKS9Y.MxX7t1EBG59WviEEJO4xL43fgdRXi4-1635823010-0-gqNtZGzNAlCjcnBszQk9.

333 Ibid.

334 Shan Herald Agency, 'CSSU Unity Proposal: Shan State's Unity Key To Establishment Of Federal Democratic Constitution', *BNI Multimedia Group*, 7 January 2022. https://www.bnionline.net/en/news/cssu-unity-proposal-shan-states-unity-key-establishment-federal-democratic-constitution.

335 'Attacks on Military on The Rise in Myanmar's Ethnic Regions After NUG Declaration of War', *Radio Free Asia*, 23 May 2021. https://www.rfa.org/english/news/myanmar/attacks-09212021185957.html.

336 Htet Myet Min Tun and Moe Thuzar, 'Myanmar's National Unity Consultative Council: A Vision Of Myanmar's Federal Future', *Fulcrum*, 5 January 2022. https://fulcrum.sg/myanmars-national-unity-consultative-council-a-vision-of-myanmars-federal-future/.

337 Ibid.

338 Nyan Hlaing Lin, 'NUCC outlines goals as it seeks to widen membership', *Myanmar Now*, 21 November 2021. https://www.myanmar-now.org/en/news/nucc-outlines-goals-as-it-seeks-to-widen-membership.

339 Min Zin, 'The Real Kingmakers of Myanmar', *The New York Times*, 4 June 2021. https://www.nytimes.com/2021/06/04/opinion/myanmar-ethnic-armed-groups.html.

340 'Suu Kyi Will Now Understand Her Mistakes: Karen National Union', *The Irrawaddy*, 6 April 2021. https://www.irrawaddy.com/in-person/interview/suu-kyi-will-now-understand-mistakes-karen-national-union.html.

341 Mikael Gravers, 'A tentative unity among Myanmar's anti-coup forces', *East Asia Forums*, 8 June 2021. https://www.

eastasiaforum.org/2021/06/08/a-tentative-unity-among-myanmars-anti-coup-forces/.

342 Naw Theresa, 'Is Mediation Even Possible in Myanmar?', *The Diplomat*, 1 December 2021. https://thediplomat.com/2021/12/is-mediation-even-possible-in-myanmar/.

343 Mikael Gravers, 'A tentative unity among Myanmar's anti-coup forces', *East Asia Forum*, 8 June 2021. https://www.eastasiaforum.org/2021/06/08/a-tentative-unity-among-myanmars-anti-coup-forces/.

344 Part of this section draws from Amitav Acharya, 'ASEAN and Myanmar: Past and Prologue', *Rising Power Initiative*, 22 April 2012 https://www.risingpowersinitiative.org/2012/04/22/asean-and-burmamyanmar-past-and-prologue/.

345 Author's interview with Surin Pitsuwan, Singapore, 27 September 2001.

346 'Worldwide Condemnation of Burmese Junta', *The Irrawaddy*, 4 June 2003 https://www2.irrawaddy.com/article.php?art_id=916.

347 'Aung San Suu Kyi questions ASEAN's stance', Deutsche Presse-Agentur, 31 July 1995. Cited in Amitav Acharya, *Constructing a Security Community in Southeast Asia: ASEAN and the Problem of Regional Order*, 3rd edition (London: Routledge 2014), p. 116 (note 64).

348 'Hassan Claims there is Progress in Myanmar', *Jakarta Post*, 29 June 2004.

349 Cited in *New York Times*, 29 September 2005, https://www.nytimes.com/2005/09/29/world/asia/briefly-landslides-and-floods-leave-57-dead-in-north.html; and Acharya, *Constructing a Security Community in Southeast Asia*, p. 223.

350 Cited in Acharya, *Constructing a Security Community in Southeast Asia*, p. 223.

351 'Southeast Asian Nations Express "Revulsion" at Myanmar's Violent Repression of Demonstrations', Ottawa, Canada,

27 September 2007. http://www.indonesia-ottawa.org/information/details.php?type=news_copy&id=4765.

352 Ibid.

353 Than Win Hlaing, 'The Role Of Internal And External Forces In Myanmar Political Reform', 2016. http://ethesisarchive.library.tu.ac.th/thesis/2016/TU_2016_5727040122_5623_4119.pdf.

354 'Message from ASEAN Secretary-General', in Pavin Chachavalpongpun and Moe Thuzer, eds., *Myanmar: Life After Nargis* (Singapore: Institute of Southeast Asian Studies, 2009), vii.

355 Than Win Hlaing, 'The Role Of Internal And External Forces In Myanmar Political Reform', 2016.

356 Chairman's Statement of the 34th ASEAN Summit Bangkok, 23 June 2019, p.10. https://asean.org/storage/2019/06/Final_Chairs-Statement-of-the-34th-ASEAN-Summit-rev.pdf.

357 Kilian Spandler, 'Lessons from ASEAN's Rakhine response', *East Asia Forum*, 5 February 2020, https://www.eastasiaforum.org/2020/02/05/lessons-from-aseans-rakhine-response/.

358 World Integrated Trade Solution (WITS) https://wits.worldbank.org/countrysnapshot/en/MMR.

359 'Singapore, China and Thailand: Key investors in Myanmar in 2020', Undated https://www.reportingasean.net/top-investors-in-myanmar-in-2020-singapore-first-then-china-and-thailand/.

360 *The ASEAN Charter.* https://asean.org/wp-content/uploads/images/archive/publications/ASEAN-Charter.pdf.

361 'ASEAN chair Brunei calls for "dialogue reconciliation and return to normalcy" in Myanmar', *Channel News Asia*, 1 February 2021. https://www.channelnewsasia.com/asia/myanmar-asean-aung-san-suu-kyi-military-coup-296211.

362 'Indonesia's Foreign Minister in Diplomatic Push for ASEAN Action on Myanmar Coup', *Radio Free Asia*, 17

February 2021. https://www.rfa.org/english/news/myanmar/push-02172021164525.html.

363 'Indonesia president urges halt to Myanmar violence as support for ASEAN talks grows', *Reuters*, 19 March 2021. https://www.reuters.com/article/us-myanmar-politics-indonesia/indonesia-president-urges-halt-to-myanmar-violence-as-support-for-asean-talks-grows-idUSKBN2BB0NM.

364 Sebastian Strangio, 'Myanmar Junta Could be Excluded From ASEAN Summit: Malaysia', *The Diplomat*, 5 October 2021. https://thediplomat.com/2021/10/myanmar-junta-could-be-excluded-from-asean-summit-malaysia/.

365 Ronna Nirmala and Shailaja Neelakantan, 'Indonesian Envoy: ASEAN Bars Myanmar Junta Chief from Upcoming Summit', *Benar News*, 15 October 2021. https://www.benarnews.org/english/news/indonesian/myanmar-asean-junta-10152021091954.html.

366 'Indonesia president urges halt to Myanmar violence as support for ASEAN talks grows', *Reuters*, 19 March 2021. https://www.reuters.com/article/us-myanmar-politics-indonesia/indonesia-president-urges-halt-to-myanmar-violence-as-support-for-asean-talks-grows-idUSKBN2BB0NM.

367 Niniek Karmini, 'Indonesia, Malaysia urge ASEAN to hold talks on Myanmar coup', *ABC News*, 5 February 2021. https://abcnews.go.com/International/wireStory/indonesia-malaysia-urge-asean-hold-talks-myanmar-coup-75704929.

368 'Timeline: ASEAN tries to tackle Myanmar's worsening crisis', *Aljazeera*, 26 October 2021. https://www.aljazeera.com/news/2021/10/26/asean-myanmar-timeline.

369 Indonesia's Foreign Minister in Diplomatic Push for ASEAN Action on Myanmar Coup', *Radio Free Asia*, 17 February 2021. https://www.rfa.org/english/news/myanmar/push-02172021164525.html.

370 Kirsten Han, 'Myanmar's Protest Movement: What's up With Singapore's Response To the Myanmar Coup?', *The News*

*Lens*, 12 March 2021. https://international.thenewslens.com/feature/myanmar-protest-movement/148353.

371 'Minister for Foreign Affairs Dr Vivian Balakrishnan's Oral Reply to Parliamentary and Supplementary Questions on the Situation in Myanmar', Ministry of Foreign Affairs Singapore, 16 February 2021. https://www.mfa.gov.sg/Newsroom/Press-Statements-Transcripts-and-Photos/2021/02/20210216-Oral-Reply-to-PQ-on-Situation-in-Myanmar.

372 Ibid.

373 Tan Hui Yee and Arlina Arshad, 'Asean countries urge Myanmar military to end violence and work towards reconciliation', *The Straits Times*, 2 March 2021. https://www.straitstimes.com/asia/se-asia/asean-countries-urge-myanmar-military-to-end-violence-and-work-towards-reconciliation.

374 Aradhana Aravindan, 'Analysis: Quiet Singapore turns up volume on Myanmar as regional fears grow', *Reuters*, 31 March 2021. https://www.reuters.com/article/us-myanmar-politics-singapore-diplomacy/analysis-quiet-singapore-turns-up-volume-on-myanmar-as-regional-fears-grow-idUSKBN2BN0VS.

375 Tan Hui Yee and Arlina Arshad, 'Asean countries urge Myanmar military to end violence and work towards reconciliation', *The Straits Times*, 2 March 2021. https://www.straitstimes.com/asia/se-asia/asean-countries-urge-myanmar-military-to-end-violence-and-work-towards-reconciliation.

376 'Thailand Has Told Myanmar to Reduce Violence, PM Says', *Radio Free Asia*, 7 April 2021. https://www.rfa.org/english/news/myanmar/disapprove-04072021160552.html.

377 'Myanmar junta leader asks Thai counterpart for help on democracy', *Reuters*, 10 February 2021. https://www.reuters.com/article/us-myanmar-politics-thailand/myanmar-junta-leader-asks-thai-counterpart-for-help-on-democracy-idUSKBN2AA0V7.

378 'Thailand Has Told Myanmar to Reduce Violence, PM Says', *Radio Free Asia*, 7 April 2021. https://www.rfa.org/english/news/myanmar/disapprove-04072021160552.html.

379 Marwaan Macan-Markar, 'Thai PM and Myanmar junta chief stay engaged via back channels', *Nikkei Asia*, 12 May 2021. https://asia.nikkei.com/Spotlight/Myanmar-Crisis/Thai-PM-and-Myanmar-junta-chief-stay-engaged-via-back-channels.

380 'New ASEAN chair Cambodia urged to maintain bloc's firm stance on Myanmar', *Radio Free Asia*, 29 October 2021. https://www.rfa.org/english/news/myanmar/asean-10292021194903.html.

381 Duy Nguyen, 'Myanmar coup: Vietnam calls for end of violence', *Hanoi Times*, 11 March 2021. http://hanoitimes.vn/myanmar-coup-vietnam-calls-for-end-of-violence-316629.html.

382 'Indonesia president urges halt to Myanmar violence as support for ASEAN talks grows', *Reuters*, 19 March 2021. https://www.reuters.com/article/us-myanmar-politics-indonesia/indonesia-president-urges-halt-to-myanmar-violence-as-support-for-asean-talks-grows-idUSKBN2BB0NM.

383 'ASEAN chair Brunei calls for "dialogue reconciliation and return to normalcy" in Myanmar', *Channel News Asia*, 1 February 2021. https://www.channelnewsasia.com/asia/myanmar-asean-aung-san-suu-kyi-military-coup-296211.

384 'Malaysia Defends Envoy's Meeting With Myanmar Military Government', *Radio Free Asia*, 8 April 2021. https://www.rfa.org/english/news/myanmar/defends-04082021173942.html.

385 'Chairman's Statement on the ASEAN Leaders' Meeting', *Online Burma/Myanmar Library*, 24 April 2021. https://www.burmalibrary.org/en/chairmans-statement-on-the-asean-leaders-meeting.

386 Niniek Karmini, 'ASEAN leaders tell Myanmar coup general to end killings', *Associated Press*, 25 April 2021. https://apnews.com/article/aung-san-suu-kyi-global-trade-

indonesia-myanmar-singapore-2959338f61cbe0b0b7c6dd75
99ee6e2c.

387 Ibid.

388 'Can ASEAN help end the crisis in Myanmar?' *Al Jazeera TV*, 24 April 2021. https://www.aljazeera.com/program/inside-story/2021/4/24/can-asean-help-end-the-crisis-in-myanmar.

389 'Singapore says ASEAN aims to speed up plan to end Myanmar crisis', *Reuters*, 6 July 2021. https://www.reuters.com/world/asia-pacific/singapore-says-asean-aims-speed-up-plan-end-myanmar-crisis-2021-07-07/.

390 'Singapore says ASEAN not as effective as hoped in Myanmar', *Aljazeera*, 21 August 2021. https://www.aljazeera.com/news/2021/8/21/singapore-says-asean-not-as-effective-as-hoped-in.

391 'Myanmar junta says no ASEAN envoy visit until stability restored', *Reuters*, 7 May 2021. https://www.reuters.com/world/asia-pacific/myanmar-junta-says-seeks-stability-before-allowing-asean-envoy-visit-2021-05-07/

392 Grant Peck, 'Myanmar leader says ASEAN blind to opposition's violence', *Associated Press*, 18 October 2021. https://apnews.com/article/business-television-asia-myanmar-global-trade-3e6bcdcb69d681578d08cd24202c129b

393 Ibid.

394 Michael Yong, 'No "significant progress" in implementing ASEAN's Five-Point Consensus on Myanmar: PM Lee to PM Hun Sen', *Channel News Asia*, 15 January 2022. https://www.channelnewsasia.com/singapore/asean-five-point-consensus-myanmar-no-significant-progress-pm-lee-hun-sen-2437921.

395 Eileen Ng and Jim Gomez, 'ASEAN leaders hold summit with Myanmar's general shut out', *Associated Press*, 25 October 2021. https://apnews.com/article/joe-biden-business-myanmar-global-trade-southeast-asia-a4ceef105a9b278365c6b8165cc10184.

396 Sebastian Strangio, 'Malaysian FM Calls for 'Soul-Searching' Over ASEAN Non-Interference', *The Diplomat*, 22 October 2021. https://thediplomat.com/2021/10/malaysian-fm-calls-for-soul-searching-over-asean-non-interference/.

397 'Myanmar frees hundreds of political prisoners after ASEAN pressure', *ABC News*, 19 October 2021. https://www.abc.net.au/news/2021-10-19/myanmar-frees-hundreds-political-prisoners-asean-pressure/100551558.

398 Gwen Robinson, 'Can ASEAN overcome the "Myanmar curse"?', *Nikkei Asia*, 1 November 2021. https://asia.nikkei.com/Spotlight/Comment/Can-ASEAN-overcome-the-Myanmar-curse.

399 Toru Takahashi, 'If ASEAN cannot pull Myanmar in line, how can it progress?' *Nikkei Asia*, 11 November 2021. https://asia.nikkei.com/Spotlight/Comment/If-ASEAN-cannot-pull-Myanmar-in-line-how-can-it-progress?msclkid=3b68906aac3e11ec957549745994885e.

400 Ben Bland, 'ASEAN Muddles Though on Myanmar', *The Lowy Institute*, 22 October 2021. https://www.lowyinstitute.org/the-interpreter/asean-muddles-through-myanmar.

401 Bhavan Jaipragas, 'Asean in uncharted waters as it snubs Myanmar junta chief Min Aung Hlaing', *South China Morning Post*, 25 October 2021. https://www.scmp.com/week-asia/politics/article/3153625/asean-uncharted-waters-it-snubs-myanmar-junta-chief-min-aung.

402 Gwen Robinson, 'Can ASEAN overcome the "Myanmar curse"?', *Nikkei Asia*, 1 November 2021. https://asia.nikkei.com/Spotlight/Comment/Can-ASEAN-overcome-the-Myanmar-curse.

403 Sukegawa Seiya, 'ASEAN and Myanmar: Crisis and Opportunity', *The Diplomat*, 2 January 2022. https://thediplomat.com/2022/01/asean-and-myanmar-crisis-and-opportunity/.

404 'Cambodia PM says Myanmar junta welcome at ASEAN if progress made', *Reuters*, 25 January 2022. https://www.reuters.com/world/asia-pacific/cambodia-pm-says-myanmar-junta-welcome-asean-if-progress-made-2022-01-25/.

405 'ASEAN Says Myanmar "part of the family" as summit concludes', *Aljazeera*, 29 October 2021. https://www.aljazeera.com/news/2021/10/29/asean-says-myanmar-part-of-the-family-as-summit-concludes.

406 This phrasing echoes my 2005 article: Amitav Acharya, 'Democracy in Burma: Does Anybody Really Care?', *YaleGlobal*, 1 September 2005.

407 Joseph Biden, Jr., 'Statement by President Joseph R. Biden, Jr. on the Situation in Burma', *The White House Briefing Room*, 1 February 2021. https://www.whitehouse.gov/briefing-room/statements-releases/2021/02/01/statement-by-president-joseph-r-biden-jr-on-the-situation-in-burma/.

408 Ibid.

409 Antony J. Blinken, 'Burmese Military Arrests of Civilian Government Leaders', *U.S. Department of State Office of the Spokesperson Press Release*, 31 Janaury 2021. https://www.state.gov/burmese-military-arrests-of-civilian-government-leaders/.

410 Ned Price, 'Department Press Briefing—February 3, 2021', *U.S. Department of State Press Briefings*, 3 February 2021. https://www.state.gov/briefings/department-press-briefing-february-3-2021/.

411 Ned Price, 'Department Press Briefing—February 2, 2021', *U.S. Department of State Press Briefings*, 2 February 2021. https://www.state.gov/briefings/department-press-briefing-february-2-2021/.

412 'Briefing with Senior State Department Officials on the State Department's Assessment of Recent Events in Burma', 2 February 2021. https://www.state.gov/briefing-with-senior-state-department-officials-on-the-state-departments-assessment-of-recent-events-in-burma/.

413 'Briefing with Senior State Department Officials On the State Department's Assessment of Recent Events in Burma', 2 February 2021. https://www.state.gov/briefing-with-senior-

state-department-officials-on-the-state-departments-assessment-of-recent-events-in-burma/.

414 Executive Office of the President, 'Executive Order 14014: Blocking Property With Respect to the Situation in Burma', *National Archives*, 10 February 2021. https://www.federalregister.gov/documents/2021/02/12/2021-03139/blocking-property-with-respect-to-the-situation-in-burma.

415 'United States Targets Leaders of Burma's Military Coup Under New Executive Order', *U.S. Department of the Treasury*, 11 February 2021. https://home.treasury.gov/news/press-releases/jy0024 https://home.treasury.gov/news/press-releases/jy0024.

416 Antony J. Blinken, 'Promoting Accountability for Those Responsible for Violence Against Protestors in Burma', *U.S. Department of State Office of the Spokesperson Press Releases*, 22 February 2021. https://www.state.gov/promoting-accountability-for-those-responsible-for-violence-against-protestors-in-burma/.

417 'United States Targets Leaders of Burma's Military Coup Under New Executive Order', *U.S. Department of the Treasury*, 11 February 2021. https://home.treasury.gov/news/press-releases/jy0024 https://home.treasury.gov/news/press-releases/jy0024.

418 Joseph Biden, Jr., 'Remarks by President Biden on the Administration's Response to the Coup in Burma', *The White House Briefing Room*, 10 February 2021. https://www.whitehouse.gov/briefing-room/speeches-remarks/2021/02/10/remarks-by-president-biden-on-the-administrations-response-to-the-coup-in-burma/.

419 Executive Office of the President, 'Executive Order 14014: Blocking Property With Respect to the Situation in Burma', 10 February 2021. https://www.federalregister.gov/documents/2021/02/12/2021-03139/blocking-property-with-respect-to-the-situation-in-burma.

420 Antony J. Blinken, 'Designating Officials and Entities in Connection with the Military Coup in Burma', *U.S. Department of State Office of the Spokesperson Press Releases*, 11 February 2021. https://www.state.gov/designating-officials-and-entities-in-connection-with-the-military-coup-in-burma/.

421 Jake Sullivan, 'Statement by National Security Advisor Jake Sullivan on Violence Against Peaceful Demonstrations in Burma', *The White House Briefing Room*, 28 February 2021. https://www.whitehouse.gov/briefing-room/statements-releases/2021/02/28/statement-by-national-security-advisor-jake-sullivan-on-violence-against-peaceful-demonstrations-in-burma/.

422 'US and UK blacklist sprawling Myanmar military-controlled companies', *Nikkei Asia*, 25 March 2021. https://asia.nikkei.com/Spotlight/Myanmar-Crisis/US-and-UK-blacklist-sprawling-Myanmar-military-controlled-companies..

423 'United States Targets Family Members Profiting from Connection to Burmese Coup Leader', *U.S. Department of the Treasury*, 10 March 2021. https://home.treasury.gov/news/press-releases/jy0051.

424 Antony J. Blinken, 'Designating Officials and Military Units in Response to Escalating Violence in Burma', *U.S. Department of State Office of the Spokesperson Press Releases*, 22 March 2021. https://www.state.gov/designating-officials-and-military-units-in-response-to-escalating-violence-in-burma/.

425 'Treasury Sanctions Military Holding Companies in Burma', *U.S. Department of the Treasury*, 25 March 2021. https://home.treasury.gov/news/press-releases/jy0078.

426 'US and UK blacklist sprawling Myanmar military-controlled companies', *Nikkei Asia*, 25 March 2021. https://asia.nikkei.com/Spotlight/Myanmar-Crisis/US-and-UK-blacklist-sprawling-Myanmar-military-controlled-companies.

427 Marise Payne, 'Statement on Myanmar', *Minister for Foreign Affairs,* 1 February 2021. https://www.foreignminister.gov.au/minister/marise-payne/media-release/statement-myanmar.

428 Marise Payne, 'Statement on Myanmar', *Minister for Foreign Affairs,* 7 March 2021. https://www.foreignminister.gov.au/minister/marise-payne/media-release/statement-myanmar-0.

429 Ibid.

430 Joint Staff, 'Joint Statement of Chiefs of Defence', *Ministry of Defense Joint Staff Japan,* 28 March 2021. https://www.mod.go.jp/js/Press/press2021/press_pdf/p20210328_02.pdf.

431 U.S. Mission Burma, 'Joint Statement on Attacks on Civilians in Karen State', *U.S. Embassy in Burma,* 24 December 2021. https://mm.usembassy.gov/joint-statement-on-attacks-on-civilians-in-karen-state/.

432 Marise Payne, 'Joint statement on increasing violence in Myanmar', *Minister for Foreign Affairs,* 26 November 2021. https://www.foreignminister.gov.au/minister/marise-payne/media-release/joint-statement-increasing-violence-myanmar.

433 Council of the EU, 'Myanmar: Declaration by the High Representative on behalf of the European Union', *Council of the European Union Press Release,* 2 February 2021. https://www.consilium.europa.eu/en/press/press-releases/2021/02/02/myanmar-declaration-by-the-high-representative-on-behalf-of-the-european-union/.

434 Council of the EU, 'Myanmar/Burma: Council adopts conclusions', *Council of the European Union Press Release,* 22 February 2021. https://www.consilium.europa.eu/en/press/press-releases/2021/02/22/myanmar-burma-council-adopts-conclusions/.

435 'Myanmar/Burma: EU imposes sanctions on 10 individuals and two military-controlled companies over the February military coup and subsequent repression', *Council of the European Union Press Release,* 19 April 2021. https://www.

consilium.europa.eu/en/press/press-releases/2021/04/19/
myanmar-burma-eu-imposes-sanctions-on-10-individuals-
and-two-military-controlled-companies-over-the-february-
military-coup-and-subsequent-repression/.

436 'Myanmar/Burma: EU sanctions 11 people over the recent
military coup and ensuing repression', *Council of the European
Union Press Release*, 22 March 2021. https://www.consilium.
europa.eu/en/press/press-releases/2021/03/22/myanmar-
burma-eu-sanctions-11-people-over-the-recent-military-
coup-and-ensuing-repression/.

437 'Council Decision (CFSP) 2021/482', *Official Journal
of the European Union*, 22 March 2021. https://eur-lex.
europa.eu/legal-content/EN/TXT/?uri=CELEXper
cent3A32021D0482..

438 'Myanmar/Burma: Council extends sanctions for another
year', *Council of the European Union Press Release*, 29 April
2021. https://www.consilium.europa.eu/en/press/press-
releases/2021/04/29/myanmar-burma-council-extends-
sanctions-for-another-year/.

439 'Council Decision (CFSP) 2021/1000', *Official Journal
of the European Union*, 21 June 2021. https://eur-lex.europa.eu/
legal-content/EN/TXT/?uri=uriservper cent3AOJ.LI.2021.
219.01.0057.01.ENG&toc=OJper cent3ALper cent3A2021
per cent3A219Iper cent3ATOC.

440 The details of the initiatives including the 'Five-Point
Consensus' is described in Chapter... The ASEAN Response.

441 'Myanmar/Burma: Declaration by the High Representative
on behalf of the European Union to support the work of
the ASEAN Special Envoy', *Council of the European Union
Press Release*, 13 October 2021. https://www.consilium.
europa.eu/en/press/press-releases/2021/10/13/myanmar-
burma-declaration-by-the-high-representative-on-behalf-
of-the-european-union-to-support-the-work-of-the-asean-
special-envoy/.

442 Mohan Malik, *Regional Reverberations from Regime Shake-up in Rangoon* (Honolulu: Asia-Pacific Center For Security Studies, 2005).

443 Cao Desheng, 'China asks Myanmar parties to resolve differences peacefully', *China Daily*, 7 March 2021. https://www.chinadaily.com.cn/a/202103/07/WS60449b63a31024ad0 baad655.html.

444 Wang Wenbin, 'Foreign Ministry Spokesperson Wang Wenbin's Regular Press Conference on February 1, 2021', *Embassy of the People's Republic of China in the United States of America Foreign Ministry Spokesperson's Remarks*, 1 February 2021. http://www.china-embassy.org/eng/fyrth/202102/t20210202_4475653.htm.

445 Ibid.

446 Chinese Embassy in Myanmar, 'Chinese Ambassador to Myanmar H.E.Mr. Chen Hai gives interview to Myanmar Media on the current situation in Myanmar', *Global Times*, 16 February 2021. https://www.globaltimes.cn/page/202102/1215672.shtml.

447 'Foreign Ministry Spokesperson Wang Wenbin's Regular Press Conference on June 7, 2021', *Consulate-General of the People's Republic of China in Mumbai*, 7 June 2021. https://www.fmprc.gov.cn/ce/cgmb/eng/fyrth/t1881926.htm.

448 'Wang Yi: China Supports ASEAN's Appointment of Special Envoy on Myanmar Affairs', *Embassy of the People's Republic of China in the United States of America*, 5 August 2021. http://us.china-embassy.org/eng/zgyw/202108/t20210805_9015393.htm.

449 'Ambassador Zhang Jun Elaborated on China's Position on the situation in Myanmar', *Permanent Mission of the People's Republic of China to the UN*, 5 March 2021. http://chnun.chinamission.org.cn/eng/hyyfy/202103/t20210306_10026726.htm.

450 'Chinese Ambassador to Myanmar H.E.Mr. Chen Hai gives interview to Myanmar Media on the current situation in Myanmar', *Embassy of the People's Republic of China in the Republic of the Union of Myanmar*, 16 February 2021. https://www.mfa.gov.cn/ce/cemm//eng/sgxw/t1854268.htm.

451 'Foreign Ministry Spokesperson Zhao Lijian's Regular Press Conference on May 20, 2021', *Embassy of the People's Republic of China in the United States of America*, 20 May 2021. http://www.china-embassy.org/eng/fyrth/202105/t20210520_9016369.htm.

452 'Ambassador Zhang Jun Elaborated China's Position on the Situation in Myanmar in the Security Council', *Permanent Mission of the People's Republic of China to the UN*, 31 March 2021. http://chnun.chinamission.org.cn/eng/hyyfy/t1866062.htm.

453 'Foreign Ministry Spokesperson Zhao Lijian's Regular Press Conference on March 15, 2021', *Ministry of Foreign Affairs of the People's Republic of China*, 15 March 2021. https://www.fmprc.gov.cn/mfa_eng/xwfw_665399/s2510_665401/2511_665403/202103/t20210315_9721227.html.

454 Ibid.

455 Koya Jibiki, 'Myanmar's isolation from West opens door for China and Russia', *Nikkei Asia*, 28 January 2022. https://asia.nikkei.com/Spotlight/Myanmar-Crisis/Myanmar-s-isolation-from-West-opens-door-for-China-and-Russia.

456 Kelley Currie, 'Can a Dam Deal Buy Beijing's Support for Myanmar's Junta?', *Foreign Policy*, 23 February 2021. https://foreignpolicy.com/2021/02/23/myanmar-china-dam-deal-junta-democracy/.

457 'Myanmar coup: China blocks UN condemnation as protest grows', *BBC*, 3 February 2021. https://www.bbc.com/news/world-asia-55913947.

458 Ibid.

459 'China Boosts Support for Myanmar Army, Countering U.S. Sanctions', *Bloomberg*, 10 June 2021. https://www.bloomberg. com/news/articles/2021-06-09/china-boosts-support-for-myanmar-army-countering-u-s-sanctions.

460 Mira Patel, 'A complex history and layered present: What determines India's response to military rule in Myanmar', *Indian Express*, 20 May 2021. https://indianexpress.com/ article/research/a-complex-history-and-layered-present-what-determines-indias-response-to-military-rule-in-myanmar-7321626/.

461 Government of India, 'Question No. 2651 Military Rule in Myanmar: Rajya Sabha', *Ministry of External Affairs Parliament Q&A*, 18 March 2021. https://mea.gov.in/ rajya-sabha.htm?dtl/33672/QUESTION_NO2651_ MILITARY_RULE_IN_MYANMAR.

462 Government of India, 'Transcript of Special Press briefing by Foreign Secretary before Prime Minister's visit to Bangladesh', *Ministry of External Affairs Media Briefings*, 25 March 2021. https://mea.gov.in/media-briefings. htm?dtl/33760/Transcript_of_Special_Press_briefing_ by_Foreign_Secretary_before_Prime_Ministers_visit_to_ Bangladesh_March_24_2021.

463 Government of India, 'Official Spokesperson's response to media queries on the ASEAN initiative on Myanmar agreed to at the ASEAN Summit held on April 24', *Ministry of External Affairs Response to Media Queries*, 25 April 2021. https://mea.gov.in/response-to-queries.htm?dtl/33822/ Official_Spokespersons_response_to_media_queries_on_ the_ASEAN_initiative_on_Myanmar_agreed_to_at_the_ ASEAN_Summit_held_on_April_24.

464 Uday Bhanu Singh, 'Post-Coup Myanmar and India's response', *Manohar Parrikar Institute for Defence Studies and Analyses*, 21 May 2021. https://idsa.in/idsacomments/post-coup-myanmar-indias-response-ubsingh-210521.

465 Mira Patel, 'A complex history and layered present: What determines India's response to military rule in Myanmar', *Indian Express*, 20 May 2021. https://indianexpress.com/ article/research/a-complex-history-and-layered-present-what-determines-indias-response-to-military-rule-in-myanmar-7321626/.

466 Motegi Toshimitsu, 'The internal situation in Myanmar (Statement by Foreign Minister MOTEGI Toshimitsu', *Ministry of Foreign Affairs Japan Press Release*, 1 February 2021. https://www.mofa.go.jp/press/release/press3e_000161.html.

467 Satoshi Sugiyama and Tomohiro Osaki, 'Japan's ties with Myanmar put to the test after military coup', *The Japan Times*, 25 February 2021. https://www.japantimes.co.jp/ news/2021/02/25/national/myanmar-japan-ties/.

468 Philip Heijmans and Kwan Wei Kevin Tan, 'Japan's Refusal to Sanction Myanmar Undermines Biden's Strategy', *Bloomberg*, 19 June 2021. https://www.bloomberg.com/news/ articles/2021-06-19/japan-s-refusal-to-sanction-myanmar-over-abuses-undermines-biden-s-strategy.

469 Reuters Staff, 'Japan defence official warns Myanmar coup could increase China's influence in region', *Reuters*, 2 February 2021. https://www.reuters.com/article/us-myanmar-politics-japan/japan-defence-official-warns-myanmar-coup-could-increase-chinas-influence-in-region-idUSKBN2A20PX.

470 Peter Morris, 'Japan struggles to have it both ways on Myanmar', *Asia Times*, 2 March 2021. https://asiatimes.com/2021/03/japan-struggles-to-have-it-both-ways-on-myanmar/.

471 Keiho Sasamori, 'Japan's Myanmar Missteps Are Damaging Its Image', *The Diplomat*, 10 March 2021. https://thediplomat.com/2021/03/japans-myanmar-missteps-are-damaging-its-image/

472 'Emergency Grant Aid for humanitarian assistance to the populations affected by the coup in the south east area of

Myanmar', *Ministry of Foreign Affairs of Japan Press Release*, 13 July 2021. https://www.mofa.go.jp/press/release/press3e_000210.html.

473 'Violence, Intimidation, Harassment by Myanmar Security Personnel Unacceptable, Secretary General Says, Also Expressing Concern over Restrictions on Internet', *United Nations*, 14 February 2021. https://www.un.org/press/en/2021/sgsm20581.doc.htm.

474 'Humanitarian Support, Coherent Global Action Still Needed 100 Days after Deadly Military Takeover in Myanmar, Secretary-General Says', *United Nations*, 11 May 2021. https://www.un.org/press/en/2021/sgsm20722.doc.htm.

475 'Statement by the President of the Security Council', 10 March 2021. https://www.securitycouncilreport.org/atf/cf/per cent 7B65BFCF9B-6D27-4E9C-8CD3-CF6E4FF96FF9 per cent7D/s_prst_2021_5.pdf.

476 'Statement by the President of the Security Council', *United Nations*, 10 March 2021. https://www.securitycouncilreport.org/atf/cf/per cent7B65BFCF9B-6D27-4E9C-8CD3-CF6E4FF96FF9per cent7D/s_prst_2021_5.pdf.

477 'Resolution adopted by the General Assembly on 18 June 2021', General Assembly https://digitallibrary.un.org/record/3930690?ln=en#record-files-collapse-header.

478 'Stop weapons supply to Myanmar, rights expert urges', *UN News*, 22 February 2022. https://news.un.org/en/story/2022/02/1112422.

479 The United Nations, 'Meetings Coverage and Press Release', 18 June 2021. https://www.un.org/press/en/2021/ga12339.doc.htm#:~:text=Theper cent20Generalper cent20Assemblyper cent20todayper cent20unanimously,andper cent20allowper cent20theper cent20sustainedper cent20democratic.

480 'Secretary-General Strongly Condemns Continuing Violence by Myanmar Military as "Utterly Unacceptable",

Urging Unified International Response', United Nations, 19 March 2021, https://www.un.org/press/en/2021/sgsm20639.doc.htm

481 'Myanmar: Bachelet deplores conviction and sentencing of Aung San Suu Kyi', *United Nations Human Rights Office of the High Commissioner*, 6 December 2021. https://reliefweb.int/report/myanmar/myanmar-bachelet-deplores-conviction-and-sentencing-aung-san-suu-kyi.

482 Security Council, 'Security Council Press Statement on the Situation in Myanmar', United Nations, 2 February 2022. https://www.un.org/press/en/2022/sc14785.doc.htm.

483 'This Is Not 'Just Another Coup'': Ex-US Ambassador to Myanmar', *The Irrawaddy*, 8 April 2021. https://www.irrawaddy.com/in-person/interview/not-just-another-coup-ex-us-ambassador-myanmar.html.

484 Megha Bahree, 'For foreign investors in Myanmar, coup adds new uncertainties', *Aljazeera*, 18 February 2021. https://www.aljazeera.com/economy/2021/2/18/for-foreign-investors-in-myanmar-coup-adds-new-uncertainties.

485 'Myanmar Economic Monitor: Progress Threatened; Resilience Tested', The World Bank, July 2021. https://pubdocs.worldbank.org/en/525471627057268984/Myanmar-Economic-Monitor-July-2021.pdf.

486 International Labour Organization (ILO), 'Employment in Myanmar since the military takeover: A rapid impact assessment', 19 July 2021. https://www.ilo.org/yangon/publications/WCMS_814681/lang--en/index.htm.

487 'If There's No Recovery, All Businesses Will Be in Trouble', *Frontier Myanmar*, 3 July 2021. https://www.frontiermyanmar.net/en/if-theres-no-recovery-all-businesses-will-be-in-trouble/.

488 'Agriculture', US International Trade Administration, 27 September 2021. https://www.trade.gov/country-commercial-guides/burma-agriculture.

489 Debby Chan, 'Business as Usual: Chinese Investments After the Myanmar Coup', *The Diplomat*, 2 September 2021. https://thediplomat.com/2021/09/business-as-usual-chinese-investments-after-the-myanmar-coup/.

490 'Myanmar Economic Monitor July 2021: Progress Threatened; Resilience Tested', The World Bank, 23 July 2021. https://www.worldbank.org/en/country/myanmar/publication/myanmar-economic-monitor-july-2021-progress-threatened-resilience-tested.

491 'Humanitarian Needs Overview Myanmar', *United Nations Office for the Coordination of Humanitarian Affairs*, December 2021. https://reliefweb.int/sites/reliefweb.int/files/resources/mmr_humanitarian_needs_overview_2022.pdf.

492 'Humanitarian Needs Overview Myanmar', *United Nations Office for the Coordination of Humanitarian Affairs*, December 2021. https://reliefweb.int/sites/reliefweb.int/files/resources/mmr_humanitarian_needs_overview_2022.pdf.

493 'Myanmar: Analysis of the Economic Fallout & Food Insecurity in Wake of the Takeover - 2021', World Food Programme, 21 April 2021. https://www.wfp.org/publications/myanmar-analysis-economic-fallout-and-food-insecurity-wake-takeover-2021.

494 Ibid.

495 Maggi Quadrini, 'Myanmar's Coup Has Put Women in Harm's Way', *The Diplomat*, 3 September 2021. https://thediplomat.com/2021/09/myanmars-coup-has-put-women-in-harms-way/.

496 Grace Tsoi and Moe Myint, 'Covid and a coup: The double crisis pushing Myanmar to the brink', *BBC News*, 30 July 2021. https://www.bbc.com/news/world-asia-57993930.

497 'COVID cover up: third wave death toll may be in hundreds of thousands', *Frontier Myanmar*, 14 January 2022. https://

www.frontiermyanmar.net/en/covid-cover-up-third-wave-death-toll-may-be-in-hundreds-of-thousands/.

498 Ibid.

499 Reuters COVID-19 Tracker, 'Myanmar', 13 May 2022. https://graphics.reuters.com/world-coronavirus-tracker-and-maps/countries-and-territories/myanmar/.

500 'Project Information Document (PID), Myanmar COVID-19 Emergency Response Project (P173902)', The World Bank, 9 April 2020. https://documents1. worldbank.org/curated/en/178971586428026889/pdf/ Project-Information-Document-Myanmar-COVID-19-Emergency-Response-Project-P173902.pdf; 'Virus Surges in Myanmar, Where Generals Control Vaccines', *The New York Times*, 1 August 2021. https://www.nytimes. com/2021/07/01/world/asia/covid-myanmar-coup.html; 'Coup, COVID fuelling 'perfect storm' in Myanmar, UN expert warns', United Nations, 14 July 2021. https://news. un.org/en/story/2021/07/1095822.

501 Maung Bo, 'COVID and the coup: Myanmar in the grip of double crisis', *Deutsche Welle (DW)*, 26 July 2021. https:// www.dw.com/en/myanmar-covid-coup/a-58644545.

502 Helene Maria Kyed, 'The military junta in Myanmar weaponizes COVID-19 against its opponents', 31 August 2021. https://www.diis.dk/en/research/the-military-junta-in-myanmar-weaponizes-covid-19-against-its-opponents.

503 'Burma', https://coronavirus.jhu.edu/region/myanmar (accessed 13 May 2022).

504 'Myanmar death toll exceeds 1,500 with nearly 8,800 in custody—UN', *Reuters*, 1 February 2022. https://www. reuters.com/world/asia-pacific/myanmar-death-toll-exceeds-1500-with-nearly-8800-custody-un-2022-02-01/.

505 The authors of the report include Mary Callahan, Priscilla Clapp, Robert Conrad, Christina Fink, Brian Joseph, Derek Mitchell (former US Ambassador to Burma), Jason Tower,

Daniel Twining, and Min Zin. 'Anatomy of the Military Coup and Recommendations for U.S. Response: Myanmar Study Group Final Report' (Washington, DC, The United States Institute of Peace, February 2022). https://www. usip.org/publications/2022/02/myanmar-study-group-final-report

506 Bertil Lintner, 'Myanmar Military Struggles to Adapt to New Kind of Conflict', *Irrawaddy*, 18 October 2021, https://www.irrawaddy.com/opinion/guest-column/myanmar-military-struggles-to-adapt-to-new-kind-of-conflict.html

507 Anders Kirstein Moeller, 'Peering under the hood: Coup narratives and Tatmadaw Factionalism', *Tea Circle Oxford*, 10 January 2022. https://teacircleoxford.com/politics/peering-under-the-hood-coup-narratives-and-tatmadaw-factionalism/

508 'Senior Myanmar Military Officials Replaced in Surprise Move'. *The Irrawaddy*, 10 January 2022. https://www.irrawaddy.com/news/burma/senior-myanmar-military-official-replaced-in-surprise-move.html

509 Hannah Beech, 'Inside Myanmar's Army: "They See Protesters as Criminals"', *The New York Times*, 28 March 2021, at https://www.nytimes. com/2021/03/28/world/asia/myanmar-armyprotests.htm

510 Fanny Potkin and Wa Lone, 'Insight-'Information Combat': Inside the Fight for Myanmar's Soul', *Reuters*. 1 November 2021. https://www.reuters.com/article/myanmar-politics-socialmedia-idCNL4N2R41Z1

511 Anonymous. 'Myanmar Defectors Describe Military Culture of Abuse, Fear', *Al Jazeera*, 8 March, 2022. https://www.aljazeera.com/news/2022/3/8/myanmars-army-defectors-describe-a-culture-of-abuse-and-fear.

512 'Interview: Captain Who Left Myanmar Army Estimates 800 Troops Have Defected Since Coup', *Radio Free Asia*, 17

June 2021, at https://www.rfa.org/english/news/myanmar/
militarydefector-06172021183614.htm

513  Billy Ford and Zaraci Oo, 'Myanmar Coup: Military Regime
Seeks to Weaponize Religion', USIP Publications, United
States Institute of Peace, 21 December 2021. https://www.
usip.org/publications/2021/12/myanmar-coup-military-
regime-seeks-weaponize-religion.

514  Much of the information in this paragraph is based on
International Crisis Group, 'Myanmar's Coup Shakes Up Its
Ethnic Conflicts', 22 Jan 2022, https://www.crisisgroup.org/
asia/south-east-asia/myanmar/319-myanmars-coup-shakes-
its-ethnic-conflicts

515  Much of the information in this paragraph is based on
International Crisis Group, 'Myanmar's Coup Shakes Up Its
Ethnic Conflicts', 22 Jan 2022, https://www.crisisgroup.org/
asia/south-east-asia/myanmar/319-myanmars-coup-shakes-
its-ethnic-conflicts

516  'Myanmar's civilian president claims resistance controls nearly
half the country - The Interview', 10 May 2022, https://
www.france24.com/en/tv-shows/the-interview/20220510-
myanmar-s-civilian-president-claims-resistance-controls-
nearly-half-of-country

517  USIP Report, *Anatomy of the Military Coup and
Recommendations for U.S*, p. 4 https://www.usip.org/
publications/2022/02/myanmar-study-group-final-report
Nay Yan Oo, 'Don't Give Up on Myanmar', 16 December
2021, https://www.brookings.edu/blog/order-from-chaos/
2021/12/16/dont-give-up-on-myanmar/Tragic

518  Nay Yan Oo, 'Don't Give Up on Myanmar', 16 December
2021, https://www.brookings.edu/blog/order-from-chaos/
2021/12/16/dont-give-up-on-myanmar/Tragic

# List of Abbreviations

AA – Arakan Army
AAPP – Assistance Association for Political Prisoners
ABRF – Army of Burma Reserve Organization
ABSDF – All Burma Student's Democratic Front
ACLED – Armed Conflict Location and Event Data
ADB – Asian Development Bank
AFPFL – Anti-Fascist People's Freedom League
AHA Centre – ASEAN Coordinating Centre for Humanitarian Assistance
ALA – Arakan Liberation Army
ALP – Arakan Liberation Party
ANFREL – Asian Network for Free Elections
ANP – Arakan National Party
APC – Armored Personnel Carrier
ARSA – Arakan Rohingya Salvation Army
ASEAN – Association of Southeast Asian Nations
BDA – Burma Defence Army
BGF – Border Guard Force
BIA – Burmese Independence Army
BSPP – Burma Socialist Programme Party
CCP – Chinese Communist Party
CDM – Civil Disobedience Movement
CG – Concerned Group
CMEC – China-Myanmar Economic Corridor

CNF – Chin National Front
CPB – Communist Party of Burma
CRPH - Committee Representing Pyidaungsu Hluttaw
CSO – Civil Society Organization
CSSU – Committee for Shan State Unity
DASSK – Daw Aung San Suu Kyi
DC – District of Columbia
DKBA – Democratic Karen Buddhist Army
EAO – Ethnic Armed Organization
EU – European Union
FDI – Foreign Direct Investment
FPNCC – Federal Political Negotiation and
Consultative Committee
G-7 – Group of 7 Nations
G-20 – Group of 20 Nations
GAD – General Administrative Department
GDP – Gross Domestic Product
HRW – Human Rights Watch
ICC – International Criminal Court
ICJ – International Court of Justice
INS – Indian Naval Ship
KIO/A – Kachin Independence Organization/Army
KMT – *Kuomintang* (National People's Party)
KNDO – Karen National Defence Organization
KNDP – Kaman National Development Party
KNDP – Karen National Democratic Party
KNPP – Karenni National Progressive Party
KNU – Karen National Union
MAH – Min Aung Hlaing
MBT – Main Battle Tank
MEC – Myanmar Economic Corporation
MEHL – Myanmar Economic Holdings Ltd
MNDAA – Myanmar Nationalities Democratic Alliance Army
MNDO – Mon National Defence Organization
MOGE – Myanmar Oil and Gas Enterprise

MPF – Myanmar Police Force
MRAP – Mine-Resistant Ambush Protected
NAM – Non-Aligned Movement
NATO – North Atlantic Treaty Organization
NCA – Nationwide Ceasefire Agreement
NCCT – Nationwide Ceasefire Coordination Team
NCGUB – National Coalition Government of the Union of Burma
NDAA – National Democratic Alliance Army
NLD – National League for Democracy
NUCC – National Unity Consultative Committee
NUG – National Unity Government
NUP – National Unity Party
P-5 – Five Permanent Members of the United Nations
Security Council
PBF – Patriotic Burmese Forces
PDF – People's Defence Force
PLA – People's Liberation Army
PM – Prime Minister
PNLO – Pa-O National Liberation Army
PPST – Peace Process Steering Team
PVO – White Band People's Volunteer Organization
RCSS – Restoration Council of Shan State
RIT – Rangoon Institute of Technology
SAC – State Administration Council
SEATO – Southeast Asia Treaty Organization
SLORC – State Law and Order Restoration Council
SNLD – Shan Nationalities League for Democracy
SOE – Special Operations Executive
SPDC – State Peace and Development Council
SPGF – Southern Pauk Guerilla Force
SSA-N – Shan State Army-North
SSA-S – Shan State Army-South
STEP – Support to Electoral Processes
STOL – Short Take-off and Landing
TNLA – Ta'ang National Liberation Army

UEC – Union Election Commission
UK – United Kingdom
UG – Urban Guerrillas
ULA – United League of Arakan
UN – United Nations
UNFC – United Nationalities Federal Council
UNHCR – United Nations High Commissioner for Refugees
UNICEF – United Nations International Children's Emergency Fund
UPWC – Union Peacemaking Work Committee
USDP – Union Solidarity and Development Party
USA/US – United States of America
USD – US Dollar
USIP – United States Institute of Peace
USSR – Union of Soviet Socialist Republics
UWSA – United Wa State Army
WFP – World Food Programme
WWI – World War I
WWII – World War II